ALSO STARRING:

- RAMSEY CAMPBELL—author of *The Parasite, The Influence* and *The Hungry Moon*
- DOUGLAS E. WINTER—horror critic, author of *Faces of Fear*, editor of *Prime Evil*
- KATHERINE RAMSLAND—author of *Prism of the Night: A Biography of Anne Rice*
- GARY BRANDNER—author of *Cameron's Closet* and *The Howling*
- JOHN FARRIS—author of *The Fury* and *Fiends*
- CRAIG SHAW GARDNER—bestselling author of *Batman* and *Bride of the Slime Monster*
- JOE R. LANSDALE—author of *The Drive-in* and *Savage Season*
- CHELSEA QUINN YARBRO—author of *Hotel Transylvania* and *Beastnights*
- THOMAS F. MONTELEONE—author of *Night Train* and editor of *Borderlands*
- KATHRYN PTACEK—author of *Shadoweyes* and editor of *Women of Darkness*
- CHARLES L. GRANT—author of *In a Dark Dream* and *The Pet*
- STANLEY WIATER—author of *Dark Dreamers: Conversations with the Masters of Horror*
- PAUL M. SAMMON—editor of *Splatterpunks* and *Blood and Rockets*
- ED GORMAN—author of *A Cry of Shadows* and editor of *Mystery Scene* magazine
- NANCY HOLDER—author of *Rough Cut*
- STEPHEN R. BISSETTE—editor of *Taboo* and *Carnosaurs*
- MELISSA MIA HALL—author of short stories appearing in *Shadows, Women of Darkness* and *Blood Is Not Enough*
- T. LIAM McDONALD—author of *Night Without Morning* and editor of *Shadowplays*
- PHILIP NUTMAN—author of *Wet Work*, British correspondent for *Fangoria*

CUT!
Horror Writers on Horr

CUT!
HORROR WRITERS ON HORROR FILM

Edited by Christopher Golden

BERKLEY BOOKS, NEW YORK

Every effort has been made to properly credit those stills, publicity shots, and other photographs included herein. Any errors are purely unintentional and, if brought to our attention, will be corrected for future editions. Special thanks to Gary Brandner for access to his private collection.

PHOTO CREDITS:
AIP, Allied Artists, Astor Pictures, Avco Embassy Pictures, Carolco Pictures, Columbia Pictures, Embassy Home Entertainment, Embassy Telecommunications, Hammer Film Productions, Jerry Gross Organization, Lightning Pictures, Lorimar Pictures, Lynch Frost Productions, Mahler (Italy), Maniac Productions, The Mantle Clinic II, Ltd., MGM, MPI Home Video, New Line Cinema, Paramount Pictures, United Artists, Universal Pictures, Vanguard, Vestron Pictures, Video Yesteryear, Warner Brothers.

CUT! HORROR WRITERS ON HORROR FILM

A Berkley Book / published by arrangement with
the editor

PRINTING HISTORY
Berkley trade paperback edition / April 1992

ISBN: 0-425-13282-X

A BERKLEY BOOK ® TM 757,375
Berkley Books are published by The Berkley Publishing Group,
200 Madison Avenue, New York, New York 10016.
The name "BERKLEY" and the "B" logo
are trademarks belonging to Berkley Publishing Corporation.

PRINTED IN THE UNITED STATES OF AMERICA

10 9 8 7 6 5 4 3 2 1

This book is dedicated to my mother, who always indulged my peculiarities, and in memory of my father, who woke us up late at night to watch *Kolchak, The Night Stalker*.

The editor would like to thank:

Connie, of course.

The writers and filmmakers who inspired me, who showed me the door.

Craig Shaw Gardner, who opened that door just a crack.

Phil Nutman and Lori Perkins, who pulled me through, kicking and screaming.

And Ginjer, who bought it.

Contents

CUT!
HORROR WRITERS
ON HORROR FILM

Introduction

Christopher Golden

Long a student of horror fiction and film, Chris is currently adapting Joe R. Lansdale's *The Drive-In* to comic book form and has a number of other comic book projects on the way. His short fiction is slated to appear in several coming anthologies including Paul M. Sammon's *Die, Elvis, Die!* and Ed Gorman and Martin Greenberg's *Stalkers 3*. His novel in progress is titled *Of Saints and Shadows*.

An employee of BPI Communications, Inc., publishers of *Billboard* and *The Hollywood Reporter*, among many others, Chris is also a columnist for the Entertainment News Wire, a service with hundreds of print and broadcast subscribers worldwide. His nonfiction has also appeared in magazines such as *Starlog* and *High Voltage*. As a marketing and publicity consultant, he has worked with The William Morris Agency and Kevin Eastman's Tundra Publishing.

Other than the obvious, he has a great passion for the Allman Brothers Band, Ben & Jerry's ice cream and Cajun food. He lives in Tarrytown, New York, with his wife, Connie, and their fish.

First Cut

1

Who are these guys and what the hell do they know about horror movies?

Who are they? If you bought the book, you'll know most of them. But just in case, there's a bio on each of the men and women in this book on the following pages. But that's not the real question, is it? The

1

real question is, if you'll allow me: Why should you give a damn (and a few bucks besides) to read what they've got to say about a subject near and dear to your heart? Am I right?

We are all, you and they and I, lovers of the macabre and often ass-kicking ritual of losing ourselves in images on a screen (preferably a large one) for the sole purpose of having our spines chilled, our brains fried, our knuckles whitened, and the proverbial shit scared out of us.

We're fans. Horror fans. We've all been affected in our own way by the terror and humor and bloodlust and disgust brought about in the twenty percent of our brains that human beings use (and I'm being generous). We've all been touched in some way by these films. But the people in this book are different; they're special in a way. The horror film is part of a foundation for these creepy folks who make their living doing just what the films do, only in print.

The foundation of fear.

Who knows what it is? Most of these folks claim to have had pretty normal childhoods. (My mother tells me I was conceived on Halloween— this is the only reason she can offer for my . . . eccentricity.) But for them, the love of the bizarre has been taken one step further than most. Rather than absorb it in all its many forms, they have found a way to create fear anew in their own hearts and therefore in ours. Using their natural skills and a talent for terror garnered from real life, from books, comic books, and movies, they weave horror far more effective than most of what you can find on the screen.

You'll find that few horror writers do not number among their influences a certain director, or film, or scene.

The point to all this—horror writers know a good horror story when they read one, or see one, as the case may be. Our friends in Hollywood often appear to be ignorant of the treasure they have in authors of horror fiction, and when they do lower themselves to adapting a paltry paperback horror novel, they almost always screw it up. This is not to suggest that the authors could do it better themselves. Indeed, when this is attempted, the results are often worse than *Friday the 13th, Part XIII* could ever be.

But the stories, ah, there's a rub. They forget that the story and its atmosphere are what made the book so popular in the first place.

And now, back to the point. The authors who have created these very effective horror tales may nor may not be able to write good screenplays or make good films, but that's not what matters here. What matters is that they, perhaps more than anyone, can recognize what makes a good horror story, and therefore, a good horror film.

2

What was requested and what was received:

What really affected these writers, inspired them, impressed them . . . what scared them? To discover this, the broadest possible guidelines were given for the chapters of this book. Choose a director, his films, a single film, a series of unrelated films with a unifying theme; discuss your influences, your tastes, your adventures in the trade; expound upon a related subject, political or personal.

You get the idea. They could talk about whatever they wanted to talk about, and that was the point. They wrote about what they wanted, what they were passionate about. For the most part, it comes back to the same subject.

What scared them?

Some of the chapters are far more detailed, far longer than others; some are shorter, lighter. Though the subject matter is quite diverse, it is fascinating to see which films come up again and again. It is no accident that these writers cover films like *The Cat People* (1942), *The Leopard Man, Night of the Living Dead,* and *Bride of Frankenstein* over and over, with no idea that their comrades have been so deeply affected by the same films. Chapters with completely different themes manage to bring up many of the same films, offering a glimpse of what makes those films great in the first place. They *can* be included under so many different subjects.

We're talking about horror in film here, not just horror films. That really opens it up. We could certainly include everything from *Snow White* to *Ghost* without losing *Henry: Portrait of a Serial Killer* or the unfortunate line of slasher films that have come to represent horror in the minds of the general public. (I am inspired to note here that authors in the genre, including those in this book, have been struggling for years to rename horror. Well, call it what you want, dark fantasy, H/DF, suspense, splatter, thriller. Bullshit semantics, we all know what we're talking about.) This book is intended to enrich not only your knowledge of such films, but your passion for them.

Speaking of which . . .

3

Why do we watch them?

We're weird. Let's face it, it's true. But for a moment cast your objective eye (no, no, it's just a figure of speech) on what passes for normality these days. Who'd want to be that?

So, yeah, you've got to be a little touched to like horror movies enough to buy this book (or write in it, or edit it) but I honestly don't think that's a problem.

But what about the rest of them? You know who I mean; the normal people. The ones who are only slightly weird, enough so that *The Silence of the Lambs* recently hit $100 million. Why do they go? What made all those terrible movies in the early eighties such wonderful box-office hits? What makes the dread-full oldies show up on television time and time again?

I mean, we know why *we* go, but what about them? When you catch the latest horror flick, look around you. How many of those people are *really* into horror movies? How many go to video stores where the clerks know their names and call when the latest vid comes in? Come on. Really. How many of these guys and gals with fistfuls of popcorn and Junior Mints have seen anywhere near as many fright flicks as you have?

Not too damn many.

So, why do they go?

Catharsis, say the psychologists. A really scary or funny (or both) movie is the best way to relieve your frustrations, they say. The movie ends and you let out that breath you've been holding, your knuckles aren't white anymore, your spine warms up, your brain is now only slightly poached, and yes, you've actually got some shit left in you. All your pent-up fears and frustrations are gone, you're Atlas relieved of his burden.

All right, well, perhaps it's not that great. But the point remains. Catharsis is a wonderful thing, and whether or not that is *the* reason the casual horror fan heads for the darkened theaters is unimportant. It's surely *one* of the reasons they go, and one of the reasons we go as well. As a matter of fact, it's a fundamental human need! So they enjoy it, but we, the weird, have found catharsis to be addictive. We love to be scared—love it in a manner nearing the perverse.

The first time I saw *Frankenstein* throw the little girl in the lake, tears streamed down my face as I howled in terror. I was seven. I was sitting on the porch with Mom and Dad. It was a sunny afternoon and the TV was black-and-white, but so was the movie. It was one of the best and most important moments of my life. After crying, I felt great. But don't you always? That's catharsis.

4

There's no accounting for taste:
Or is there?
It's interesting to note the generational differences among the book's contributors. Though their ages are not included in their biographies, it's not difficult to discern who saw which film as first-run theatrical releases.

How old were they when they sat in that darkened theater and were terrified by Boris or Bela, creatures from space, Norman Bates, Christopher Lee, the Living Dead, Michael Myers, Linda Blair, or heaven forbid, Freddy?

Did they escape to the theater down the corner where the movies were a quarter and you got a newsreel and a couple of cartoons, and Saturday a double feature? Or did they take their best girl (or boy) to the local drive-in and "neck," only to shove their date aside when the onscreen terror became more arousing than the backseat action? Did they pay an increasing dollar amount to sit in a sticky multiplex (which no longer has discount matinees) and wander around the mall afterward, maybe get a slice of pizza from Papa Gino's? Or did they, philistines that they are, rent some piece of direct-to-video low-budget gore trash, or maybe see it on cable?

Some of the authors in this book fit in the category "E: All of the above." But no matter where they come in, the films they feel the most passionate about are often those from their childhood.

Writers who grew up in the thirties, forties, fifties, and sixties usually cop the following plea: "That stuff I watched growing up was shit, but it was great and I still love it."

The new crop of twentysomething writers on the other hand, who grew up mostly in the seventies, are the first to say: "That stuff I watched growing up was shit, and it's still shit."

Though at times it keeps us home from the theater in the form of, "Well, I'll catch that on video (or cable)," the video industry has in its favor one major point—it has and will continue to enable the younger audience to see what the big stink was all about back then, even if back then was only a few years ago. In twenty years, it will allow the new generation to view the cream of today's crop. Today's creators of all ages are incredibly lucky to be able to go back and view the films that influenced their progenitors, and figure out why.

It's possible that each generation has had an equal amount of junk to wade through before getting to the good stuff. Maybe it just seems like good horror films are getting more and more rare every year? Perhaps in a few years we'll all realize how wrong we are and look more favorably on the present? Maybe . . .

Nah. For the most part, it's still you know what.

5

What isn't in here:

Actually, there's a lot that isn't in here. It would have been physically impossible to cover everything, especially with the guidelines I gave the book's contributors. The longer the book, the more films included, and yet the book could easily be quadrupled in length and number of contributors with no end in sight.

Some of my favorites that are touched on only briefly, if at all, include *The Exorcist, The Shining, The Hunger, The Stepfather, Halloween, Near Dark, River's Edge,* and *Beetlejuice.* I wish that they and hundreds of others (including all those great movies I saw on *Creature Double Feature* as a kid) could have had more in-depth treatment, but that is for another time.

Thankfully, contributors to *Cut!* did put their passions and their questions down on paper. It is a great starting point to further our education and investigation of the horror film, and we gain some serious insight into the writers themselves—their personalities, their influences.

As for me, two of my favorite horror films, two of the best, fall under a topic not touched on herein, and as they are so important to me, I feel it my duty to cover them briefly here. The topic is "Science in Horror."

There are plenty of science-fiction films referred to in *Cut!*, as you'll see, especially in chapters by Monteleone and Lansdale. After all, a large portion of the horror films of the forties and fifties were really scary science fiction in the first place. But the films I refer to are from much later than that. They are *Alien* and John Carpenter's *The Thing.*

Ridley Scott's *Alien* is without question one of the most suspenseful and atmospheric films ever to grace the screen. Craig Shaw Gardner covers certain aspects of it in his piece, but I would like to note several facets of the film here.

First, you barely see the monster. In a film that is legendary for its bloody terror, most people forget that it harkens back to an earlier time when the monster is nearly always offscreen. In effect, you are as frightened as the crew of the *Nostromo* because you, like them, have no idea where the f---ing alien is.

Second, it's claustrophobic. Even when the astronauts are outside, they are stuck in those suits, making even the deepest, most remote corner of space seem close and crowded. This feeling exponentially increases the tension in the film.

Third, and perhaps most important from a certain point of view, the science itself is frightening. The thought of being that far away from Earth with only that ship and the people around you, some of which you may not be able to trust, is chilling in itself. But a distress call in deep space? The aliens themselves, the ultimate warriors, actually existing and being so completely unstoppable? The larger, elephantine alien whose stomach-burst skeleton sits as the ghost pilot of a long-dead vessel? Where the hell did that big thing come from? Why did it have the aliens aboard? And if it could kill those giants, how could Ripley and Jones the Cat stand a chance?

The science. The imagination. The two can create scenarios of wonder or, as in this case, of terror. Such is also the case with John Carpenter's *The Thing*.

Far closer to John W. Campbell's original story than the 1951 version, though both have their good points, Carpenter's film was way ahead of its time. The amount of alien gore in the film turned off the 1982 audience, though had it been released six or seven years later, it would probably have been a blockbuster.

The Thing, like the original, takes place in an Antarctic wasteland— the film's atmosphere similar in its way to Ridley Scott's depiction of space in *Alien*. A monster is destroying the people who live on the base one by one, absorbing them. But again, it's the science that terrifies.

Below the tension and between the special effects, you cannot help but—indeed Carpenter forces you to—take notice of the *implications* of what is going on here. Never mind that this creature can replicate any being it comes into contact with. It can replicate any being it has *ever* come into contact with. It's been frozen under the ice for hundreds of thousands of years. It could have absorbed "a thousand different creatures on a thousand different planets. It could become any of them at any time." But whoa, wait a minute. If that's true, then it could be the guy next to you. It could be you!

And that's when the paranoia sets in. It's the pseudo-science that starts it off. Blake goes nuts because he knows from the very beginning that what the thing wants to do is to get to civilization, and what will happen when it gets there. The computer projects the number of *hours* it will take for the world's population to be completely overtaken. Only at the end do MacReady (Kurt Russell) and Chiles (Keith David) realize what Blake knew all along and decide to blow up the compound, leaving us with an uncertainty as to whether the thing has been truly destroyed, and the certainty that they will both freeze to death.

All of this is not to say that the suspense and special effects and excellent acting, writing, and directing have not created spectacular horror in these films, only that the use of science, which has so often caused films to be separated by genre, here enhances the terror to an almost unbearable point. The presence of the science helps to raise these two films to the heights of terror and earn them the brand "classic."

I would also like to note that in any full-length examination of science fiction/horror, Scott's *Blade Runner* could not be ignored. The horror is not so evident here, but many scenes, especially those revolving around Roy Batty (Rutger Hauer), are incredibly chilling. The science is terrifying and the film pays great tribute both to Mary Shelley and James Whale in its *Frankenstein* motifs.

So now I have served my passion.

6

Horror stories on page and screen:

In an interview I dimly remember, Robert R. McCammon explained why he wrote horror. The gist of it was that with horror as an umbrella, you can write about anything: life, death, truth, falsehood, blood, sperm, love, hate. And in any genre from comedy to suspense to western to musical (remember *Sweeney Todd*?). Horror is the literature of life, and horror stories can really be about anything that's a part of life. It's the proximity to reality, the closeness to life that makes the terror real.

Onscreen, there are many tricks of the trade that can be used to enhance the horror: special effects, makeup, music, camera angle, lighting, etc. However, when the studio relies on those techniques at the expense of the story, they create a false horror, a worthless scare. The prime examples of this misfortune are a majority of the filmed works of Stephen King. It's unfortunate that it took so long for people to get around to treating King's work with the correct touch—a lot of good material was wasted. But this happens all the time.

As I write this, movie studios are hoping to make vampire films based on the work of three women in this book: Nancy A. Collins, Anne Rice, and Chelsea Quinn Yarbro. Not to mention the myriad other past and future films by and based upon works by writers in this book. We can only hope that by the time their new films get around to happening, Hollywood will have shaped up, will have learned a lesson that is so implicit in past mistakes.

A message to the film community: Please take full advantage of the wealth of excellent stories that can be found in horror fiction. The people who wrote them knew what they were doing. They know a lot about horror stories or they wouldn't be able to sell books. Believe it or not, they may even know more than you directors and producers.

End of today's lesson.

And now these writers sit in judgment over the celluloid stories. What do they know that the Hollywood types don't? What do they know that you don't?

Turn the page and find out.

Chapter

1

Clive Barker

Yes, but can he sing and dance?

Clive Barker first made a name for himself as a playwright, producing such works as *Frankenstein in Love* and *The Secret Life of Cartoons*. He has since become an industry unto himself: novels, films, comic books, etc. He is also a gifted illustrator. As writer/director, his films include *Hellraiser* and *Nightbreed*, and his books include the six-volume *Books of Blood* (the latter three of which appeared in this country under the titles *The Inhuman Condition*, *In the Flesh*, and *Cabal*) as well as *The Damnation Game*, *Weaveworld*, *The Great and Secret Show*, and *Imajica*.

The first time I met Clive was at a press screening of *Hellraiser*, after which I interviewed him for a local paper. He spoke quite a bit about how film, not only horror film mind you, influenced him. Even claimed not to have nightmares, did Mr. Barker.

"They're all up there," he said, pointing at the screen.

So, really, he's passing those nightmares on to us. Which, in a roundabout way, brings us to the point. How was Clive affected by sharing other people's celluloid nightmares growing up? Did the movies help shape this bizarre mind? Almost certainly.

And how does he feel about it?

"I'm about as depraved as anyone is ever going to get," he gleefully admitted in the above-mentioned interview, "and I'm happy."

Peter Atkins

Born in Liverpool, England, on November 2, 1955, Peter has about him an extraordinarily pleasant manner. Ever helpful and cooperative, supportive and earnest, his personality certainly belies the twisted interior that has produced the screenplays for *Hellbound: Hellraiser 2* and *Hell on Earth: Hellraiser 3*. Since receiving his degree in English literature, he has never held what the Brits would call a "proper" job. He spent five years as an actor with the fringe theater group the Dog Company, alongside his old friend Clive Barker, and another five as a rock-and-roll musician with his band the Chase. These days he writes full-time in fiction, TV, and film. His short fiction has appeared in *Fear* magazine and his comic-book work in Epic Comics' "Hellraiser" series. Two of his teleplays, "The Leda" and "The Freak" have been filmed for the cable-TV show *Inside Out*. His first novel, *Morningstar*, is to be published by Grafton in the UK in the early summer of 1992. Its U.S. release is eagerly awaited.

A personal note: Peter is the author of what is certainly my most oft-quoted piece of film dialogue and what may be my favorite. It's from *Hellbound*. "If you're lying," says Pinhead, "your suffering will be legendary, even in hell." Quite a concept.

Other Shelves, Other Shadows:
A Conversation
(An Interview with Clive Barker)

by Peter Atkins

CLIVE BARKER: Why don't we talk about horror movies which are not horror movies? Movies which ostensibly belong in another category, but which are embraced by the genre? Or that we might want to push kicking and screaming into the genre! There are some very obvious ones—Cronenberg was asked by the Toronto Film Festival to list his top ten horror movies and amongst them he put *Taxi Driver*.

PA: As did Ramsey Campbell for the English magazine *Shock Express*.

CB: Yeah. Same principle.

PA: So—Clive Barker will widen the definition of the horror movie?

CB: Well, he'll list some exceptions to the rule, at least.

PA: And by listing the exceptions, we may come to know the rule, to achieve a definition?

CB: To see some essential elements which might seem important. There's an easy kind of nonhorror horror movie. *Silence of the Lambs:* the thriller that's also a horror movie. Or *Alien:* the SF movie that's also a horror movie.

The crossovers there are very obvious. I'd like to arrive at a list of less obvious examples. Into that list could go a lot of the late Peckinpah pictures. *Bring Me the Head of Alfredo Garcia* is, I think, an extraordinary horror movie: the obsessive elements of the characters, the constant preoccupations with the extremes of physicality and sweat and dirt and filth and degradation and humiliation and all those things which are such a part of so many horror movies.

Then there's something like *The Night Porter*—again, arguably a horror movie. Or *In a Glass Cage*. A Spanish movie. Very grim. Pederasty, Auschwitz . . . A very disturbing movie. Such a weird thing. Not graphic at all. Blood hardly flows, but I think it very clearly has the sensibility of a horror movie. It intends to horrify you. It intends to chill you. It certainly has Hitchcockian moments in it. It has that twisted thing, you know?

PA: In both those films we're being asked to confront the variety of human response to massive horror, to the Holocaust. I agree with your claiming of them for the horror genre, but we need to find a distinction between them and a very violent action thriller.

CB: Well, I'd like to make another distinction first which is between those and *The Pawnbroker* and that distinction is how other movies in what we'll call the atrocity subgenre are *not* horror movies, while those two clearly are. The sensibility behind *The Night Porter* and *In a Glass Cage* is touched by a pleasure being taken by the creators in horrifying people which is entirely admirable. Doug Winter said in his horror/antihorror thing that something has to *intend* to horrify you. But I think there's a further twist on that. There's a kind of horror—the horror of *The Killing Fields,* for example—where they clearly mean you to be horrified but they don't want you to take pleasure in that.

PA: Right. That's the kind of movie—and I don't mean to be reductionist—that confronts you with horror and hopes to produce a *political* response. They want to make you ask political or sociological questions, to look for ways in which it can be put right. The movies you're talking about are different.

CB: Yes. Because they are tinged—dare I say it—by perversity. There's a lot more ambiguity in their response.

PA: And in the response they elicit from us the audience. *The Killing Fields* wants to make you vote correctly while *The Night Porter* wants you to admit something about yourself—admit that perhaps you, too, might respond in the same perverted way in the same circumstances as the characters in the movie.

CB: I think *The Night Porter* also wants . . . There's a certain level at which horror movies toy with you—I've always said that stories are good traps; they trap you into going into a place physically where otherwise you wouldn't go. It's true of horror stories, it's true of erotic stories. They take you somewhere and you look around and say, "Here I am. Whoever would have thought it," you know? And when you do that, you are a little renewed by that experience. They, too, may serve political ends, but they're a lot more buried, a lot more concealed. Anyway, I just wanted to offer that up as a particularly interesting area of . . . We could talk at great length about the thriller and where it abuts the horror arena, but that's not a terribly interesting area to talk about because there are creators there—Hitchcock's the prime, De Palma's another—who are very aware that they're crossing back and forth between genres, between thriller, suspense, and horror, and they make it so obvious that a dialogue about it is going to illuminate nothing. Whereas I don't think people have really examined this art-house picture crossover anywhere near as much. Both *The Night Porter* and *In a Glass Cage* are art-house movies with a veneer of acceptability, but in their gut they're horror movies.

So that's one area, the art-house atrocity picture. Actually, of course, there's also the *Ilsa, She-Wolf of the SS* pictures or whatever they're called. I haven't seen any of those. Are they terrible?

PA: Well, they're certainly badly made. And morally indefensible. The interesting thing, though, is that they would complete the arc I think you're suggesting. If at one end we have *The Killing Fields*, in which there's an assumed consensus of outraged liberalism, and in the middle we have *The Night Porter,* which says "Well, let's examine our response," then at the other end we'd have *Ilsa* and her ilk frankly saying, "We *love* this stuff."

CB: Right, right. Let's try and find other arcs. Let's start with Jodorowsky. I finally saw *Holy Mountain* the other day and it's got some amazingly good things to offer. It's a mescaline movie for sure, but it has some extraordinary things in it. And like *El Topo* and like *Santa Sangre*—which I'm a huge admirer of—it has this unapologetic mingling of religious imagery with the wild stuff and a sprinkling of sociological concerns—the latter shown mostly by its characters being drawn either from the very rich and very decadent or the peasants, the poor, whores, pimps, dwarves, etc. So it's a physical, Fellini-esque, representation of part of its subject.

PA: The absence of the middle class . . . that's interesting. It's a Shakespearean approach—peasants and kings and nothing in between.

CB: Yes. The middle class are redundant to the story because there's no drama in them. One of the most stunning cinematic images of the last five years in my view is the disposal of the elephant corpse in *Santa Sangre*. When the ceremony is over, this great horde of peasants comes down the hill, tears the sarcophagus apart, and begins to merrily dismember the elephant. There's an epic heroic quality to the imagery which is missing in so much else that's out there.

PA: And do you think that dramatic division into the very rich and the very poor is what *allows* the movie the kind of grand poetic symbolist statements that are denied to the middle-class thriller? I mean, thrillers are always middle class because their *audience* is middle class. . . .

CB: Right. And if the thriller *didn't* occupy the middle, it wouldn't thrill. . . .

PA: Because we couldn't identify with it. Sure. And it's true we don't identify with *Santa Sangre* the way we would with . . . I don't know . . . *Jagged Edge* or something but . . .

CB: Well . . . I *do* identify with *Santa Sangre*! (laughs)

PA: Yeah, but it's a poetic identification—the empathy is imaginative, not neurotic. You're identifying with archetypes.

CB: Archetypes is unfair to the movie. The performance he pulls from his son is a delicate, clever, Perkinsesque one—Perkinsesque because the movie is clearly a *Psycho*-riff—and I think we sympathise with him just like we sympathise with Norman.

PA: Right. You know—this is probably a sidebar but we're talking about crossover stuff anyway—I personally prefer *Santa Sangre* to *El Topo,* and I suspect one of the reasons, with all due respect to Jodorowsky, who I venerate as much as you do, is Claudio Argento's involvement. I can almost see him telling Jodorowsky that those arty things are fabulous but can't . . .

CB: Can't we turn it into a *Psycho* riff! Yes! (laughs) Because we do see more "human," more delicate performances in *Santa Sangre* and that probably is to do with its thriller aspects. What's great is the mutual enrichment of that with the almost Mystery-play–like nature of the drama. I always loved the idea of Mystery plays. Of very ordinary, prosaic people conversing with angels. Or playing angels, or God. Anyway, let's spread this argument from just Jodorowsky. Other poetic horrors? Other Mystery-play horrors?

PA: Cocteau? Herzog? Wenders' *Wings of Desire*?

CB: Herzog . . . arguably *Aguirre, Wrath of God* is a horror movie. Certainly *Nosferatu* is a horror movie. These are movies that are very seldom approached the way horror movies are. Herzog kind of went off the boil for me with *Fitzcarraldo*. Wenders I never got.

PA: But *Wings* would fit in with what you're talking about, surely.

CB: But it's a fantasy, not a horror movie.

PA: Sure, but picking up from your Mystery-play comments—you know, the ease of insertion of the miraculous into . . .

CB: Of the metaphysical into the mundane, yeah.

PA: Ordinary people meeting angels who look like ordinary people.

CB: Conversations with the divine in grey Berlin cafés. Absolutely. But sticking with horror, I don't think Wenders connects. Fassbinder, arguably, did produce a couple of pictures which at least tangentially have the flavour of horror movies.

PA: Well, he certainly produced angst movies. You'd say some were more than that?

CB: I think something like *Fox and His Friends* for instance, which is *so* grim, *so* relentless . . . you know, if *Taxi Driver* is a horror movie, then *Fox* should certainly fall into that category. As a vision of hell on earth, *Fox* will do quite nicely, thank you very much. *Querelle,* too, in its way; it's physically a hellish movie. An infernal movie. It's great. An artificial set, a harbour full of phallic forms, and people overtaken by a kind of soporific sexuality—homosexuality in that case—and lounging around sweating, being beaten, and dying violently.

There are more. Jodorowsky. Herzog. Fassbinder. The European art movie is full of stuff that tangentially connects with horror. Franju should be in there, I guess.

PA: Yeah. The obvious ones are *Les Yeux Sans Visage* and *Judex,* but the documentary *Blood of the Beasts* certainly has . . .

CB: An *amazing* movie. Let's bring Bergman in. *Hour of the Wolf* is a horror movie. And one of the grimmest movies I know, a movie that made a profound impression on me, was *Shame;* when they take the boat out at the end and they go through the water and they're pushing the bodies away from the boat, this is the kind of grim, angst-ridden black-and-white stuff which makes *Night of The Living Dead* look like a Marx brothers comedy.

PA: Well, it certainly makes it look more like a drive-in movie, which is what it was. But do I sniff controversy here? Are you saying that that European tradition is "better" than the American horror movie?

CB: No, not at all. All of this is a personal response. I'm simply saying that in its power to disturb *me,* that sort of thing is stronger.

PA: Okay. Then, without being judgmental, can we arrive at some notion of differentiation? Can we, rather than construct a hierarchy, at least *classify*? For example, you mentioned *Taxi Driver* when talking about Fassbinder. Now, *Taxi Driver* is without doubt a bleak vision, at least as bleak as *Fox,* and yet one way we could differentiate between the two would be to acknowledge the catharsis of *Taxi Driver*'s *explosive* climax. Is it more an American tradition to embrace the catharsis, to enjoy the explosion?

CB: I'm not sure. Bergman, in other movies, certainly does give space to a kind of catharsis, to the healing, cleansing climax. Most of his movies have at their heart a solution. *Shame,* though, I chose because it does leave you with the impression that this grim grey landscape goes on *forever*. I guess I must just respond to that more. I must be more moved by that. There's a kind of movie that isn't great fun to *watch*, but leaves you deeply changed. Bergman's pictures fall into that category. They're movies I don't enjoy watching, I've never enjoyed watching, but *boy*, do they leave their mark, you know? Their power lies in . . . at their best they operate in a kind of no-man's-land which American movies tend not to do. American movies tend to be very particular—this year, that place, this day, that dinner, etc.—and their power comes from that particularity. But curiously that also dates them very quickly. European movies—art-house movies, that is—tend to be less specific. They operate in a kind of mythic space.

So what we're doing is talking about horror movies that aren't filed as horror movies. When you go to the video store and you've seen every single adaptation of every single Stephen King book available, when you've seen every Freddy, every Jason, every Hellraiser, what else can you look for to get the same frisson?

PA: Well, is it the *same* frisson? That's why I'm trying to pin you down to definitions or classifications. What *is* it that we're looking for that you think can be found in these wildly disparate movies?

CB: I don't know. Maybe we can arrive at some analysis of it, but all I'm doing is naming those that do it for me. I'm scanning world cinema and picking out personal favourites that seem to me to be in some way *related*. I'm offering enthusiasm, rather than evaluation.

We've looked at European art house, we've looked at the atrocity subgenre. Maybe we should touch upon very extreme forms of thrillers.

And I'm trying to avoid the middle-class-jeopardy pictures. Let's leave Hitchcock out of this. I mentioned *Alfredo Garcia, Taxi Driver*. That's the kind of extreme vision I'm looking for. I'd say that *Marathon Man* is well on its way to being a horror movie. I saw it again recently and I'd forgotten how brutal it is. There's the appalling death of Roy Scheider and there's the scene at the end when Olivier is being pursued through the jewelry district and pulls that blade from his sleeve and slashes the guy. There's also torture—one of the most memorable torture scenes in movie history.

PA: Yes. Specifically because Dustin Hoffman has nothing to offer. He doesn't know what Olivier wants to hear. Traditionally—in war movies, for example—we can admire the stoicism of the hero as he chooses not to give the information. Here, Hoffman has nothing to offer, nothing to make the pain stop.

CB: And it's horrifying because it could be us. We, too, are ignorant and couldn't make the pain stop.

PA: I agree it's a great scene. And a great thriller. But a horror movie? I don't know. *Taxi Driver* I can see. *Marathon Man* is too . . . contained, too specific. Too classical, almost. It's an adventure in which horrifying things may happen. It's a closed world and *we* remain safe. *Taxi Driver* is a hideous vision in which we get lost. It's not just Travis Bickle, it's *everything*. New York is the monster—big, incomprehensible, and malicious. *Taxi Driver*'s horror breaks the bounds of its narrative, while that of *Marathon Man* remains contained.

CB: But I think something else is going on in *Marathon Man*. Here's this innocent guy whose brother is involved in some very unpleasant shit and the innocent is dragged slowly into a recognition that the ordinary world which he's taken for granted can be lethal. His bathroom window is suddenly a means of escape. And he's running along a highway in his pyjamas, terrified, surrounded by cars driven by other ordinary people. Taking William Goldman as the connection—is it any less a horror picture than *Misery,* which is basically about the consequences of a guy having a bad time on the road? What I think Goldman and Schlesinger do brilliantly in *Marathon Man* is show the stain spread—show how big this thing is, how many people are involved. There's another great scene when William Devane arrives; Hoffman and the girl are in a room with several other people and by the end of the scene there are four corpses on the floor. It's this eruption of violence into his little life that I think makes it work. But you're right to differentiate between it and the Scorsese. One is a brilliant entertainment and the other is a genuine deeply felt vision.

PA: Fine, but let's leave that kind of *qualitative* difference alone. It's whether it's a *horror* entertainment or a *thriller* entertainment I'm arguing about. You said you wanted to avoid the middle-class-in-jeopardy and cited Hitchcock, but surely Hoffman's character is absolutely an analogue for Cary Grant in *North by Northwest*? The innocent man gradually caught up in a growing mystery, in growing violence? But perhaps you're right and we should leave analysis to the academics. You've touched on something else very interesting—this notion of the innocent delivered into mystery. That's another area of crossover, isn't it? The hero discovering not only a mundane mystery he has to solve by the end of the picture, but a wider mystery, a metaphorical, perhaps even metaphysical one. What other movies deliver the message that the world is not as simple as we thought it was?

CB: There're all kinds of movies that do that. We could think, for example, of the westerns in which a dead cowboy returns to put things right. *Jacob's Ladder*, too, would fall into that category.

PA: That would be a textbook example, in fact; by solving the mystery of these haunting visions, he solves the mystery of his own life.

CB: Let's stay with the thriller that takes us into far more outlandish territory than we suspect at the outset it's going to and see where the definition of a thriller finishes and the definition of a horror movie begins. It's clear we disagree on *Marathon Man*. Do we disagree on *Boys from Brazil*?

PA: Well, plainly, there's an easier crossover there simply because the premise is slightly *fantastique,* slightly science fictional, but again I'd come back to this concept of . . . imaginative safety. This is in no way a comment on the efficacy or the quality of the movie, but I the viewer, as in *Marathon Man*, feel relatively safe. I'm tense, I'm on the edge of my seat, I respond the way one does to a good thriller, but . . .

CB: I don't disagree with any of that, but I feel that way about most horror movies, sadly. Most horror movies don't invade that personal safety either. Most *movies* don't. The bulk of movies just give you excitement, a good time. It's very rare that they get under your skin. I mean, of all Hitchcock's movies, I can only think of two that get under my skin—*Psycho* and *Vertigo*.

If I have to think about movies that really horrify me . . . De Palma's *Scarface*. If we go to Doug Winter's definition—that something must *intend* to horrify you—then, my God, does that movie work! I broke out into a cold sweat. I didn't want to go into that bathroom, I didn't want to hear those chainsaws. *Chinatown*, too, as well as having elements of classic film noir, also has elements of the horror movie. We talked earlier of the stain spreading, of the mystery getting bigger, and by the end of that movie the whole world seems to be tainted, every power broker horribly corrupt. The violence is notoriously particularised—the nose-slashing, the shooting of Dunaway at the end. *Scarface* is even more horrifying. Simply horrifying, in fact—it doesn't scare, it horrifies. To be scared you have to care about the characters. *Scarface* doesn't ask us to care, it just asks us to watch as these monsters visit cruelties upon one another. It's that relentlessness that forms the bridge, I think. So it's the relentless thriller we're looking for.

PA: Ferrara's *King of New York* seems the latest example. Phenomenally vicious. And phenomenally gleeful in its presentation of that viciousness.

CB: No more gleeful than *Taxi Driver*, I'd say.

PA: Oh, I wouldn't. We made an arc earlier and I think we could make another here. At one end would be *Taxi Driver* with its obsessively observed violence, in the middle *King of New York* with its mix of observation and gleeful indulgence, and at the other end something like *The Cop and the Killer,* one of those fabulous Hong Kong thrillers, which is pure glee, pure indulgence.

CB: That's interesting, but I don't think it quite works. Those Hong Kong movies—which I love as much as you do—are as stylised as cartoons. Both Scorsese and Ferrara would at some level claim to be realists, to be telling it the way it is. So to really complete the arc you'd need some morally indefensible piece of realism, not something as close to pantomime as *The Cop and the Killer*. In fact, I'd say it was *Scarface* that completed the arc. Because there you have the recognisable social milieu, the realism, but it's all padding for genuinely indulgent violence.

But I'm glad you brought the Chinese stuff up because that's a whole other area in our imaginary video store. You can certainly go to that stuff for horror. There's some extraordinary horror images in *Chinese Ghost Story*, for example. That is an amazing movie. All the ones we've talked about are amazing movies. But all different. *In a Glass Cage* could not be more different from *Scarface*, which could not be more different from *Shame*. All I'm saying to our imaginary browser is keep your options open—look everywhere. By classifying yourself as a genre fan, you're probably denying yourself all kinds of different pleasures. We can take this to almost absurd lengths. Let's look at kids' movies, for example. There are movies I saw as a child—and that were made for children—that still produce chills. One thinks of Monstro the whale in *Pinocchio* or the Night on Bald Mountain sequence from *Fantasia*, which is absolutely extraordinary. That's the one piece of pure cinema which I love beyond all others. It contains everything I ever wanted to see in the movies.

PA: Interesting—because, arguably, that's an art-house sequence too. Is *Fantasia* really a kids' movie at all?

CB: It's very art house, true. . . .

PA: Though Mickey's in there, of course. And including him was a stroke of genius on Disney's part; I love *Fantasia,* but I suspect if Mickey wasn't in there to break it up, I'd love it less.

CB: I'd love it for the dancing hippos if nothing else.

PA: Sure. Actually, to pick up on something we talked about earlier, the Mickey sequence is pretty damn nightmarish, too. He's another Cary Grant or Dustin Hoffman—the innocent caught up in a nightmare beyond his understanding or control. But you wanted to talk about Night on Bald Mountain?

CB: I just wanted to celebrate it as a great moment of chilling cinema. And it *is* art house—I mean it was based on drawings by Kay Nielsen, after all, so it is very much in a European tradition.

PA: It was also based on sketches the Disney artists made of Bela Lugosi swirling round in a cape, so it really is a great example of the kind of conflation of ideas and influences you've been talking about.

CB: Right. So the horror fanatic, the lover of the dark, who is fixated on Tom Savini's special effects and passes over *Fantasia* is missing a significant amount. Let me just list other great images to be found on the kids' shelves. The massed flying monkeys from *The Wizard of Oz*. Malificent turning into the dragon in *Sleeping Beauty*. The first emergence of the massive beast in *Dragonslayer*. The massed skeletons in *Jason and the Argonauts*. Talos, the bronze giant from the same movie—wonderfully terrifying.

So Harryhausen is a source for this kind of stuff. Disney is a source for this kind of stuff. Unfortunately, kids' movies of today tend to be too knowing for their stuff to work on that fundamental level—though I would like to give an honourable mention to Large Marge's transformation in *Pee Wee's Big Adventure*! It's comic, of course, but it's tremendous. There were comic elements in tales by Poe. There's nothing to say that the comic and the horrific can't go hand in hand. And that's the one genre that we haven't looked at—comedy. There must be movies which manage successfully to combine the funny and the horrific—though the shelves are full of those terrible self-conscious crossovers which are neither. Can we think of one that works?

PA: *Dead of Night*? The old one, not the recent thing with the same title. It makes it easy for itself by being an anthology, of course, but nevertheless pulls the combination off, I think. The golfing story is merely funny, the ventriloquist story is "merely" terrifying—absolutely bloody terrifying, in fact—but the "room for one more inside" is both funny and chilling.

CB: Yes, I'd agree. And I'm sure there are others we could think of, but frankly, I'm exhausted! (laughs)

PA: Okay. I think you've given us video junkies enough pointers for a few interesting double bills. *In a Glass Cage* and *Pinocchio*, *Bring Me the Head of Alfredo Garcia* and *Fox and His Friends*, *The Wizard of Oz* and *Shame*, *The Night Porter* and *The King of New York*. Clive Barker's guide to what to rent when the horror shelves are empty.

CB: Or what to rent when you've seen every last bugger *on* the horror shelves! My message—as it always was—is don't contain your explorations.

PA: "There are no limits"?

CB: Exactly.

Chapter

2

Stephen R. Bissette

Phil Nutman commonly refers to Steve Bissette and me as "mutated Care Bears." I'd rather not dwell on the implications of that statement. Suffice to say that Steve is a large, furry kind of guy, and I must admit (at the risk of alienating him) that the man's a saint.

The comic-book artist turned writer is best known for his work on "Swamp Thing" and "Taboo," which he edits and publishes, and has recently completed a fantastic "Aliens" novella for Dark Horse Comics. His analysis of film has a clarity of thought that even the most educated film journalist will find enviable.

Now then . . .

To get to Steve's house, you have to drive miles into nowhere, on dirt roads, and know by intuition which turns are right. His house is set back in the woods in a spot reminiscent of half of any random dozen horror movies you might choose. Okay, nothing really abnormal about this. He's a country boy, after all, with his wife and two adorable kids, who love the outdoors. You go inside, everything seems pretty normal—until you see the memorabilia.

Stills, posters, comics. Everything. And then you start talking movies. Literally, Steve has seen thousands of films. Horror, mystery, suspense . . . anything sick from any nation. You name it, Steve's seen it.

And then you think, "I'm miles from anything resembling civilization. . . ." It's not a comforting thought.

Higher Ground: Moral Transgressions, Transcendent Fantasies

by Stephen R. Bissette

"I want to return to horror, but in a spiritual way . . . in the study of horror movies, I don't discover this: they don't know they are in a spiritual sense. They are! We are! You are! Through the madness, through the monster of the unconscious, through death . . . transcendence through death. If somebody could do that, it would be of great importance."

—Alejandro Jodorowsky

The 1980s closed with a number of horror-fantasy films that stand in marked contrast to the nihilism of the modern horror film, particularly the corporeal "splatter" wave that opened the decade. *Flatliners, Jacob's Ladder,* and *Ghost* (all 1990) form a triad that indicated a significant shift in the winds of the pop culture. Constructivist and life affirming in nature, these films moved away from the puritanical ethics of their roots, finding solace and potential in the warmth of the human hand and heart, rather than the cold, impassive frontiers of the stars above.

While hardly profound, for Hollywood product their aspirations were unusually moral. However superficial their accomplishments compared with the deeper resonances of their continental brethren, from Jean Cocteau's *Orphée* (*Orpheus*, 1950) to Wim Wenders' *Wings of Desire* (1987), these vehicles marked an ill-defined but genuine romantic genre movement, exploring the schism between flesh and spirit, aching for transcendence while yearning to cling to the precious emotions of the mortal coil. As we move into the nineties, the final dance into the new millennium, the genre has sought higher ground.

It is time to define and assess this new wave. While fantasy and horror have always been among the most moral of genres (despite the cries from their detractors), this current wave has for the most part eschewed the sacred objects and religious iconography so vital to the gothic traditions. Nor do they address directly the presence of a God or Savior. Unlike the humanistic theology proffered by Martin Scorsese's adaptation of Nikos Kazantzakis' *The Last Temptation of Christ* (1988) or the incarnations of God proposed in the polar extremities of Pier Paolo Pasolini's *Teorema* (*Theorem,* 1968) and Carl Reiner's *Oh, God!* (1977, spawning two sequels, 1980–84), the 1990 triad was concerned with transcendence of the mortal individual rather than belief in God or issues of organized religion. They were Hollywood productions, Judeo-Christian archetypes were inevitably invoked, but these references remain peripheral to the nonsectarian context of the films themselves.

Portraying concepts of heaven and hell that will be identifiable and palatable to both Christian fundamentalists and New Age acolytes, they attempt an opening of the eye and heart, moving from the secular to a spiritual quest for godhead in distinctly humanist terms. The Grim Reaper no longer holds dominion over all. Via the Star Child of Stanley Kubrick's *2001: A Space Odyssey* (1968), the comforting anima mother of David Lynch's *The Elephant Man* (1980), and the angelic chiropractor of Adrian Lyne's *Jacob's Ladder* (1990), the specter of death has given way to redemption via the affirmation of the afterlife and the passion of rebirth.

Why have these fantasies become imperative at this time? David Desser asserts that it is "always in the best interests of the ruling class of succeeding generations to encourage a transcendental view of life," which "can encourage a disbelief in the validity of individual action, a devaluation in the idea of change. Much like the strategy of the medieval Catholic Church, the transcendental promise of a better life in the next world (heaven, nirvana) could defuse cultural tensions and political actions in this one." [1]

The 1980s afterlife fantasies were fueled by societal forces we can now, in hindsight, recognize as being in part *pre*–Gulf War tensions, an emotional wave the carefully orchestrated war effort (and its media coverage) effectively manipulated and sublimated. That effort was terrifyingly successful, and this sublimation informs and suffuses the afterlife fantasies that anticipated and were contemporary to the Gulf War and the current climate of political malaise.

However, the current wave as embodied by *Flatliners* and *Jacob's Ladder* was quite different from that which accompanied World War II, or those current films that slavishly emulate that earlier wave (such as *Ghost* and *Always,* discussed below). Whereas the World War II fantasies were sectarian (overtly Christian) and nonhorrific in their

1. David Desser, *Eros Plus Massacre*, Indiana University Press, 1988, p. 20.

orientation, sharing very specific wartime agendas as their dramatic focus, the current trend is unable to galvanize similar emotions and concerns because America's *denial* of those emotions and concerns is so pervasive. Hence, the fictional (i.e., fantasy and horror movies) and nonfictional (the news) media are unable to work with the smooth, cooperative precision of the World War II propaganda machine. While the militaristic fantasies of the *Star Wars* trilogy, *Rambo* machismo, and the specified recruitment fantasy of Tony Scott's *Top Gun* (1986) have proven effective propaganda, many of the afterlife fantasies peculiar to the nineties have quietly become, perhaps, subversive to the ends Desser describes.

While *Ghost* and *Always* certainly fit Desser's definition, *Jacob's Ladder, Flatliners,* and eighties precursors like *Resurrection* and *Brainstorm* do not. *Jacob's Ladder* was particularly subversive in this regard: its subplot concerning military experimentation upon U.S. infantrymen with psychosis-inducing hallucinogens overtly fed on jaundiced post–Vietnam War and Watergate fears that are contrary to the patriotic propagandistic goals Desser refers to, even as it empha-sized the helplessness of the individual in the grip of authoritarian power. "Sometimes I think it would be a lot easier being dead," observes one of the dispassionate teenagers of Tim Hunter's *River's Edge* (1988), an observation *Jacob's Ladder* and its ilk (including black comedies like *Beetlejuice*) obsessively refute, undermining the populist narcotic Desser accurately defines.

The most conventional, regressive, and successful film of the trio was Jerry Zucker's *Ghost:* as such, it rigorously avoids any confronta-tion with questions of God or religion, or antiauthoritarian subtexts. *Ghost*'s romantic fantasy shares common roots with *Wings of Desire* and especially Steven Spielberg's *Always* (1989), while the divine retribution inherent in its shadow demons and the fates of its villains touches the more horrific bedrock *Flatliners* and *Jacob's Ladder* spring from. As Bruce Joel Rubin wrote both *Ghost* and *Jacob's Ladder*, their shared precepts were no surprise.

Ghost tells the tale of an unmarried couple, Sam Wheat (Patrick Swayze) and Molly Jensen (Demi Moore, on the heels of averting a biblical apocalypse through personal sacrifice in Carl Schultz's *The Seventh Sign,* 1989). Young, affluent, and very much in love, their relationship is emotionally and physically strong (emphasized by Molly's tactile profession as a potter and sculptor, linked with the film's lovemaking sequence). However, Molly remains troubled by Sam's aversion to commitment, or even declarations of love. They are tragically separated by Sam's murder, unknowingly provoked by his discovery during accounting duties of $4 million in illegal laundered drug funds his friend and bank coworker Carl Brunner (Tony Goldwyn) had secreted in various accounts.

Now an intangible, invisible presence, Sam struggles to communicate with Molly and protect her from yuppie Carl and his impoverished hired assassin (Rick Aviles). Sam is aided by an ugly subway spirit (Vincent Schiavelli) who teaches Sam how to physically interact with the material world, and by a phony spiritualist (Whoopi Goldberg) whose latent medium abilities allow Sam to contact Molly. With the medium's help, Sam rescues Molly, causing the death of both Carl and his hired killer (whose own spirits are then dragged screaming into oblivion by formless shadow beings), savoring a final dance and kiss with his beloved before being spirited away into the afterlife.

Ghost streamlined and reinterpreted one of our most venerable cultural fairy tales, that of a love between man and woman that transcends death itself. Rubin's script avoided the fatalism of Fritz Lang's *Der Mude Tod* (*Weary Death*, a.k.a. *Destiny* and *Between Worlds*, 1921) and *Liliom* (1934), and tempered the ethereal, sorrowful romanticism of Henry Hathaway's *Peter Ibbetson* (1935), William Dieterle's *A Portrait of Jennie* (1949), Jeannot Szwarc's *Somewhere in Time* (1980, from Richard Matheson's novel *Bid Time Return*), and their kind into a gratifying immediacy that obviously satisfied contemporary audiences (though Sam awaits Molly in the afterlife, they are not denied a final kiss). *Ghost*'s upbeat, passionate confection of romantic fantasy and manipulative suspense thriller proved surprisingly effective. Despite the transparency of intent and content, the persuasive synthesis of story, performers, and director intoxicated the masses.

Ghost was a pop synthesis of elements cannibalized from the past, recalling nonhorrific romantic ghost comedies like Norman Z. MacLeod's *Topper* (1937, spawning two sequels, 1939–41, a TV series in the 1950s, and a remake, 1980) and its kind. *Ghost* also tapped the World War II and post-war romanticism of Alexander Hall's *Here Comes Mr. Jordan* (1941) and Victor Fleming's patriotic *A Guy Named Joe* (1943; both produced by Everett Riskin), and their angelic ilk, from *I Married an Angel* (1942), *The Horn Blows at Midnight*, *The Angel Comes to Brooklyn* (both 1945), and Frank Capra's *It's a Wonderful Life* (1946) to Jan Kadar's *The Angel Levine* (1970) and Michael Landon's 1980s TV series *Highway to Heaven*.

Though the popularity of the 1940s' ghost and angel romances was obvious, "Hollywood fantasy of this period was . . . bland and cosy. Instead of the wonder, the exaltation and sometimes the real menace that characterizes the best of fantasy, Hollywood was offering ersatz substitutes that neither disturb nor exhilarate." [2] *Ghost* complemented its derivative nature with tantalizing glimmers of imagination (the point-of-view perceptions of passing through organic flesh-and-blood human bodies or the fibrous wood of doors, the out-of-body death experiences, etc.), but it essentially remained as ersatz as its predecessors.

Steven Spielberg's *Always* (1989) was, in fact, a remake of Fleming's *A Guy Named Joe,* reincarnating and reinventing the attitudes and specifics of the World War II fantasies with self-referential obsessiveness. The urgency of the original (which was otherwise a slight affair, despite its "classic" status) was lost when shorn of its wartime setting, trivializing Spielberg's remake. *A Guy Named Joe*'s dead fighter pilot (Spencer Tracy) returned to invisibly train his replacement and romantic rival (Van Johnson) for war; Spielberg's conceit replaces the wartime scenario with daring forestry service pilot Pete (Richard Dreyfuss) losing his life while fighting a forest fire and returning to train *his* nominal replacement and romantic rival (Brad Johnson).

Both versions reflect the desire to provide their audiences with spiritual comfort during troubled times, but Fleming's concoction was fueled by its wartime audience's *need* to vicariously confront the toll of the war, assuring them that there was *not* a futile finality in the loss of loved ones, alleviating the guilt of women who nurtured relationships after the loss of their husbands or boyfriends, deifying the spirit of the American warrior and the necessity for teamwork. Spielberg, however, was unable to create a suitable replacement for these concerns; though completed in an atmosphere of tensions that led to the Gulf War, the fire-fighting scenario (Spielberg's ineffectual surrogate for World War II) failed to galvanize such volatile tensions in any manner. The result proved a more remote experience than *Ghost,* reflected by its box-office failure: *Ghost* clearly provided a more accessible mirror and balm for the fears and longings that concerned a generation facing the specter of AIDS and the impending closure of the century.

A more specific comparative scrutiny of the two films is telling. Where *Always* was inherently *selfless,* an elegiac and comparatively

2. Peter Nicholls, *The World of Fantastic Films: An Illustrated Survey*, Dodd, Mead & Co., 1984, p. 24.

introspective meditation on the regret and relinquishing of love lost, *Ghost* was an aggressive and extroverted *selfish* fantasy, reveling in the consummation of spiritual and physical love with a tangible interactive immediacy. *Ghost* was virile, violent, told in broad strokes, where *Always* was leisurely, layered, and nuanced with its melancholy romance essentially passive in nature despite the intensity of its fire-fighting sequences. These fiery highlights were tempered by the inherent *selflessness* of such a profession. The occupations informing *Ghost* were less incendiary, but the world of banking, money, and covertly laundered criminal dollars was more readily identifiable to yuppie audiences, the struggle against human greed and avarice more vicariously exciting than battling the elemental force of fire in a profession that promised no tangible material gain.

The narrative devices in *Ghost* and *Always* were remarkably similar, though consistently to opposite ends: the ritualistic celebration of the lovers' dance, their beloved song (both nostalgic standards), and the hunger for the male partner to say "I love you"—spoken but never heard in *Always* (drowned out by Pete's aircraft's engines as he departs on the fatal flight), tearfully spoken, heard, and reciprocated in *Ghost*'s finale. The ghost lore was identical: both see the recently deceased, both can be seen by cats (which react with pleasure in *Always* and with fear in *Ghost*). Since the cats weren't proper familiars (an implicit rejection of the supernatural devices of witchcraft), living humans must act as mediums, accomplished in *Always* during an eerie interlude with a crazed hobo (Roberts Blossom) able to hear and repeat Pete's statements, while *Ghost*'s medium is a pivotal character providing the means for the lovers' reconciliation and consummation. Pete's rival and replacement was a decent, handsome, sympathetic fellow, deserving of Pete's behind-the-scenes efforts to bring the living lovers together; *Ghost*'s romantic rival was scum, with Sam struggling to warn Molly of his evil nature and ultimately (if inadvertently) killing him.

The values embodied in *Always* were arguably those belonging to an earlier generation, anachronistic to audiences of the nineties. *Always*'s guardian angel Hap (Audrey Hepburn) proclaims "anything you do for yourself is a waste of spirit," and assures Pete he's "such a *good* man . . . we don't send back the other kind." *Ghost* opted for clear-cut and confrontational melodrama, depicting the horrifying damnation of "the other kind" (Carl and his hit man) as a judgmental comeuppance, and replacing the radiantly feminine Hap and her doctrine with the grotesque subway ghost who teaches Sam how to interact with the material plane with often violent consequences—a more satisfying male fantasy. Sam's efforts to protect Molly and to cement their love was also a gratifying patriarchal fantasy; Pete's unobtrusive aid to his lover (Holly Hunter) and decision to free her to live with the man she gravitates to after Pete's death ("I'm releasing you. . . . I'm moving out of your heart. Go on") were sentiments *Ghost* vigorously refuted. Pete's farewell statement—"The love we hold back is the only pain that follows us here"—was contradicted by Sam's possessive declaration: "It's amazing . . . the love inside . . . you take it with you." *Ghost* had its cake and ate it, too, a doctrine the nineties audiences preferred to *Always*'s selfless code.

A richer contemporary of *Ghost* was Anthony Minghella's *Truly, Madly, Deeply* (1991); the premise was, in fact, identical, though its ambience and conclusions proved refreshingly contrary to *Ghost*'s conventional bid for audience tears and catharsis. Central to their differences is *Truly, Madly, Deeply*'s commitment to its heroine Nina (Juliet Stevenson), who is obsessed and grieving for her dead lover Jamie (Alan Rickman), nurturing the solitude that allows her obsession to become all-encompassing. While *Ghost*'s drama revolved around Molly, much of it happened apart from her, or *to* her; she is the focus of Sam's obsession, from whose spirit of view *Ghost* is told.

Nina's story maintains its focus with its female protagonist: when Jamie's spirit is manifested playing his cello to her piano rendition of Bach, he becomes the corporeal embodiment of her own fantasy of his return. Thereafter, he (and a bevy of spirit friends) become an intrusive presence in Nina's life, and Minghella lovingly, humorously details Nina's gradual disenchantment with their relationship, as her dream-come-true becomes a banal, domestic reality: "She's forced to confront, in the most concrete way, what it would really mean to live the rest of her life with a dead guy as her significant other."[3] *Truly, Madly, Deeply* turns the romantic conceit of *Ghost* over to reveal its underbelly, performing a necessary and truly adult dissection with the disarming precision and charm of a drawing-room comedy. At one point, Nina is confronted by a group of Jamie's undead friends gathered around her television, watching videos of classic Hollywood romances and mouthing the dialogue: an accurate caricature of the audiences who wallowed in the regressive romanticism of the eighties afterlife retreads.

3. Terrence Rafferty, "The Current Cinema: Romantic," *The New Yorker*, May 6, 1991, p. 83.

Wim Wenders's *Wings of Desire* provided similarly tender revisions of the archetypal angel fantasies, reinventing the form with revelatory depth and texture. In modern Berlin, the citizenry is overseen by benevolent angels who lovingly tend their mortal flock, easing human burdens with passive intervention: their presence is felt as a "sense of well-being." Touching their foreheads to mortals, they offer encouragement, introspection, consolation, and love.

Wings of Desire's guardian angel Damiel (Bruno Ganz) tires of doing "no more than observe, collect, testify, and preserve," longing to *become* a human being. "I'd like to feel there's some weight to me," he confides to his fellow eternal Cassiel (Otto Sander), "to end my eternity and bind me to earth." Damiel forsakes eternity after nurturing a deep affection with Marion (Solveig Dommartin), an acrobat in a poverty-stricken circus, and discovering an actor (Peter Falk) who was once an angel himself and harbors no regrets over his decision to become human. Damiel "dies" and is reborn on the streets of Berlin as a derelict, possessing a coat of armor (which he promptly pawns for clothes and a little money) and able to see colors for the first time, as angels can only see in black-and-white. He seeks out and finds Marion, while Cassiel broods—for his inability to rescue a suicide, for the loss of his fellow angel, an eternal friendship suddenly transformed and rendered finite. Wenders's conclusion bonds Damiel with Marion, savoring humanity and the consummation of his love for her ("I . . . know now what no angel knows"), as a disconsolate Cassiel looks down on his former ally and his beloved city.

"I've always imagined that it had to be rather terrible to be an angel . . . [how] privileged people are that they can taste, feel the rain on their faces, drink coffee, touch somebody; whereas the poor angels cannot,"[4] Wenders said, a perspective reinforced by both Ganz's performance and the plasticity of the medium itself. The film is predominantly in black-and-white, limiting our perceptions to those of the angels: Damiel's merging with the human plane is shared by the film, first blossoming into color when Marion bares her shoulders (she thinks, "desire to love!"), subtly interweaving fleeting moments of color (some of which emphasize the banality of human existence: one color shot lingers upon a laundromat, savoring its ordinariness) until Damiel makes his irrevocable transition into human existence. After the

4. Quoted from Vincent J. Bossone's review of *Wings of Desire* in *Cinefantastique* (19:1–2), January 1989, p. 110.

transformation, only Cassiel's interludes return to black-and-white, rendered impressionistic and frightening after his failure to prevent the suicide.

In a marvelous climactic sequence, the orchestration of black-and-white and color condenses and reasserts itself as Cassiel watches Damiel moving toward his fateful romantic meeting with Marion in a noisy, crowded Berlin rock nightclub. The stage lights flickering over the band spill over the audience, their strobing rendering Damiel and the crowd monochromatic until he moves into the warm, orange light of the bar Marion frequents. Where *Ghost*, *Always*, and *Jacob's Ladder* rely on nostalgic pop songs to emphasize their unions and reunions, *Wings of Desire*'s lovers unite to the dirgelike strains of Nick Cave and the Bad Seeds' "From Her to Eternity," counterpointing both their bonding and Cassiel's melancholy.

Wenders appropriately dwells on the pleasures of the tactile: touch, and the longing to touch, quietly define the pulse of the narrative. Falk's humanized angel voiced Wenders's little joys: a cup of coffee, the touch of a hand, even of one's own, all to be savored. Telling, too, that the consummation of Damiel and Marion's love remained offscreen: Wenders prefers us to hear of the experience in Damiel's words ("I learned amazement last night . . . only the amazement about the two of us—the amazement about man and woman—only that made a human being of me"), savoring the transformation rather than the consummation.

Wenders's angels only occasionally manifest wings (as in the opening images, and during Marion's dream of Damiel) and are able to see into the past, like Nicholas Roeg's *The Man Who Fell to Earth* (1976), himself a fallen angel in fashionable seventies science-fictional guise. Cassiel continually glimpses the war-torn Berlin of the Second World War—an evocative and caustic reference to the era that popularized the American angel fantasies *Wings of Desire* drew from, contrasting the propagandistic vigor of those films with glimpses of dead infants and children lying in the rubble, imagery distinctly adverse to the pop-cultural subtext Desser ascribes to the genre. At another point, however, Damiel and Cassiel muse over the memory of the first protohuman ("Do you remember how, one morning, out of the savanna . . . the biped appeared, our long-awaited image?"), delighting in its minutiae. Their wistful existence is punctuated by the moments children and old people *do* see them, and by their omniscient listening to the ever-flowing stream of human thought: a marvelous narrative device by turns moving and hilarious, lending a novelistic depth of insight into even the sketchiest characterizations. The warmth and depth of *Wings of Desire* set it apart from the rest of its *fantastique* kin, its rich, bemused, and sensual assessment of what it is to be human communicated with heartfelt and poignant conviction.

Though *Wings of Desire* and *Truly, Madly, Deeply* were clearly superior accomplishments, they were atypical of their time. *Ghost* and *Always* typified the romantic fantasies dominating the close of the eighties, recalling those of the forties and embracing their nostalgic yearnings with an adolescent zeal. The seventies had closed with similar derivations, with Warren Beatty and Buck Henry's *Heaven Can Wait* (1978), a witty remake of *Here Comes Mr. Jordan*, probably the best of them. Most were vapid retreads of the earlier generation's angel and ghost fare, including *Kiss Me Goodbye* (1982), *The Heavenly Kid*, *Bliss* (both 1986), *Date with an Angel, Da* (both 1988), *Made in Heaven, Chances Are* (both 1989), *Almost an Angel, Ghost Dad* (both 1990), and Bo and John Derek's inevitable *Ghosts Can't Do It* (1990).

Others proffered revisionist visions of the afterlife borrowed from *Outward Bound* (1930) and its remake *Between Two Worlds* (1944), Shangri-la's heaven-on-earth in Frank Capra's marvelous rendition of James Hilton's *Lost Horizon* (1937), or Michael Powell's remarkable *A Matter of Life and Death* (1946, U.S. title: *Stairway to Heaven*), a quirky and original fantasy romance that reflected the WWII British tensions, hopes, and fears with more visionary audacity than *A Guy Named Joe* could hope to muster. Their descendants, however, were a strangely diffuse breed, preferring to reflect the Reagan era's nostalgic "promise" of a return to a prior generation's values (still a balm during the imperialist George Bush regime) rather than reflecting and confronting the real issues of their *own* generation. *A Guy Named Joe* and *A Matter of Life and Death* were fantastic confections, but they were more honest mirrors of their time than the eighties breed.

W. P. Kinsella's *Shoeless Joe* was the source novel for Phil Alden Robinson's giddy slice of fantasy Americana, *Field of Dreams* (1989). Evocative of Frank Capra, Ray Bradbury, and Rod Serling, the film was almost fey in its wistful devotion to America's most beloved sport as Everyman's heaven-on-earth: the pitcher's mound as higher ground. An ethereal voice prompts Iowa farmer Ray Kinsella (Kevin Costner) to court financial ruin for himself and his family, plowing prime cash-crop corn under to build a professional baseball field in its place. The baseball diamond becomes a Shangri-la for long-dead scandalized baseball legends: Shoeless Joe (Ray Liotta) and his fellow White Sox materialize to enjoy games denied them in life, melting into the bordering rows of corn between afterlife innings. *Field of Dreams* was brash and buoyant enough to brace its peculiar (if shared) male baseball fantasies against the grim realities of Midwestern farm foreclosure evictions and the melancholy of squandered dreams, a soothing inversion of John Sayles's embittered *Eight Men Out* and Costa Gavras' scathing *Betrayed* (both 1988). Kinsella indeed succeeds in building heaven and is allowed to savor a handshake and game of catch with his dead father, resurrected in his youthful prime and finally fulfilling his dream of playing ball with the majors. *Field of Dreams* personified the afterlife fantasy as wish fulfillment, just as the unusual coda of Robert Benton's otherwise nonfantasy *Places in the Heart* (1984) presented an ethereal church communion uniting characters torn by the racism, poverty, and violence inherent in its 1930s Depression Texas. Such gratification is, of course, implicit in the very concept of heaven.

Other cinematic afterlives were more caustic, blurring the comforting distinctions between heaven and hell. There was little reassurance to be found in the dreamy cloudscape a romantic clerk (Jonathan Pryce) escaped to after being tortured by the dystopian police state of Terry Gilliam's *Brazil* (1985), or the welfare office horrors of Tim Burton and Michael McDowell's *Beetlejuice* (1988), wherein suicides are condemned to work *behind* the counters. The sterile, anxiety-ridden bureaucratic judgment system imposed upon all souls in Albert Brooks's *Defending Your Life* (1991) and the buffoonery of *Bill and Ted's Bogus Journey* (1991) tempered their revisionist afterlives with broader humor, but the undertones were no less cynical.

The disorienting variety of perspectives presented in Diane Keaton's *Heaven* (1987) are even more remarkable. *Heaven*'s impressionistic collage of film clips and interviews chronicled the rapture attached to afterlife fantasies with an amusing, absurdist affection. More typical were the banal pseudo-documentaries that cheaply dramatized "true life" after-death experiences, which *Heaven*, *Defending Your Life*, and *Beetlejuice* gleefully roasted. Rolf Olson's *Journey into the Beyond* (1973) typified the tabloid sensibilities shared by *Beyond Belief* (1976), *Beyond and Back* (1978), *Death: The Ultimate Mystery* (1975), *The Occult Experience* (1987), and the like. The stock imagery of these testimonials—moving through a dark passageway toward and into a divine light, the beckoning presence of other souls, etc.—were appropriated by shrill exercises like Tobe Hooper's *Poltergeist* (1982), enhanced by the state-of-the-art special effects breathlessly melding genuinely affecting evocations of the afterlife (at that time, trademarks of producer Steven Spielberg's cinematic style) with grisly explosions of the horrific. Ultimately, *Poltergeist* renders such manifestations and intrusions of the spirit world as a source of horror, the emotional trappings of the traditional ghost story writ large as a Spielberg spectacle.

In contrast to *Poltergeist*'s undigested fear and awe of the afterlife, the coda of David Lynch's fictionalized biography of John Merrick, *The Elephant Man* (1980), was truly transcendent. Lynch's chronicle of the life of Merrick (John Hurt), a hideously deformed young man who harbored a sensitive, intelligent sensibility that was allowed to blossom once he was rescued from a lifetime of freak-show exploitation, vaulted the audience through Merrick's eyes into the afterlife at the moment of his death. It was a startlingly visionary finale to a predominantly naturalistic narrative, though anticipated by Lynch's first feature *Eraserhead* (1976)—in which the title character (Jack Nance) escapes the film's nightmare world through apparent death and joins the deformed Radiator Lady (Laurel Near) in a radiant, if perverse, afterlife—and echoed in Lynch's later *Twin Peaks* (1989–91) and *Wild at Heart* (1990). Precedent also lay in Kubrick's *2001: A Space Odyssey*, and particularly Luis Buñuel's volatile *Los Olvidados* (1951; U.S. title *The Young and the Damned*): as one of Buñuel's brutalized urchins dies, an image of flowing water rushes over his face as his statement, "I am alone," is answered by a woman's voice, "As always, my son." The moment is punctuated by the superimposed image of a dog scurrying into the darkness, a transition anticipated (as in *The Elephant Man*) by a subjectively presented dream that interrupts the otherwise harrowing realism of the film. Unlike Buñuel, Lynch grants his hero solace in the beyond: clouds give way to stars rushing past us and a woman's indistinct features, as the tender voice of his anima, the mother he never knew but always loved, whispers a verse to him:

> When will the clouds be aweary of fleeting?
> When will the heart be aweary of beating—and nature die?
> Never, oh never, nothing will die.

The stream flows, the wind blows,
The cloud fleets, the heart beats,
Nothing will die.[5]

Daniel Petrie's extraordinary drama *Resurrection* (also 1980) reflected and amplified the quiet humanism of Lynch's coda and stands as a heartfelt sui generis classic. Its only special effects proffered an afterlife identical to that of *Beyond and Back*'s testimonials: when Edna Mae McCauley (Ellen Burstyn) dies in a car accident that also claims her husband's life, she is drawn down through the darkness to a blinding light harboring deceased friends and relatives who welcome her, until she's wrenched back into her now-crippled body to awaken in a hospital bed. After her resurrection, Edna is taken by her solemn father (Roberts Blossom) back to rural Kansas, stopping on the way at the remote Last Chance gas station, where its dreamy-eyed, impassioned owner, Esco Brown (Richard Farnsworth), stirs her spirits. They continue to her family home, where Edna manifests a mystical ability to heal, using it to heal herself and opening it to others during weekly sessions. Though she invokes scripture at times, Edna refuses to exploit her gift to preach the gospel; "If there's anything holy here," she insists, "it's just the simple holiness of *love*, that's all." The narrative appropriately dwelled on the apparent divinity of her powers, but in a nonsectarian manner that refutes organized religion's proprietary claim upon or condemnation of manifestations of human divinity. Whereas Edna's grandmother considers Edna's powers "God's work," Edna responds, "I don't know very much about God," and her actions confirm this. Her refusal to adopt conventional, dogmatic religious perspectives in questioning and utilizing her healing abilities, offering them in the name of love rather than the patriarchal God, brings down the ire of her father and eventually provokes the murderous wrath of her slightly unbalanced lover (Sam Shepard) in the film's more melodramatic affectations.

Edna abandons her attempts to cope with such rigid dogma, and her cooperation with medical research proves equally destructive, nearly claiming her life after the traumatic healing of a woman (Sylvia

5. I am sorry to say, I have been unable to identify the author or source of this verse in time for this publication. Note how this verse reverberates through the haunting, enigmatic verse recited by the ethereal child-woman Jennie (Jennifer Jones) in *Portrait of Jennie* (1949): "Where I come from/ Nobody knows;/ And where I'm going/ Everything goes./ The wind blows,/ The sea flows—/ Nobody knows."

Walden) contorted by muscular disease. In the moving epilogue, Edna has found a haven in her autumn years as the lone owner of the Last Chance gas station. Her brief interaction with a vacationing family whose young boy is ravaged by cancer tenderly ends the film: she hugs the child, secretly healing his fatal illness with a loving, selfless embrace.

Grounded throughout by Burstyn's compelling portrayal of Edna, *Resurrection* self-effacingly maintained an earnest dignity, refusing to martyrize its heroine. The Dionysian struggle between religion and science was played out in strictly humanistic terms on a personalized arena, avoiding the genre flourishes usually imposed on such material. In fact, *Resurrection* implemented a sly understated reversal of genre archetypes: the Texan Last Chance gas station harbored a spiritually centered hermit (Farnsworth) rather than the fiends of *The Texas Chainsaw Massacre* (1974) or *The Hills Have Eyes* (1977), promising sanctuary and redemption rather than dread and sudden death. Edna is resurrected not as the soulless, vengeful zombie of a Boris Karloff thirties or forties horror vehicle, but as a warm, loving woman gifted with healing powers, miraculously in tune with the mysteries of life and death as a restorer, not a destroyer, of health and life. Ultimately, *Resurrection* was seminal in its rejection of traditional religious and generic values, embracing an ennobling, courageous vision of life's— and the afterlife's—potential.

In marked contrast to *Resurrection* and the implicit optimism of the wartime and postwar fantasies, the horror and science-fiction genres clung to the somber, moralistic dread invoked by the God of the Old Testament, values *Resurrection* confronted and rejected through the characters of Edna's fundamentalist father and fanatical boyfriend. The same year that *Resurrection* was released to indifferent box office, Ken Russell's sensationalistic eye-drugging rendition of Paddy Chayefsky's *Altered States* (1980) was a popular success. As in *Resurrection*, the "message" was that selfless love grounds and binds spirit and flesh, but Chayefsky's moral rings hollow in the wake of his own pastiche of Robert Louis Stevenson's *Dr. Jekyll and Mr. Hyde* and New Age novels like Michael Murphy's *Jacob Atabet* (1977), by way of John C. Lilly, Carlos Casteñeda, lurid fifties fare like *The Neanderthal Man* (1953), and *Monster on the Campus* (1958), and *The Outer Limits'* episode "The Sixth Finger" (October 14, 1963). Chayefsky vehemently disowned Russell's film, but the fault does not lie with Russell, who properly embraced the novel's excesses with operatic zeal, making the delirious visions and visceral organic transformations Dr. Eddie Jessup (William Hurt) endures the spectacular core of the narrative. The fault lies rather with Chayefsky's moralist conclusion: Jessup's introspective visionary quest ends in the inhuman, absolute zero of the void. He would be damned and destroyed were it not for the unconvincing and glib finale, differing from the tragic end Dr. Jekyll met only in that Jessup is redeemed by the love of his devoted woman (Blair Brown). For all the lip service paid to progressive spiritual transformation of the self, *Altered States* still bound the human spirit to a puritanical dogma; the author's conviction that Jessup's quest was inherently *wrong* fettered its narrative to Victorian moral attitudes as old as Stevenson's *Dr. Jekyll and Mr. Hyde* or Mary Shelley's *Frankenstein*.

The almost divine retribution exacted against Dr. Frankenstein (Colin Clive) in James Whale's *Frankenstein* (1931) for daring to create new life from the dead embodies the fervor and convictions that would dominate both genres well into the sixties, as a vengeful and jealous God punished all mad visionaries—mad scientist and faith healer alike—who dared tread where angels feared to go. The success of *Frankenstein*, and the guidelines imposed by the Motion Picture Production Code until 1967, perpetuated the genre's rigid moral structure, with Boris Karloff, the actor forever identified with the role of Frankenstein's monster, the iconic teacher of the pop culture's morality lessons. In film after film his tampering with (or falling victim to others' tampering with) God's dominion over life and death exacted a procession of grievous punishments.

Of all the Karloff films, Edward Dmytryk's eerie *The Devil Commands* (1941) is most relevant here, foreshadowing both *Flatliners* and especially *Brainstorm*, as well as Peter Newbrook's compelling *The Asphyx* (1972). Based on William Sloane's novel *The Edge of Running Water, The Devil Commands* stars Karloff as a widowed college professor who invents a device that electronically records human brain activity, allowing communication with the dead through living human subjects used as "psychic conductors," with the goal, of course, to establish contact with his dead wife. The process kills its host subjects: Karloff keeps the bodies encased in their helmet devices in a seancelike circle. Desperation drives him to use his own daughter (Amanda Duff), who escapes in the predictably cataclysmic finale as unleashed electrical and occult energies destroy Karloff and his experiments. Dmytryk sustained an atmosphere of dread and sorrow before the formulaic contrivances asserted themselves (complete with a lynch mob for the climax). Conceptual predecessors to the technologies of *Brainstorm*, the iron maiden–like helmets eloquently embodied the fusion of science and occultism. The climactic violence reinforced this thematic ambience with an effective display of otherworldly energies, suddenly coalescing into a palpable, kinetic vortex that consumes Karloff and his cadaverous conductors.

Though they are separated by over twenty years, there is little difference between the punitive message delivered by *The Devil Commands* and Roger Corman's moralistic science-fiction horror film *X— The Man With the X-Ray Eyes* (1963). Again, a scientist dared to trespass on God's domain (cynically manifest in the evangelist's tent of the finale) and suffered terribly for his transgressions. Like the later *Altered States*, the introspective quest of *X* ends with the perception of a cold, inhuman void. (Production Code restrictions and Corman's cynical worldview allowed no redemption through love.)

Professor Xavier (Ray Milland) creates a chemical that enhances vision itself. Able to peer deeper into the world around him, Xavier is forced into seclusion, isolated from friends, associates, and human society. His visionary capabilities evolve further until he is virtually blind to the tactile world around him, eventually unable to perceive anything but its furthest reaches: suns, moons, the cosmos itself. He finally stumbles into a Christian revival tent speaking of his visions, the horrified preacher (John Dierkes) responding to his plaintive heresies with the biblical invocation, "If thine eye offend thee, pluck it out!" In a shocking final freeze frame, Milland does just that (an apocryphal rumor postulates that Corman cut a chilling coda line, "I can *still see!*"—though there is no real evidence to support the claim).

Incredibly, nothing produced during the two decades that separate *The Devil Commands* and *X* dared to propose any alternative to such moral platitudes: horror and science fiction remained a regressive bastion for fearful Christian religious dogma. That the obsession, transgression, and penalty in *X* involved *visionary* ability rather than Frankensteinian life after death elevated the theme to a provocative new level and marked the digression that would allow cinematic science fiction to celebrate the rebirth of man through the fetal Star Child of *2001: A Space Odyssey* the same year the horror genre mired itself in the dread birth of *Rosemary's Baby* (1968), emblematic of damnation rather than redemption.

Corman's *The Trip* (1967) was a nominal thematic extension of *X*, reflecting (though unable to fully embrace) the Aquarian aspirations of its target counterculture youth audience. Sadly, *The Trip*'s attempts to bring LSD-spawned psychedelic visions to the screen were crude and archaic at best, ultimately alienating or provoking derisive laughter from "experienced" young audiences. If *The Trip* embodied a healthy thematic progression (in Corman's original cut, Peter Fonda's hero benefits from his "trip," though the film's distributors tampered with the film before release), it also typified an inherent inability to share and sensually visualize that progression. The filmmakers would have to become as visionary as their fictional protagonists.

The necessary cinematic gestalt exploded from a group of film artists who shared the countercultural fascination with altered perceptions and mysticism, laboring in relative obscurity to create truly visionary nonnarrative "trips." Anticipated by and growing out of the underground cinema movement (particularly the films of Maya Deren, Kenneth Anger, Stan Brakhage, and animations by Harry Smith and Stan VanDerBeek), the "expanded cinema" of Jordan Belson, Scott Bartlett, and the Whitney family is most relevant, if only for the impact their abstract animation shorts (and the ground-breaking use of computers to achieve these meditative visions) had upon mainstream American cinema. Belson's *Allures* (1961), *Re-Entry* (1964), *Phenomena* (1965), *Samadhi* (1967), and *Momentum* (1969), specifically paved the way for *2001*'s most breathtaking nonnarrative passages.[6]

Stanley Kubrick's *2001: A Space Odyssey* was *the* visionary breakthrough production in mainstream narrative cinema, an audacious melding of pragmatic science fiction and experiential metaphysics. The contact with extraterrestrial intelligence postulated by *2001* successfully embodied the dictum of its author, Arthur C. Clarke, that a truly advanced technology would be indistinguishable from magic—herein, it was indistinguishable from the afterlife, the delirious voyage through the Stargate ending in a heaven portrayed as a sterile white Edwardian environment, the stage for astronaut Bowman's (Keir Dullea) final death and rebirth, by implication the literal evolution of the human spirit and species. *2001* became its generation's religious "trip" of choice, defining the new frontier of science-fiction cinema: while the horror

6. For an overview of this movement and its creators, see Gene Youngblood, *Expanded Cinema*, E. P. Dutton, 1970.

Note that Belson contributed sequences to two mainstream features, Robert Parrish's *Journey to the Far Side of the Sun* (1969) and Philip Kaufman's *The Right Stuff* (1983).

genre wallowed in the wake of *Rosemary's Baby*'s demonic Antichrist progeny, science fiction struggled to sustain the genuinely innovative transcendental experience *2001* provided. While Kubrick and Clarke moved on to other unrelated projects, *2001*'s special-effects creator, Douglas Trumbull, took up the torch and consciously began to crystallize its energies.

Choosing to work within the confines of mainstream narrative cinema, Trumbull crafted the visionary imagery that stretched the parameters of the medium in *2001*, continuing with Robert Wise's *The Andromeda Strain* (1970) and *Star Trek: The Motion Picture* (1979), Steven Spielberg's *Close Encounters of the Third Kind* (1978), Ridley Scott's *Blade Runner* (1982), and others. Trumbull pursued his own visionary quest (emphasized by the ecological parable he chose to make his directorial debut, *Silent Running*, 1972) while his peers worked on militaristic war fantasies. There is a clear cause and effect between *Star Wars* (1977), its sequels and imitations—such as *Battlestar Galactica* (1979)—and films like *Firefox* (1982), *Top Gun*, and the video-game phenomenon which defined and refined the attitudes and technologies that informed the laundered, manipulative telecasting of the Gulf War, as well as short-circuiting the visionary potential the mainstream cinema might have fully embraced in the wake of *2001*. Trumbull's career charted a course in clear moral opposition to such destructive fantasies.

Spielberg's *Close Encounters of the Third Kind* achieved a certain transcendent intensity, realized with triumphant clarity and impact through Trumbull's effects. However, its fantasies were ultimately Gnostic rather than humanistic and transformative. Anticipated by Pierre Kast's *Les Soleils de L'Ile de Paques* (*The Suns of Easter Island*, (1972) and countless precedents in science-fiction literature, *Close Encounters* literalized and suburbanized *2001*'s notion that the heavens harbored mankind's transcendence via evolution or cosmic redemption.

Spielberg's conceit was that the aliens had already come for us, mysteriously choosing individuals like his hero (Richard Dreyfuss) out of our midst, implanting the image of the prescribed rendezvous location (the ironically named Devil's Tower in Wyoming) with the promise of a trip to the heavens and potential rebirth. The film's only conceptual innovation lay in sympathetically plunging its mass audiences into vicariously experiencing the creative process, and the toll it exacts: Dreyfuss's rebirth is experienced through the process of externalizing the implanted vision itself, the climactic rendezvous its reward. The central passages of the film convincingly detail the process: though he appears mad to his family and neighbors, all of whom ultimately abandon him, he struggles with whatever medium is at hand in his suburban environment—clay, mashed potatoes, the debris of his ruined home—to give shape to the imagery that obsesses him, allowing him to recognize the actual locale of the aliens' intended rendezvous with their "chosen."

The finale at Devil's Tower is flawlessly orchestrated by Spielberg and Trumbull, but it does ultimately personify a Gnostic Christian longing for redemption. If "the fundamental difference that separates the Gnostic from their contemporaries is that, for them, their native 'soil' is not the earth, but that lost heaven which they keep vividly alive in their memories,"[7] then *Close Encounters* was surely a Gnostic parable, and as such oddly sectarian in its origins. Its childlike aliens are shimmering, backlit beings who ethereally step out of the impossibly outsized mothership: surrogate angels from a portable mechanized afterlife blessing man with a visitation, mysteriously judging and spiriting a chosen few to the heavens. The Christ analogy relevant to Robert Wise's *The Day the Earth Stood Still* (1951) on through to Spielberg's *E.T. The Extraterrestrial* (1982) is more typically Christian, and separate from the Gnostic yearnings that fuel all of *Close Encounters*' successors. *Liquid Sky* (1983) and *Repo Man* (1984) evinced a caustic nihilism while John Binder's *UFOria* (1980/86) was an uneasy parody. More pervasive values were popularized by *Wavelength* (1983), *Starman* (1984, itself a romantic science-fictional dry run for *Ghost*), *Cocoon* (1985, and its 1989 sequel), and even Arthur C. Clarke and Peter Hyams's *2010* (1984), which manages to be both a competent sequel to and sad trivialization of *2001*. No less Gnostic, though more intimate and downbeat, were the parables offered by Nicholas Roeg's adaptation of Walter Tevis's *The Man Who Fell to Earth* and Eliseo Subiela's *Man Facing Southeast* (1986).[8]

Such parables reinforced the notion that deliverance awaited mankind from outside of ourselves. What was unique about *Resurrection* was the passionate belief in redemption as a spiritual potential that lies *within* the human spirit, demanding an introspective journey rather than unquestioning faith in religious dogma, an externalized quest for the

7. Jacques Lacarriere, *The Gnostics*, translated by Nina Rootes, E. P. Dutton, 1973, p. 29.
8. See David Lavery's essay "Gnosticism and the Cult Film," J. P. Telotti, ed., in *The Cult Film Experience*. University of Texas Press, 1991, pp. 187–99.

heavens (embodied in the sixties space program), or the even more regressive longing for divine intervention from the stars. Apparently Trumbull shared this belief: shortly after the completion of *Close Encounters*, Trumbull read *The George Dunlap Tape*, a screenplay completed in 1973 by Bruce Joel Rubin, who would later script both *Ghost* and *Jacob's Ladder*, and found the structure for just such an introspective fantasy adventure. "It is about exploration into the human mind rather than exploration *mechanically* into outer space," he explained prior to its troubled production under the title *Brainstorm* (1983). "It will be . . . the ultimate special effects trip."[9]

Rubin's story proposed a recording device capable of recording, storing, and playing back brainwaves as sensory perceptions: sound and sight as well as taste, smell, sensation, and emotion, a stimulation of the senses Trumbull simulated in selected theaters by actually expanding the parameters of the 35mm screen to create a wider 70mm peripheral vision. The creators of the device, Dr. Lillian Reynolds (Louise Fletcher) and Michael Brace (Christopher Walken), quickly find the sponsoring corporation's plans to package and market the invention for darker military applications, edging into "toxic" recordings of "physical pain thresholds," "negative memory retrieval," and "psychotic episodes" in specialized "extreme versions," all under the secret code name "Brainstorm." The ultimate "toxic tape" is that storing Reynolds's death via cardiac arrest, which Brace and the audience experience in sections, moving ever closer to the divine afterlife.

The first movement of the film is most effective, savoring the scientific team's exploration of the device's capabilities and discovering its powerful potential for personal transformation. A playful sexual experience is recorded and swapped among the men: looping of the tape induces a near-fatal ecstatic overload in an older team member (Joe Dorsey), who embraces the experience to reevaluate his life and pursue new goals. Michael's antagonistic relationship with his wife, Karen (Natalie Wood, who tragically drowned during filming), changes when the device allows them to share intimate memories, emotions, and perceptions, rekindling their bond as lovers and, in the film's rather contrived second half, as strong allies united against the Machiavellian corporate/military forces after their son is traumatized by accidental experiencing of a "toxic" tape.

9. Quoted from an interview with Trumbull in "Close Encounters of the Third Kind," *Cinefantastique* (6:4–7:1), Spring 1978, p. 36.

The core of the film is Reynolds's taped death-and-afterlife experience. Frustratingly, this was cumulatively undercut by the narrative's interruptive melodramatic espionage elements, as Brace successfully fights to retrieve and experience Reynolds's after-death experiences (with the physical stimulus disconnected, thereby avoiding cardiac arrest himself). The experience itself opens with a remarkable sequence that abandons the usual afterlife trappings—the dark tunnel, bright light, beckoning specters of long-lost loved ones—for what Rubin referred to as "bubble memory mode." Drawn from an earlier script idea involving "people who had just died speed[ing] . . . alongside their memories . . . intersecting with them in a kind of chromosomic network,"[10] Trumbull beautifully captured the concept in its initial stages. Reynolds's agonizing death spasms lead to an out-of-body perception enveloped and overwhelmed by geometric patterning of mercurial spheres, "bubbles" that harbor her stored shards of memory and allow them to be fleetingly reexperienced.

Here, however, Trumbull's directorial miscalculations began to take their toll: the memories were filmed in an objective, rather than purely subjective, manner, compromising the concept (which is properly realized during her initial out-of-body perceptions) on its most basic cinematic level. This distancing also colored Trumbull's rendition of the "bubble mode" with the perfection of mathematical geometry, creating a cold, aloof abstraction that seems alien: indeed, "an ultimate special effects trip" rather than a recognizably human experience.

Reynolds's memories briefly explode with organic horrors—evocations of the hellish prison of the flesh, emphasizing the illness that plagues Reynolds throughout—and move beyond, plunging into the cosmos and an ethereal light harboring formless but literalized "angels," an interpretation enhanced by James Horner's insistent musical score. Michael's vicarious experience of Reynolds's afterlife continues *after* the tape had ended, nearly claiming his own life as it affords him an intimate brush with infinity.

Trumbull's heartfelt embracing of humanist themes in an admittedly clumsy science-fiction drama were creditable, but *Brainstorm* does not share the dignified status of *Resurrection*. Consider Christopher Walken's profoundly moving performance in David Cronenberg's adaptation of Stephen King's *The Dead Zone* (1983), a tragi-horror variation of

---

10. Rubin quoted in Sheldon Teitelbaum, "Bruce Joel Rubin: Movie Metaphysician" *Cinefantastique* (21:5), April 1991, p. 50.

Resurrection, suggesting the depths Trumbull might have achieved had he maintained his focus on characters rather than contrived plot machinations, maladroit romantic sequences, broad slapstick (during the remote-controlled vandalism that undoes the corporate/military villains), and the sometimes effective Cinerama showmanship of the sensory simulations. That Trumbull completed the film at all in the wake of costar Natalie Wood's death was a testimony to his fierce devotion to the project, but *Brainstorm* clearly fails to realize its potential.

Trumbull's film was nevertheless a key transitional work, though Rubin maintains his disappointment with *Brainstorm*, saying it "was . . . everything I had feared it would become . . . the ideas were there, but the story barely touched the depths that had once been on the page."[11] Rubin himself may not have realized the portent of his own material: in earlier drafts of the script, Michael died during his climactic experience of Reynolds's afterlife tape, hence "paying" for his visionary arrogance with the genre's traditional retribution. Trumbull had promised *Brainstorm* would "make *Altered States* look like pablum";[12] though it is dramatically inferior to Russell's spectacular hokum, *Brainstorm* was conceptually the more progressive film. Michael's survival in the final cut represented a thematic step forward, an extension (however pedestrian its dramatics) of the direction Corman and Kubrick had indicated.

Rubin's most vocal criticism of *Brainstorm* concerned Trumbull's Christian literalization of the "angels," interesting given Rubin's initial objections to director Adrian Lyne's eschewing of the Apocalyptic Christian imagery that pervaded the original drafts of Rubin's controversial *Jacob's Ladder* screenplay, replete with classical devils, demons, angels, hell, and a literal stairway to heaven. "I was very disturbed by Adrian's response," Rubin recalls, "since I had been fascinated by the idea of introducing archetypal imagery into twentieth century experience . . . [which was] exactly what Adrian did not want. . . . He wanted to create images that challenged or expanded those ideas."[13] Lyne wisely eschewed the traditions of *Dante's Inferno* (1924, 1935), the Judeo-Christian devils and angels evident in countless

---

11. Bruce Joel Rubin's "Jacob's Chronicle" in *Jacob's Ladder*, Applause, 1990, p. 162.
12. "Trumbull returns to directing with *Brainstorm*," sidebar by P. B. Beene, *Cinefantastique* (11:2), Fall 1981, p. 11.
13. Rubin, "Jacob's Chronicle" in *Jacob's Ladder*, p. 179.

films from D. W. Griffith's *The Sorrows of Satan* (1925) to Rubin's own *Ghost* and its ilk. Indeed, Rubin had originally conceived the film in the apocalyptic mode of *The Omen* series (1976–81), *The Seventh Sign* (1989), or Mike Hodges's *Black Rainbow* (1990, still unreleased in the United States), but Lyne wisely shaped it to a more intimate and affecting scope. Had Lyne embraced the clearly Christian iconography of Rubin's script, *Jacob's Ladder* would have stood regressively apart from its contemporaries.

Jacob's Ladder's precedents were readily apparent and, for many viewers, obtrusive. The central conceit was immortalized by Ambrose Bierce's short story "An Occurrence at Owl Creek Bridge," and Rubin pinpointed director Robert Enrico's 1961 version of the story as his inspiration.[14] *Jacob's Ladder* shared the tactile sensuality unique to Enrico's version, along with the jarring dynamics of Charles Vidor's earlier experimental film version, *The Bridge*, a.k.a. *The Spy* (1931), and a similar avant-garde short, Paul Fejos's *The Last Moment* (1927). Bierce's tale of the "escape" a Confederate spy savors in the split second before the hangman's noose snaps his neck—the escape, of course, is a doomed man's fancy—has inspired many derivations in all media, including Herk Harvey's *Carnival of Souls* (1962; restored version, 1990), John Boorman's *Point Blank* (1967), and Mary Lambert's *Siesta* (1987). Narratively, it is a shell game, and once a viewer has read or experienced either Bierce's original story or one of its derivations, a rather transparent one at that. *Jacob's Ladder* was, essentially, the same shell game, told subjectively from the point of view of its protagonist, Jacob Singer (Tim Robbins), who we meet in a Vietnam battlefield.

Singer and his fellow infantrymen are apparently attacked by an unseen enemy, and Jacob is grievously wounded; he awakens in a subway train, on his way home from work at the post office. The

14. Robert Enrico's film adaptation of Bierce's story *La Rivière du Hibou*, won an Academy Award as Best Short Subject and was subsequently shown in abridged form in an episode of Rod Serling's *The Twilight Zone*. Enrico's version was not, however, produced as a short film; it was, in fact, one of three Bierce stories realized by Enrico in his feature film *Au Coeur de la Vie* (*In the Midst of Life*, 1961/63), an anthology that also included Bierce's "Chickamauga" and "The Mockingbird."

    "An Occurrence at Owl Creek Bridge" was also filmed by director Robert Stevenson as a Christmas episode of *Alfred Hitchcock Presents* (December 20, 1959).

ensuing narrative chronicles Singer's alternating perceptions, from being mortally wounded in Vietnam, to working as a New York City postal-service employee, a disorienting juxtaposition of what might be past, present, future, or even imagined lives. Consistent throughout were the hideous beings stalking him, his relationships with his lover Jezzie (Elizabeth Pena) and philosophical chiropractor Louis (Danny Aiello), and the grief and loss harbored over the accidental death of his youngest son (uncredited Macauley Culkin). Convinced that demons stalk him and fellow survivors of the enigmatic battle in 'Nam, Jacob discovers that members of his division were in fact the subjects of a military experiment with hallucinogens that induced psychopathic violence. He had been mortally wounded by one of his friends, suffering a private hell in the tenuous moments *between* life and death. Accepting his death, he returns "home," where his youngest son takes him by the hand and leads him up a stairway, into the light.

Lyne and Rubin played the shell game well, aided by the decision to avoid the classical Christian iconography. As interpreted by Lyne, Singer's demons consciously evoke British painter Francis Bacon's spastic, fleshy grotesques rather than the medieval archetypes of Brueghel and Bosch, truly terrifying revenants that reinforced the nonsectarian attitudes reflected in the film's final cut. Narratively, alas, it may strike audiences as being *only* a shell game, a writer's conceit privy to his whims rather than a coherent internal logic. Emotionally, however, *Jacob's Ladder* carried surprising resonance, its spiritual convictions potent enough to make it a progressive successor to Bierce's cynical tale and its "weird tale" derivations. Though both Rubin and Lyne are at times overly facile and manipulative in the obsessive drive to keep the audience off balance and its final revelation coyly hidden, *Jacob's Ladder* was a compelling masterpiece of the *fantastique*.

Just as Lynch's *The Elephant Man* coda used the same cinematic device as Buñuel's *Los Olvidados* to transcendent rather than fatalistic conclusions, *Jacob's Ladder* uses the narrative device of Bierce's fatalistic "twist ending" to a transcendent end. To Bierce, death was the final cruel joke that cut a man down, taunting him with a false dream of escape; to Rubin, death is a process. "Heaven and Hell are the same place. If you are afraid of dying, you experience demons tearing your flesh away. If you embrace it, you will see angels freeing you from your flesh":[15] the teachings of German theologian Meister Eckart as para-

15. Rubin, *Ibid.*, p. 190.

phrased by Jacob's angelic chiropractor Louis. *Jacob's Ladder* worked best when daring the tightwire walk over the abyss between the polar extremities of Buñuel and Lynch: its horror lay in the dread of the plunge, its beauty in the yearning for and attaining of redemption.

Curiously, *Jacob's Ladder* was anticipated by Brian De Palma and David Rabe's harrowing *Casualties of War* (1989). Though this film is at best peripheral to the genre, it was indeed the catalyst for this entire meditation, a fact I cannot stress enough. *Casualties of War* is a war movie, but De Palma's vital participation makes it relevant here, using the director's expertise at crafting manipulative thrillers to confrontational and decidedly moral ends, representing a definite turning point for both the director and, oddly, the horror genre he had apparently abandoned. Precedence lay in his earlier works, from *Sisters* (1973) and *Carrie* (1976) to the devastating coda of *Blow Out* (1981), as he honed his directorial tools to craft *Casualties* with startling precision of intent and effect. It seemed, on one level, a testimonial to De Palma's finally taking *responsibility* for the imaginary violence he so often reveled in, a potent dissection of the male polemic that fuels violence, war, and rape. While its themes and Vietnam setting are typical of playwright David Rabe's work (*Sticks and Bones, Streamers,* etc.), it was both a dramatic deviation from and ideal culmination of De Palma's obsessions.

David Rabe's screenplay was based on a real atrocity committed during the Vietnam War, detailed in an article (*The New Yorker*, 1969) and book by Daniel Lang, in which an American army patrol's kidnapping, gang-rape, and murder of an innocent Vietnamese woman forced the only soldier who tried to *stop* the rape and murder to extremes in his attempt to cope with, and exact moral judgment for, the horrific crime. De Palma, so often accused of misogyny for his thrillers' meticulously realized setpieces depicting violence against their female characters, crafts an angry indictment of misogyny and murder amid a xenophobic patriarchy's indulgence in the insanity of war, wherein the military authorities seem eager to dismiss and dispose of the event and its female victim as a mere "casualty of war." The Lutheran Private Eriksson (Michael J. Fox in a creditable performance) was clearly the sympathetic hero and conscience of the film, and, by proxy, of De Palma and the audience.

Casualties of War was structured as "a bad dream," a nightmare reverie, a remembrance that begins on a subway train ride. As such, its framing device and Vietnam setting echoed and anticipated *Jacob's*

Ladder, which also began its "trip to hell" on a subway. The heroes of both films are haunted and entrapped in their grueling memories of the Vietnam War, both purged in its fires and reawakened in a "better life": Jacob finds his redemption and peace reuniting with his dead son in the afterlife, while Eriksson finds tentative redemption in a brief dialogue with an American-Vietnamese woman who eerily reminds him of the raped and murdered atrocity victim (indeed, her face provokes the dream). She suggests "it was just a bad dream . . . it's over now," as if bestowing forgiveness for Eriksson's inability to save her surrogate (and for his—and our—involvement in the war?), as Ennio Morricone's triumphant score affirms the moment.

Casualties of War's urgency and longing for moral judgment and transcendence informs *Jacob's Ladder* and *Flatliners*. This urgency was summarized in Eriksson's tormented monologue at the core of Rabe's screenplay: "Just because each of us might at any second be blown way, everybody's acting like we can do *anything*, man, and it don't matter *what* we do! But I'm thinking maybe it's the other way around, you know? Maybe the main thing is just the opposite. Because we might be dead in the next split second, maybe we've got to be *extra* careful what we do—because maybe it matters *more*. Jesus, maybe it matters more than we even know."

The sentiment was echoed in *Flatliners,* when Nelson (Kiefer Sutherland) despairingly tells Rachel (Julia Roberts), "Rachel, everything matters—everything we *do* matters," before rushing to induce his own death one last time.

Joel Schumacher's *Flatliners* carried an implicit reference to Vietnam in Rachel's memory of her father's return from the war and subsequent suicide, but its moral tone properly links it to *Casualties* and especially *Jacob's Ladder*. For all of Schumacher's pious Christian iconography— lingering images of divine and deathly statuary; James Newton Howard's musical score, complete with boy's choir; the final shot's pastiche of Michelangelo's Sistine Chapel image of God the Creator—the view of the afterlife and its interface with mortal existence seemed distinctly Eastern in origin. The afterlife is clearly subjective and individualized, a deeply personal confrontation with the karma of one's past or path, a necessary coming to terms with negative emotional scars, here embodied as personal experiential demons.

Five medical students indulge in ritualized, controlled experiments with artificially induced death and resurrection. As in the old Karloff vehicles, the purpose is to pierce the veil; as in *X—The Man with the*

X-Ray Eyes, The Trip, Altered States, and *Brainstorm,* the quest is visionary. "Philosophy failed, religion failed, now it's up to physical science," Nelson the instigator (Sutherland) proclaims, "when the EEG flatlines, the brain is dead, I'll be exploring." The results are terrifying for the four active participants, and only Randall Steckle (Oliver Platt) abstains from the experience, remaining the reluctant control member of the group.

Nelson's first line in the film appropriates the Native American war cry, "Today's a good day to die," his apparent narcissism masking a genuine deathwish. His flatline journey has him reexperiencing a childhood crime, the accidental "murder" of an eight-year-old playmate (Joshua Ruddy) who was treed, stoned, and plunged to his death. Nelson's confrontation with his past spills into his waking life, as he is stalked and tormented by the dead child's "ghost." Refusing to divulge the grim repercussions of his afterlife experience to his colleagues, he allows their competitiveness to extend the periods of induced death further.

Reckless hedonist Joe Hurley (William Baldwin) enjoys flatline visions that are specifically erotic: impressions of his birth and the women in his life, from the nurse who delivered him and the mother and relatives who nurtured him to impressions of girlfriends and lovers. He is subsequently haunted by video images and specters of women he videotaped during sex without their knowledge. Dave Labraccio (Kevin Bacon), a tenacious atheist, becomes the group's lifeline, having already laid his medical career on the line to save a dying patient. His postdeath visions move from life's fetal beginnings to soar over mountainscapes, until a children's rhyme wrenches him into a confrontation with an angry little black child (Kesha Reed) before he is revived. Labraccio's waking visions of the girl assault him on a subway train, as she humiliates him with venomous curses, reciprocating his own habitual verbal abuse of the real child during their childhood.

Most affecting of all is Rachel's (Julia Roberts) painful exorcism of the past. Her character is introduced working in the hospital, enthralled by a female patient's description of her near-death experience; she later explains, "I've lost people close to me, and I want to be sure they've gone to a good place." Her morbid obsession harbors traumatizing guilt she suffers over the suicide of her father (Benjamin Mouton), an event she relives in the film's strongest flatline sequence. We see her memories of the homecoming celebration, ascending the red stairs, peering into the open bathroom door, her father's back obscuring his actions (initially disturbingly evocative of masturbation, an eerie Freudian "primal scene") before she screams, followed by her father fleeing, her's mother crying "it's your fault!", and her father's handgun suicide. Her companions are barely able to return her to life, after which she, too, is plagued by spectral visitations.

Though derivative, these visitations were atmospherically effective. The mise-en-scène and chromatic lighting of Joe's and especially Rachel's visions specifically recalled the "ghost" visitations in Mario Bava's *La frusta e il corpo* (*What!*, 1963), *Il rosso segno della follia* (*Hatchet for the Honeymoon*, 1969), and *Shock—Transfert suspence hypnos* (*Beyond the Door 2*, 1975).[16] As in these Bava features, the specters prove to be projections of deeply troubled minds, though their manifestations remain unnervingly corporeal: the revelation that Nelson's grisly penance is self-inflicted was also lifted directly from *La frusta e il corpo*.

The ghostly intrusions escalate, culminating in a series of confrontational climaxes as each character is driven by a need for redemption, a purging of the rage, regret, or guilt for their past transgressions— "atonement, gentlemen," as Nelson solemnly states. The most poignant moments belong to Labraccio (who seeks out and apologizes to his victim, now a grown woman with a family) and Rachel (left alone, she confronts her father's spirit, who was actually mainlining heroin; he tearfully asks for and receives his daughter's forgiveness in the film's most moving passage), though the the narrative anticlimactically drives Nelson to risk "flatlining" alone in order to confront his demon. His friends rescue him from his suicide attempt, the dead boy's spirit finally granting absolution only after Nelson has vicariously endured his victim's terrified last moments.

The thematic links with other films in the cycle were obvious, from Rachel's fascination with near-death experiences (in a primer for Roberts's role in Schumacher's soap opera, *Dying Young*, 1991) to Labraccio's initial visitation aboard a subway train, an urban staple that curiously provided a haven for spirits and demons in nearly all of its contemporaries (*The Heavenly Kid, Wings of Desire, Ghost, Jacob's Ladder*). Like *Jacob's Ladder*, the film clearly emerged from the horror genre, with Schumacher's imagery and Peter Filardi's script unapolo-

16. Similarly, *Flatliners'* "ghost" children recall those of Bava's classical *I tre volti della paura* (*Black Sabbath*, 1963) and *Operatione paura* (*Kill, Baby, Kill!*, a.k.a. *Curse of the Living Dead*, 1966).

getically acknowledging its sources, appropriately emphasized by the seasonal Halloween setting and dialogue toying with traditional moral obligations, its visuals redolent with *giallo* atmospherics. As in *Ghost*, wherein the villainous Carl stalks Molly only to be gorily impaled by a plunging shard of glass, the staging of Nelson's (self-)mutilations were closer to the *gialli* of Dario Argento, even lapsing into the subjective stalk-and-slash point-of-view camera during the attack on Nelson in Labraccio's jeep.

Unlike the graphic *gialli*, Schumacher and Filardi sublimated the spectacle of death endemic to the modern horror film, ritualizing such energies into the sterile but suspenseful "flatlining" operations. *Flatliners* was first and foremost a slick and stylish "brat pack" updating of the old Karloff vehicle formulas, enlivened and properly driven by its engaging characters and performances. Nelson's testimonial "I don't want to die—I want to come back with the answers to death—and life!" sets the stage for the climactic eliciting of the Karloff thrillers' venerable pontifications: Steckle's fear that "we're being paid back for our arrogance," coupled with Labraccio's "I'm sorry, God, I'm sorry we stepped on your *fucking* territory!" paid lip service to values the modern horror film had by and large abandoned.

Despite its studio-packaged veneer, *Flatliners* rigorously maintained its focus on its characters (to its credit, an uncharacteristic devotion to narrative rather than box-office requirements eschewed the usually obligatory onscreen consummation of Labraccio's sexual attraction to Rachel) and their quests—first for vision, then for redemption awakened by, rather than as a penalty for, the achievement of vision. The film disappointed only when it failed to convey its potential scope and intensity through its MTV-derivative "trips."

Just as Corman's *The Trip* was mired in the stock cinematic trappings of its time, visualizing its titular "trip" with hokey exploitation psychedelia, Schumacher's *Flatliners* settled for stylish rock-video evocations of the afterlife. This contrived approach to such rich material, coupled with its *giallo* embellishments, clearly marked the eighties trappings that characterize its flaws. *Ghost* likewise dates itself with its reliance on effects drawn from Spielberg's *Close Encounters* and *Poltergeist*—pools and halos of optically enhanced backlighting, animated Disneyesque angels of light and demons of shadow—while Spielberg himself wisely abandoned such staples in *Always*. Although most audiences still respond to such familiar chords, the banality of such stylistic indulgences and repetitive special effects seems obvious when compared with the eloquent and evocative economy of Wenders's *Wings of Desire*.

Throughout *Wings of Desire*, Wenders stresses the tactile immediacy of being human, living in real time, with the pull of gravity, age, and the elements on the flesh. Peter Falk tells the ethereal Damiel of the pleasures of hot coffee, of rubbing one's hands together for warmth on a cold day, and once Damiel manifests himself as a mere man, he delights in both sensations.

This vicarious savoring of the pleasures and the pain of the mortal flesh typifies contemporary explorations of the theme. This *tactile* insistence grounds *Ghost*, *Flatliners*, and especially *Jacob's Ladder*, and allows them to occasionally eschew the banality of their story orientations and contrived special effects. *Ghost*'s romantic craving for a lover's touch, kiss, and the consummation of love, coupled with its recognition of the power implicit in the ability to physically interact with the "real" world, lent it an irresistible drive despite its melodramatic excesses and retrograde romanticism. *Truly, Madly, Deeply* embraced such longings with deeper compassion, celebrating Nina's blossoming from self-imposed exile with her resurrected lover to daily interaction with the outside world as a healthy and necessary opening of the heart to genuine human touch. *Flatliners'* more effective vision of the tentative afterlives its protagonists explored was that of the hedonist, who bathes in a sensuous montage of female curves and skin that is warm, human, and nurturing. *Jacob's Ladder* properly shared its hero's point of view through an urgently composed and communicated immediacy. Its obsessive reveling in subjective detail carried an enthralling cumulative effect: Jacob's extreme agonies were felt, enhanced by the unexpectedly tactile pleasures—a kiss while wearing shaving cream, a finger tracing the contours of the spine, the intertwining of lovers' fingers—which also lent a disturbing reality to the organic demons. Though ultimately manipulative rather than meditative in its impact, *Jacob's Ladder* orchestrated its tactile obsessions with a calculated skill comparable to Wenders's *Wings of Desire*.

It is the imperative of the physical, the tactile, the flesh, and the sense of touch in juxtaposition with their spiritual themes and fantasies that lend these films their uncanny power. The climax of *Jacob's Ladder* ultimately relies on the tried-and-true cinematic evocation of heaven as a radiant light spilling from the top of a stairway, but its ability to genuinely stir our emotions lies in the moment father and son embrace, separated by death, reunited in the afterlife.

Like the selfless, life-restoring hug that ends *Resurrection*, Rachel's forgiving reunion with her father in *Flatliners*, Nina's reawakening to daily life in *Truly, Madly, Deeply*, or the communion of lovers that confirms an angel's love of mortal life over ethereal eternity in *Wings of Desire*, the loving embrace of Jacob and his son denies the Gnostic longings of its science-fictional brethren, and the diversionary political intent Desser ascribes to pop-culture afterlife fantasies. Though trivialized by TV sitcoms, melodramas, and commercials, perversely reduced to a dehumanizing commodity by pornography, and subverted by the horror genre's spidery vampirism or David Cronenberg's organic incarnations of sexual parasitism and disease, the embrace is still a primal gesture of love in the ever-present reality of the human experience.

It is the *embrace*, rather than Hollywood's tawdry heaven, that moves us, reaffirming the power and healing potential of the human touch.

Chapter

3

Gary Brandner

Although, as you'll see from this piece, his own feelings were mixed about it, the film version of Gary Brandner's *The Howling* completely blew me away when I first saw it. Along with *An American Werewolf in London*, it is the exception that proves a rule: that modern filmmakers can't deal with werewolves.

The point is, while I was shuddering as a half man reached into his own skull and plucked out a chunk of gray matter, I was also loving every minute of it. The film, though quite different from Gary's book, is what sent me into bookshops to seek out his work. From *Hellborn* to *Quintana Roo* to *Floater* and beyond.

Gary, who likes picking guitar, playing tennis, and drinking beer, makes his home in the San Fernando Valley. He's been a full-time writer since 1969, and in that time has produced more than thirty novels, half a dozen screenplays, and short stories nearing three digits in number. He started as a mystery writer, but has found a very comfortable niche (and some serious $$$) in horror.

Despite Gary's mixed feelings about *The Howling,* there's one thing he can't deny: I'm not the only one it drove into the bookstores. Sometimes the trials of Hollywood pay off, and as he tells us in the following piece, sometimes they don't.

No, But I Saw the Movie

by Gary Brandner

1

Where do horror movies come from? The same place other movies do—some are wrenched from a screenwriter's imagination, some are distilled from a novel. Producers like using a novel as the basis for their movie because it has a certain presold title value. They also hate using a novel because they must then deal with the author.

Even without the author factor, fashioning a motion picture from a book is a chancy endeavor. When they're done well, the result can be a classic like *From Here to Eternity*. Other times, no matter how popular the book, the film can be a dog like *Bonfire of the Vanities*.

Books in the horror genre are subject to the same disparity. The movie *Wolfen* turned Whitley Strieber's scary urban werewolf tale into a confusing message film about Indians. Conversely, the movie version of *Jaws* may have even improved on the book by dumping a tiresome onshore romance in favor of the seagoing action.

Many of the best-known horror movies, both good and bad, came from books. To name a few: *Frankenstein*, *Dracula*, *The Exorcist*, *Rosemary's Baby*, *Psycho*, and just about anything Stephen King ever wrote. Some, like *Rosemary's Baby*, are loyal to the original. Others, like *Frankenstein*, use the central idea and not much else. Sometimes that works best. James Whale's 1931 classic set the standard for monster stories, while Mary Shelley's turgid nineteenth-century novel is tough going.

No matter what kind of a job the filmmaker does with the book, you can bet that somebody is going to be unhappy with the result. Often that somebody is the book's author. Hemingway, for instance, is said to have hated everything the movies did with his stories. Many a lesser author has squirmed in his seat as he watched his story transformed for the screen. The thought is inescapable: "Jeez, if only I was in charge!"

However, giving the book writer control of the movie is no guarantee of success. Joe Wambaugh was appalled by *The Choirboys* and resolved never to let Hollywood have another of his books unless he could do it himself. For *The Onion Field* he did it himself. The result was a thoroughly professional, thoroughly depressing movie that almost nobody went to see. Stephen King wrote and directed *Maximum Overdrive*, a critical and box-office bomb.

The sensible thing for a book writer is to take the James M. Cain approach. When asked how he could let Hollywood do that to his books, he replied, "Nobody did anything to my books. They're all right there on the shelf."

Such philosophy aside, it is probably natural for an author to agonize over what happens to his literary child once it is adopted by Hollywood. The difference in the two media makes a literal transference impossible. A book is a thinking experience wherein the reader must do some interpreting. A motion picture is a passive medium where the viewer need only sit and absorb the images. Whereas you can go into a character's mind in a book, the first rule of movie making is: Show it!

The only way for the author to truly understand the transformation of his words into pictures is for him to get personally involved in the process. Easier said than done. Most producers and directors do not want the book writer anywhere near the set. Sometimes, however, the author will finagle himself into the screenplay assignment. I have seen my own books turned into movies both as a distant watcher and as a participant. Neither experience has been completely satisfying.

When I heard that my first horror novel, *The Howling*, had been purchased for a motion picture, I was euphoric. The thought of writing the screenplay never occurred to me. Nor did it occur to the producer. I signed the contract in a happy fog and strolled Sunset Boulevard feeling at one with the Hollywood community. It was a feeling that was not to last.

Although I was not involved in writing *The Howling* screenplay, I assumed I would be consulted for my opinions once the production started to roll. After all, I was in town and available, and who would have a better feeling for the essence of my werewolf story? Silly me.

The first word I had on the progress of my book into movie was an item in the *Hollywood Reporter* about the casting of the principals. I was excited to see that the movie was still alive, but a little disappointed that I was still uninvolved. But then, I am a writer, not a casting director. I waited for a call when they started the actual filming. I could still be waiting. I heard nothing more of *The Howling* until months later when my agent wangled a reluctant invitation to a screening of the finished picture. Somehow they had managed without me.

This particular screening was for exhibitors, the purpose being to persuade them they could make money by booking *The Howling* into their theaters. I sat in the dark screening room, unapplauded and unrecognized, in agonizing anticipation of seeing my work on the screen.

I did see my name on the screen: single title card, same size and screen time as the director and screenwriter, just as spelled out in the contract. For many minutes I was afraid that was going to be the only thing I would recognize.

Whereas my book opened with the rape of a young suburban wife, the movie jumped off with a female television reporter going into a porno bookstore to trap a psycho killer. That season four out of five female leads were television reporters. A couple of the character names were mine, but not much else. It took a while for me to see that my basic story line—a troubled woman menaced by a village of werewolves—remained. I was at least gratified that a sex scene by firelight between a male and female werewolf was transferred nearly intact from page to screen. My feelings were mixed when the lights went up. The basic story and the lead characters were mine, but there were long stretches of the movie where I recognized nothing. I admit, however, that when the audience of theater owners applauded with enthusiasm, I did not hesitate to accept congratulations.

In the weeks that followed before general release of the movie, my joy was tempered as I began to read interviews given by Joe Dante, the film's director. Dante's version was that he had taken a tawdry little book (mine) and created a marvelous motion picture (his). Since nobody was interviewing me at the time, I had no chance to point out that without my tawdry little book he would have had nothing to direct. If asked, I would have added that the state-of-the-art werewolves created by Rob Bottin had at least as much to do with the movie's success as Dante's direction.

When screen rights to the sequel, *Howling II*, were sold, I wangled the assignment to write the screenplay. This time it would be done right. I had a lot to learn about the ways of Hollywood.

Since my book was what the producers bought, I assumed in my innocence that my book was what they wanted on the screen. I pounded out a first draft that was a faithful adaptation of the book. The story picked up several of the surviving characters from the original and took them into new terrors. My focus for this one was on Marcia, the sexy female werewolf. Screenwriter John Sayles had thoughtfully left her alive at the end of the first movie.

The first draft was quickly finished and delivered to the producer—four hundred pages of book manuscript condensed into one hundred and ten pages of screenplay. A few days later I was introduced to a genuine Hollywood horror: The Story Meeting.

Meeting One was attended by the producer, the producer's wife, an associate producer, some guy whose function I never did get straight, and the writer—me. It was an informal affair, held in the best Hollywood tradition around the producer's swimming pool.

"Nice job," said the producer, riffling through the pages. "Good opening. Punchy dialogue."

The wife, the associate producer, and the other guy nodded in agreement. I beamed. This was easier than I had imagined.

"Just one thing . . ."

I met the producer's eye, eager, attentive, sincere.

"A Spanish connection is putting up most of the money for the production. He wants seventy percent of the picture to be shot in Spain."

There was no Spain in *Howling II*. The story moves from Seattle to Los Angeles to Mexico. But I was eager to prove myself as a screenwriter. "No problem," I said, and jogged off with the script under my arm.

Well, it *was* a problem. But by wrenching the story line out of shape and adding some unlikely coincidences, I moved my cast of characters to Spain, where I tried to save some of the flavor of the book. With the second draft of the script completed I was ready for:

Meeting Two. The producer, the wife, the associate, and the other guy were unanimous in their appraisal of my effort. They loved it.

"Beautiful job."

"Lovely script."

"Socko ending."

"Just one thing . . ."

I flinched.

"The Spanish connection with the money is a good friend of Fernando Rey. He wants a nice part in the movie for his pal."

"There isn't any Fernando Rey character in the story," I pointed out.

"You're a writer," the producer reminded me. "Write one in."

I folded my script and went away.

Fernando Rey is a fine actor, and from all reports a very nice man, but squeezing him into *Howling II* was forcing a wrong piece into a jigsaw puzzle. It was not art, but I did it. By changing the sex and adding twenty years to the age of one of my characters, I came up with a part he could play. The story now made less sense than ever, but not to worry, movie magic would cover the flaws. With much of the bounce gone from my step, I proceeded to:

Meeting Three. The faces around the producer's pool were grim. Nobody praised my writing talent. Nobody told me the latest draft was great. Nobody had read it.

"We got a problem," said the producer.

Warning bells clanged.

"The Spanish money dropped out."

"Fernando Rey?"

"Gone."

"Spain?"

"Adios. But the project is still alive. We had to cut the budget way back, but we got a deal to shoot in Yugoslavia."

I blanched.

"The good news is we've got Christopher Lee and Sybil Danning. How soon can you fix the script?"

Not soon. Not late. Not ever. I had a book deadline coming and there was simply not enough time to shift my story from Spain to Eastern Europe, write out Fernando Rey, and write in Lee and Danning. My script was turned over to another writer, who, out of charity, I will not name.

I heard nothing more of *Howling II* until it appeared for about ten minutes in the theaters before escaping to video-store shelves. If you saw the results, you can imagine my emotions. It is an indecipherable mishmash with actors never seen before or since. The werewolves were bargain basement and the dialogue was deadly. Most of the picture was filmed in Yugoslavian darkness, the better to conceal the cheap sets and Goodwill costumes. Christopher Lee sleepwalked through his brief part, and Sybil Danning did what she could. There is one outstanding scene where Miss Danning rips open her bodice to display her talents, but even they are not enough to save the movie. My name remains in the credits as coscreenwriter and author of the alleged source novel. Alas, *Howling II*, the video, is still available. Rent it at your own risk.

Inevitably, I suppose, it was followed by *Howling III, IV, V,* and *VI.* I did write a book titled *Howling III*, but it has no more connection with the movie of that name than does *Moby Dick.*

The book uses the original legend as background for the story of a young boy uncertain whether he belongs to the world of man or the beasts. The movie version of *H-III*, produced in Australia, introduced marsupial werewolves. The producers made no attempt to contact me.

H-IV was ambitiously subtitled "The Original Horror." It did have a resemblance to my original story, but with a budget of seventy-five dollars or so, the final product was forgettable. *H-V* is a werewolf movie with no werewolves.

There is no longer any attempt to put the *Howlings* into theaters, and subsequent sequels have gone directly to video. *H-VI* has been filmed, but has yet to be released. *H-VII* is under option. My connection with any of these is limited to the screen credit, "Based on the series of novels by . . ." I do receive a check for each, which I admit I have not hesitated to cash.

2

Turning *Cameron's Closet* into a movie was a happier experience. The producer, Luigi Cingolani, was actually a maker of movies rather than deals. And the director, Armand Mastroianni, made some creative contributions to the script. But in the best of circumstances, there are wrenching changes that must be made in going from page to film.

The essence of the book, in case you have not read it, is that the make-believe monster in a ten-year-old boy's closet becomes real through the power of the little boy's thoughts. Trust me, it works.

Once the contract was signed, talk turned to the changes that would have to be made. Early in the book there is a scene where Cameron's twelve-year-old brother dies a frightful death while the younger boy watches helplessly. It is a key scene, as the psychological trauma plants the seeds of horrors to come. The problem was that in the movies you do not kill children. Yes, I know there are exceptions, notably Stephen King's *Pet Sematary*, but Big Steve plays by a different set of rules. The rest of us can slaughter all the teenagers we want, but spare the tykes.

I solved this one by writing the brother out of the story entirely. This decision pleased the director, who would have one less child actor to worry about. Since the story now needed an early shock, I was allowed to decapitate Tab Hunter, who played the boy's father, so it was not a total loss.

Another philosophical point of contention between the producer and me was the nature of the monster. My idea was that Cameron's telekinetic powers were expanded by childhood trauma to the point where his imaginary playmate took on a real existence and gradually absorbed evil vibrations from those around it. However, quasi-religious demons were big that season, and the producer wanted a demon. Now I am not anti-demon, having featured one in another book a few years back, but the concept did not exactly fit the story I was telling here. However, the screenwriter, even when he is the original author, is a hired hand, and when the producer says, "Give me a demon," you give him a demon. I concocted a legend giving birth to a demon and yanked him into the story, keeping what I could of Cameron's psychological control of the beast. There remain some unexplained events in the movie as a result of mixing monsters.

Also lost in the transition were subplots and side trips by the characters to Portland and Las Vegas. I could not quarrel with this. A book has the latitude to wander off the main track here and there to enrich the overall fabric. A movie has less than two hours to get from point A to point B with no time for diversion. And even though *Cameron* was being shot on a higher budget than the later *Howling*s, there was no money to spend on location shooting in Vegas and the Pacific Northwest.

Other changes reflect differing personal tastes. There is a scene in the movie where one of the bad guys is blasted out of an upstairs window by the monster. I wanted him to land on a picket fence with the pickets graphically puncturing his torso in a neat, gory row. The director, however, recalled a recent movie where somebody was hurled from a high window and impaled on a sundial. He thought the picket-puncture scene would be too similar. We finally had the bad guy land atop a parked car. It later seemed that every falling body in that year landed on a car.

Sometimes what is available dictates a script's contents. The studio rented for *Cameron's Closet* included the mechanism for a revolving room. The most memorable example of this effect is in *Royal Wedding,* where Fred Astaire appears to dance up the walls and across the ceiling. It is the room, of course, that rotates while the camera remains stationary. There is no dancing in *Cameron*, but with a nifty effect like that available it would have been a shame not to use it. A scene was added where the demon (never mind how) slides the boy up the wall and across the ceiling toward the whirling blades of a fan. The sequence did not make much sense in the context of the story, but it looked neat on the screen.

The biggest problem with *Cameron's Closet* turned out to be the monster. A horror movie can succeed or fail on the scariness of its monster. Whereas in a book the writer can leave foggy areas for the reader to fill in with his own horrors, a movie monster has to be fully realized. When the producer signed special-effects wizard Carlo Rambaldi, everyone had high hopes for something really horrible. Rambaldi, after all, was responsible for the original *Alien*. Unfortunately, the monster he provided for *Cameron* looked like the traditional Guy in a Rubber Suit. The film was skillfully edited so you get only glimpses of the beast, but some shots are still embarrassing.

Despite the problems, *Cameron's Closet* was not a bad movie. The actors, including Mel Harris and Cotter Smith, did a solid professional job, and young Scott Curtis as Cameron gave us a kid who was likable and believable and avoided the Hollywood cutes.

Like the walking dead in horror stories, a book-into-movie can rise from apparent extinction to live again. The film rights to my book *Walkers* were originally optioned ten years ago by producer Edgar Sherrick. I also wrote a screenplay for him. The package was sold by Sherrick to ABC, which was then producing theatrical movies. When the network dropped its theatrical department, the project was shelved. While the book rights reverted to me, my screenplay remained the property of ABC. Eight years later the rights to the book were bought by NBC, and in February 1989 *Walkers* appeared as a four-hour miniseries starring Lindsay Wagner and Bruce Boxleitner. It was retitled *From the Dead of Night*, for reasons unknown to me. Again, I had nothing to do with the screenplay. It made a pretty good TV production, if a little bloated to fit the four-hour time slot.

My last adventure in the screen trade was scripting my book *Floater*, which Tobe Hooper was to direct and Empire Pictures was to produce. I found Hooper to be a joy to work with—enthusiastic and full of ideas. I had about thirty pages of the script completed when the Writers Guild called a strike. I was forced to sit on my hands for months while Empire Picture went bankrupt and Tobe Hooper found other projects. *Floater* is probably one of the scariest movies you will never see.

Chapter

4

Ramsey Campbell

He admits it.

The other writers back away from the subject, deny the allegations, vehemently oppose the stereotype. Ramsey Campbell freely admits to having had a warped childhood.

At the age of eighteen he saw a collection of his short fiction published, and his novels since have included such titles as *The Face That Must Die*, *The Doll Who Ate His Mother*, and the recent *Needing Ghosts* and *Midnight Sun*. His stories have been collected in a number of different volumes including his most recent work, *Waking Nightmares*.

As his book jackets proclaim, Ramsey has indeed won more awards for his horror fiction than any other living writer. He has been given the British Fantasy Award five times and the World Fantasy Award twice.

His book *Ancient Images* (a favorite of mine) revolves around a mythical, lost, last film for Karloff and Lugosi, and the filmmakers who become obsessed with finding it and solving the mystery of its curse. His own love of these old films is apparent in the book, and when illuminated by his comments here, a paradox becomes apparent. While Ramsey's taste in films leans toward ostensibly kinder, gentler pictures, the films are not what they seem. These films rouse within us a true fear, a disturbance in our nature to which gore is irrelevant. Ramsey knows better than most that, as emotions go, terror runs far deeper and lasts much longer than mere disgust.

The Quality of Terror

by Ramsey Campbell

As a child I suffered from sleepless nights after having seen Disney's *Snow White*. That's hardly unusual. I should think most children who saw the film in the first decades of its existence, and quite a few who encountered it later, found scenes from it invading their dreams: the old woman with the apple which is too red, the mirror from which a face peers that doesn't belong to the person in front of it. (Indeed, when the film was originally released, there was a good deal of controversy over the British censor's certificate, and later copies of the film were missing some images: the wicked queen kicking a skeleton to pieces in the dungeon, and her being struck by lightning.) However, none of these scenes was the source of my nightmare. That came in the charming interlude in which the dwarfs perform a song and dance for Snow White. The problem was simply that in the background of the scene was an open window that showed pitch darkness, and at five or six years old I *knew* something worse than I could imagine was about to appear in that window.

This was my introduction to terror in films, and more of the same was to follow. I couldn't have been much older when I saw John Ford's *Mogambo*, a romantic jungle melodrama in whose favour even Lindsay Anderson, one of Ford's earliest and staunchest defenders, could find little to say except "The shots of the gorillas must have been difficult to obtain." Towards the end of the film a boy in the row behind me told his friend that the woman in the film was about to shoot the man—"and," he said enthusiastically, "you see all blood." From that moment, approximately the whole of the last reel was transformed for me into an agony of waiting for the act of violence. It was my earliest encounter with the technique of suspense as expounded by Hitchcock.

Soon I saw *Knock on Wood*, a comedy in which Danny Kaye played a ventriloquist whose doll is used without his knowledge as a hiding place for, as I remember it, a canister of microfilm. Two groups of secret agents want the microfilm. In one scene, a member of each group enters Kaye's flat in his absence, and one spy kills the other just as Kaye returns. To hide the corpse the remaining spy hangs it on the back of a door with a hat over its face. Of course Kaye's obliviousness to the presence of something more than a coat and a hat on the hook is a protracted gag, but I found the suspense almost unbearable, and the fact that everyone around me was laughing made the situation all the more nightmarish.

Well, comedy's a funny thing, and so is terror. These early experiences suggest to me that terror can be found in many sorts of fiction, and I value it wherever it occurs. Finding it worthwhile in itself often gets horror buffs looked at askance, but I don't know why this should be the case, any more than I see anything odd about admiring a comedy for provoking mirth or a tragedy for moving its audience to tears (so much, by the way, for the specious argument which links pornography and horror fiction on the basis that both, and only both, seek to achieve a physical response). On the other hand, I'm all in favour of examining what the terror and its context mean, which is why (for instance) I dislike *The Exorcist*, book and film both. While the film certainly contains images one would previously never have expected to see on the screen, there's a sense in which the breaking of taboos can be deeply reactionary, and I think that's the case here. Just as medieval Norman church carvings often depicted obscene caricatures of sex in order to turn the faithful against their own sexuality, so *The Exorcist* presents an obscene caricature of adolescent rebellion in order to blame the devil for it, a view of rebellion which Dennis Wheatley would have applauded, God bless him.

It occurs to me to wonder when the ambition to frighten, as distinct from communicating fear as a by-product of telling the story, first declared itself in the cinema. My vote would be for Murnau's *Nosferatu*, in which the use of actual settings challenges the viewer to reject the evidence of his own eyes, the least human Dracula in all cinema. The same decade gave us a version of *Dr. Jekyll and Mr. Hyde* in which John Barrymore revels in a grisly inventiveness far beyond the demands of the narrative. The years immediately preceding the Hays Code are a trove of disturbing images: the torture by bell in *The Face of Fu Manchu*, Kong's revenge on the natives in the complete *King Kong*, the extreme sadism of the developments involving Miriam Hopkins in the Mamoulian *Jekyll and Hyde*, the sewn-up mouth and general grim humour of *Murder at the Zoo* (whose finale, along with the monster's invasion of the bride's room in Whale's *Frankenstein*, is among the earliest examples of scenes prolonged so as to make the audience sweat). Despite or perhaps because of their age, these images retain their power to shock any audience that is sensitive to their context, even if they are restrained by today's standards or lack of standards. In horror films as in many other places, less can often be more, and the greatest justification of this appeared in the forties: the films of Val Lewton.

In *The Leopard Man* (1942), a young girl is sent shopping after dark and is savaged to death. Almost every aspect of the scene is drawn from the book on which the film is based, Cornell Woolrich's *Black Alibi*. Whereas the film shows us only a trickle of blood beneath a door, however, Woolrich flings the door open. ("It was as though clots of red mud had been pelted at the outside of the door, until, adhering, they formed a sort of spattered mound up against it. There were rags mixed in with it, and snarls of hair. . . .") Reading the book after seeing the film is rather like reading "The Monkey's Paw" rewritten by a splatterpunk. All the same, one crucial similarity between the scenes in the book and the film is the willingness to be as frightening as possible.

If the Lewton films directed by Jacques Tourneur contain the finest scenes in the series, this is as much a tribute to Tourneur's delicacy as to his skill. But as well as the night walks in *Leopard Man* and *I Walked with a Zombie* and the scene in the swimming pool in *Cat People*, the finale of *The Body Snatcher* (directed by Robert Wise) and several episodes of *The Seventh Victim* (by Mark Robson) are landmarks of screen terror. Especially in the Tourneur films, the subtlety and suggestiveness of the handling raises terror to aesthetic heights which involve beauty and awe.

Other contemporary evidence of the will to frighten is less impressive, but not to be ignored. By showing victims from the killer's viewpoint in *The Lodger* and *Hangover Square*, John Brahm screws terror one notch tighter. The mummy saga of the forties (*Hand*, *Tomb*, *Ghost*, and *Curse*) contains, amidst all the chuntering about tana leaves, scenes of unexpected menace. As I recall the films of the fifties I discover that my memories of true terror are mostly of isolated scenes or images: the first glimpse (not the close-up) of a Martian in *The War of the Worlds*; the nightmarish episode in *Tarantula* where the heroine is trapped in a collapsing house with a disfigured Leo G. Carroll while the spider crouches over the roof; the Lovecraftian apparition of *The Beast from Haunted Cave* and especially its shadow as it makes for its victims, waving its tentacles, from deep in the earth; the unusually gruesome severed head in *The House on Haunted Hill* (a film enlivened, like William Castle's equally plodding *Mr. Sardonicus*, by unexpectedly disturbing images). Finest of all was the opening scene of

Bergman's *Wild Strawberries*, rendered not at all reassuring by being acknowledged at the outset as a dream, and the finale of the same director's *Magician* (*The Face* in Britain) wasn't far behind. For me the most thoroughly frightening film of the decade was the last great Jacques Tourneur, *Night* (*Curse* in America) *of the Demon*, a rare serious film about the supernatural, in my opinion compromised hardly at all by the decision to show the demon. Showing it at the beginning, however, was as much of a mistake as the voice-over in Siegel's *Invasion of the Body Snatchers* (another masterpiece of the period) which keeps informing the audience how deceptive the film's appearance of normality is.

I think it's fair to say that the ambition to frighten is more widespread in the sixties. Hitchcock gave his colleagues in the business a considerable amount to live up to in *Psycho*. A good deal of what's best about the film belongs to Robert Bloch, of course, including some of his neatest black jokes. But it is also Hitchcock's most densely constructed film in terms of images: the recurring journey into darkness (the opening track in from a cityscape into the darkness of a room leads to Janet Leigh's drive into night) becomes a plunge into darkness (the car into the swamp, Martin Balsam going down the stairs, Vera Miles's descent into the cellars; indeed, this recurrence seems to be the justification for the otherwise inexplicable unnerving track through the darkened hardware store toward Miles). The film shares with *Peeping Tom* a preoccupation with looking and with eyes, and the journeys into darkness lead into the black gaze (even blacker than the motorcycle cop's) of Mrs. Bates, who stares at us out of Norman's eyes in the final seconds of the film (in the scene where, as Robin Wood points out, the audience has become "the cruel eyes studying you" which Norman earlier described as one of the horrors of being institutionalised). It is the most poetically organised of Hitchcock's films, and a triumphant vindication of genre.

Meanwhile in *Black Sunday* Mario Bava virtually reinvented the Italian horror film and gave the genre at least one of its most unforgettable images, the insects scuttling out of the dead face of the witch as the spiked mask is pulled off. Nor am I likely to forget the disinterment of Vincent Price's wife in *The Pit and the Pendulum*, the dancing dead in *Carnival of Souls*, the bulging door and the cry of "Then whose hand *was* I holding?" in *The Haunting*, the hideous and hideously lively corpse in the first story of Bava's *Black Sabbath*, or the grinning mask which conceals worse in *Onibaba* (the last film to give me nightmares). Nevertheless all these rather pale beside *Repulsion*, the most terrifying film I've ever seen.

Some of Polanski's images of schizophrenia may derive from his own experiences with LSD (as I imagine is the case with the hieroglyphics that print themselves out on the lavatory wall in *The Tenant*), but I think that hardly matters. When I see the rooms of Catherine Deneuve's apartment growing cavernous, when the walls grow soft and hands burst out of them, these things aren't happening to an actress up there on the screen, they're happening directly to me, and to object that we aren't asked to feel sympathy for the character seems redundant. I take Polanski to be one of the cinema's most distinguished specialists in horror, and I'd like to put in a word for *Rosemary's Baby*, not least because Marvin Kaye recently dismissed the book, of which the film is an exceptionally faithful (if sinuous) adaptation. "Try to find anything the least bit ambiguous about its sweet-young-thing-brutalized-by-the-bogeyman plot," Kaye challenges, but I don't think the ambiguity he seems to want is necessary: of course Rosemary's predicament isn't "solely in her mind," any more than is Irena's in *Cat People*, but surely by the time either of these films becomes unambiguously supernatural the psychological aspects have been explored—in Rosemary's case, the expectant mother's sense of losing control of her own pregnancy and confinement (eloquent word!), of becoming the property of experts, self-styled or otherwise. I'd suggest that if either film turned out not to be supernatural, it would be much less of a film.

To return to the sixties, they were luridly illuminated by *Night of the Living Dead*, George Romero's most frightening film, though not his best. When the film opened in Britain, the critic Tom Milne rightly praised its relentlessness and refusal to compromise. None of us could have realised how quickly Romero's genuine pessimism was to be parroted by almost every minor (or worse) horror film that followed, any more than John Carpenter could have foreseen how his admirable commitment to being nothing but frightening in *Halloween* was to be imitated to excess by a horde of hacks. Between the Romero and the Carpenter came several films I can't ignore: the great delirium of *Suspiria* (a quality Argento brought to several other breathtaking films), *Don't Look Now* (a film whose every aspect the late Robert Aickman loathed, but whose last reel I still find terrifying), *The Texas Chainsaw Massacre*, and *Eraserhead*.

I always find the first half of Hooper's film almost unbearably menacing and the second something of a letdown. Some of my disappointment may have to do with a sense that the timing of shocks is slightly off, but I think the real problem is that in *Chainsaw Massacre* the urge to be terrifying gets out of control, leaving the film with nowhere to go before the end. (Lord knows my own novel *The Parasite* suffers from the same kind of uncontrollable escalation.) It's a pattern which I fear has been repeated ad nauseam since.

As for *Eraserhead*, it is the most nightmarish film I know. There are films that deal explicitly with nightmare (*Los Olvidados*, for instance, or that admirable moment in *Tristana* where the clapper of the bell turns out to be something else, leaving the audience groping in their memories for the point at which the dream must have begun); there are films whose illogic comes to seem nightmarish (*The Brain Eaters*, allegedly related in some way to Heinlein, makes no sense whatsoever, and I found my inability to predict its narrative appealingly disconcerting); the nightmarishness of some may or may not be inadvertent (for instance, Corman's *Attack of the Crab Monsters* works surprisingly well for me, perhaps because it traps its characters on a constantly shrinking island with its defiantly unlikely monsters). While we're on the subject of dream narratives, I may as well mention that I found J. S. Cardone's *The Slayer* more persuasive and more gripping than all the Elm Street nightmares. But in my experience, no film other than *Eraserhead* records nightmare in such detail—the textures, the lighting, the meanings that flicker out of reach, the utter casualness of the outrageous. *Eraserhead* can be read as a metaphor about fears of birth, but I don't find that makes the experience of the film any more manageable. The only other films that affect me similarly these days are some of the work of Andrei Tarkovsky; for whatever reason, I was unable to watch a videocassette of *Stalker* for more than half an hour at a time, and some of the images in *Mirror* seem to reach into a part of my mind darker than I can explore.

The death of the baby in *Eraserhead* is appalling—legitimately so, I think. Soon, however, the screen offered masses of images at least as atrocious, and much of this was mindless escalation. I've nothing against explicitness; I find the monstrous transformations in John Carpenter's *Thing* awesome rather than repulsive; I thought *The Evil Dead* was great scary fun; *Hellraiser* is wholly compelling, and David Cronenberg seems to display excessive images so as to challenge the audience to confront its reactions. His version of *The Fly* proves that extreme physical explicitness and terror needn't be mutually exclusive, while most of his films—*Videodrome* in particular—demonstrate that these qualities can coexist with intellectual substance. On the other hand, I find Lucio Fulci's zombies (especially those who visit the blind woman in *The Beyond*, *The Seven Doors of Death*, or whatever title it may next acquire) more unnerving before they set about their gory rending of victims, though I certainly didn't want the British censor to remove these images on my behalf. In general I think that horror films have recently been at least as guilty of the coarsening which David Aylward (writing in the sadly defunct Canadian journal *Borderland*) found in too much of today's horror fiction; whether or not they "used to strive for awe and achieve fear," certainly now they "strive for fear and achieve only disgust." *The Texas Chainsaw Massacre III* is a dispiriting recent example which struggles to be nastier than the original.

Let me not end on a pessimistic note. Terror is still capable of higher things. Despite the context of theme-park extravagance in which they occur, Julian Beck's scenes as the preacher in *Poltergeist II*—when he seems about to reveal himself as a cadaver without, as far as I can see, any makeup effects to aid him—convey a real sense of supernatural terror which is worth the whole of the rest of the series. And the most powerfully frightening scenes of the nineties for me so far are Joe Pesci's in *Goodfellas*, where he plays a psychotic who is all the more disturbing because he is so much fun to watch. It's a creation worthy to stand beside Travis Bickle in another Scorsese film, *Taxi Driver*. Horror fans who look for their horror only in films and books labeled as such are cheating themselves, and I hope that some of what I've said here makes my readers look again. After all, that's what writers are for.

Chapter

5

Nancy A. Collins

The cover, really, is what caught my eye. There was no type on the front, no title and no name. Immediately I picked it up and read the back—*Sunglasses After Dark*. Another vampire novel, I realized, and then noticed the sexy female on the cover had fangs.

I put it back on the shelf. I had enough to read at the time and I usually don't buy a book that isn't by an author I'm familiar with, either by previous books, anthology appearances, or reputation, unless of course that author comes highly recommended. At the time, Nancy didn't fit the bill.

For whatever reason, I eventually did something uncharacteristic of the older me (the teen me did this all the time). I plunked down my hard-earned bucks for a book by someone I'd literally never heard of.

I'd like to think it was intuition. *Sunglasses* won the Bram Stoker Award for Best First Novel, an award well deserved. Nancy's writing has an undeniably cinematic quality that is impossible to ignore. Her work cries out for celluloid. Her subsequent books, *Tempter* and *In the Blood*, have only borne out what most of us had realized after the first paragraph of *Sunglasses*. She's in this for the duration.

The effect of movies on Nancy's life and career wasn't only about watching the films, it was about the experience of going to the movies. Read on and see what I mean.

The Place of Dreams

by Nancy A. Collins

I love movies. I used to go to them all the time when I was a child, before the local movie theater shut its doors. But as I've grown older I

75

find myself making fewer and fewer forays to the fabled land of silver dreams, preferring to wait until they're available on home video.

Why is this, you ask?

Is it because movies aren't as good as they used to be? While movies are certainly *different* now than when I was a kid (hell, I was born in 1959! We're not talking the silent era here), I really couldn't say if your basic Hollywood studio release is any better or worse than those in the early to mid-sixties.

Is it because of the increasing use of violence and obscenity? Well, that's not something I normally worry about and I find it doesn't distract from my enjoyment of a picture—provided mindless violence and foul language are not the prime selling points of the film.

Is it the outrageous prices they're charging for tickets? Well, kind of. But since I work in my own home and have the luxury of setting my own hours, I can take advantage of the cheap(er) matinee rates whenever I feel like it.

So what is it that's keeping me away from the theaters? The answer's so simple that it eluded even me for a time. The simple reason I don't go to the movies as often as I'd like is the theaters themselves.

Whatever happened to honest-to-god managers who were something besides overglorified bookkeepers? Whatever happened to ushers who would actually eject noisy, inebriated, and otherwise obnoxious pests from the theater? Whatever became of the sense of social responsibility that existed between movie theaters and the communities they served?

You see, I was spoiled as a child. I didn't realize it at the time, but now—with the hindsight thirtysomething years provide—I can see I was spoiled big-time.

I grew up in a small rural town in southeastern Arkansas—a region renowned for rice paddies, cotton fields, mosquitoes, and little else. For a few years McGehee, Arkansas, was a thriving railroad town, bustling with activity on the weekends when the local farmers came in to do their shopping and relax from their hard labors.

McGehee had several of the amenities associated with a cultural center: there was a fancy hotel, drugstores where you could get cherry phosphates and banana splits at the soda fountains, numerous dry-goods stores, a sit-down family restaurant, and a moving-picture palace.

However, by the time I came along, most of that was gone, or in the process of disappearing.

The railroad had been seriously crippled during the fifties, when the highway system became the preferred mode of travel. The soda fountains were still operating, although the fancy hotel had been turned into a bank. The dry-goods stores located downtown were starting their long fight with discount stores like TG&Y and K Mart, located along the new highway. McGehee was beginning its decline, although its citizens didn't realize it—or weren't willing to admit it.

One of the last vestiges of the town's boom time was the local movie theater. By the time I was old enough to remember going to it, it had changed its name from the Bijou to the Malco. And it was there I was spoiled.

In order to tell the story of the Malco, I have to tell the story of its first and, in many ways, only manager: Mr. King. Charlton Birchley King, known throughout his life as "C.B.," came to McGehee, Arkansas, from Memphis, Tennessee, in the late thirties because he had married a local woman whose mother was "doing poorly" and needed attention. (The ailing mother-in-law would finally die in 1984.)

Although it wasn't widely known at the time, Mr. King owned twenty-five percent of the M. A. Lightfoot Company, Inc., better known as Malco, a southwestern concern that had started out in vaudeville and later moved into the more lucrative moving-picture venue.

Mr. King opened the Bijou in McGehee, which, according to my research material (my mother, grandmother, and great-aunt), was quite swank for its day. It boasted plush curtains, genuine leather seats, and a "retiring room" for women with nursing babies. The ushers were required to shave regularly and wear suits, while the female employees wore similar uniforms. Mr. King took the business of providing dreamstuff for his customers seriously, and ran a tight ship.

Then, during the early days of television, the old Bijou closed and a new theater was built across the street, utilizing the "fifties moderne" look. This was the Malco, and for the first twelve years of my life, it was the only movie theater my family went to.

The Malco was a single-screen theater, capable of seating two hundred, with seating for another hundred in the balcony. Up until the mid-sixties, the Malco, like every other public place of entertainment, was segregated. It had a separate entrance and ticket booth for Negro customers, and during the week they were barred from sitting anywhere but in the balcony. Although I never saw it, I assume they had their own snack bar as well.

The Malco lacked the Bijou's plush curtains and leather seats, but it still had special nights and catered to the needs and interests of the locals. Mr. King took his social responsibilities quite seriously and made a point of questioning his patrons as they left the theater as to whether they liked the evening's presentation. Would they prefer more cartoons before the feature? Would they like to see more films starring particular actors? Did they want more westerns? More thrillers? He even quizzed the children as to their preferences—which is how I became aware of Mr. King as something more than just another adult.

Since television made such a drastic change in weekly movie attendance, Mr. King decided to leave the "big" movie for the weekend shows and screen rereleases of film classics during the weeknights. Mondays were reserved for comedies, Tuesdays for silents (one of which, if I'm not mistaken, was the now-lost *London After Midnight*), Wednesdays for horror movies, and Thursdays for action films. My grandfather, a devout Boris Karloff and Lon Chaney, Sr., fan, was the one who introduced me to the pleasures of the cinema, by taking me with him on these excursions.

One of my earliest memories of being scared by anything on the screen was when my Grandfather Willoughby took me to see *Abbott and Costello Meet Frankenstein*. I can still recall my four-year-old self cowering behind one of the seats, peeking out at Lou Costello, strapped to a hospital gurney, being spun like a bottle between Frankenstein's Monster and the Wolfman. As an adult, it seems a really silly thing to be scared by; but when you're four years old, that's a situation you have no trouble identifying with!

Considering the secondhand glamour that comes with such a profession, C. B. King was not a particularly impressive man to look at—he tended to wear his pants a size too big and held them up with ubiquitous green suspenders. He wore glasses and walked with a perpetual stoop, due to a severe heart condition. My mother once described him as "looking like Peter Lorre, only four inches taller and forty pounds heavier." He was the first person I ever saw who had a pacemaker. It was one of the old-fashioned ones, worn outside the body. Mr. King kept it in his breast pocket. I can remember at the age of five thinking it was some kind of transistor radio and asking him what kind of music he got on it. He thought it was funny.

Mr. King was a good man. I can say that in retrospect, after having met many who were not.

My mother was fond of saying "If C. B. King couldn't find a dog to help over a stile, he'd find a cat, or a goat." That was just his way. He was interested in people and felt that he, as a businessman, owed something to the community that helped put bread on his table. Outside of animals, his biggest concern was the plight of needy children. Four times a year he organized food drives where you could get into the Saturday matinee for free if you donated canned food.

During my early preadolescence, I spent every Saturday at the Malco Kiddie Matinee. Tickets cost a quarter and you got to watch a triple feature, invariably consisting of a Japanese monster showdown, a reissued AIP black-and-white monster/teenager flick, and a Hammer horror movie, plus cartoons. And this was in 1970, folks.

Mr. King also arranged for "dusk-to-dawn shows," usually on summer weekends, that were aimed at the teen crowd. For a dollar you could see six—count 'em, six!—feature films, provided you didn't fall asleep halfway through. Most of these were AIP releases, along with various Amicus and American International programmers. There was always at least one biker flick (*The Leather Skirt Mob*, *She-Devils on Wheels*, *Born Losers*), a youth-oriented picture (*Hard Day's Night, The Trip, Wild in the Streets*), a beach-party movie (*Ghost in the Invisible Bikini*, *Beach Blanket Bingo*, *Muscle Beach Party*), a Vincent Price/ Edgar Allan Poe extravaganza (*Masque of the Red Death*, *The Pit and the Pendulum*, *The Raven*), and a gritty spaghetti western (*The Good, the Bad and the Ugly*, *A Fistful of Dollars*, *For a Few Dollars More*).

I loved the dusk-to-dawn shows, looking on them as something of an endurance challenge. Sometimes I managed to stay awake all the way to the biker picture, usually the last on the program. Most of the time I nodded off during the Poe flick.

McGehee's parents didn't worry about their children sitting up until four or five in the morning because they knew the Malco to be clean, safe, and staffed with actual ushers who would bounce you from the theater if you talked too loudly or were bothering the other patrons. In many ways, it served as home-away-from-home for several generations of McGehee's youth.

While Mr. King was a goodhearted man, it was his heart that proved to be his undoing. In 1972, after three open-heart surgeries and two pacemakers, his heart exploded, killing him instantly. No one realized it at the time, but his passing marked a turning point in McGehee's history, and not for the better.

After C. B. King's death, the Malco fell into the hands of an outsider with little interest in serving the community as anything besides a ticket taker. The kiddie matinees quickly became a thing of the past, as did the dusk-to-dawn shows.

The quality of the films continued to slip until the only shows it played were *Swedish Stewardesses* and *The Corpse Grinders*.

Drunken riffraff took to vandalizing the seats and threatening the other customers. On one occasion, a particularly drunken patron ripped an entire row of seats from their moorings and *threw* them at one of the ushers. Rats, always a problem at theaters, proliferated until it wasn't safe to keep your feet on the floor during the screening. Finally, after three years of decay and decline, the Malco closed its doors in 1975.

Looking back, I can see how big a role the movie theater played in my hometown's social life. During its heyday, it was a safe, respectable place for a family to leave its kids for an afternoon. It was also the only place in town the teenagers could socialize without fear of being branded delinquent.

Once the Malco was closed, things in McGehee grew worse. Outside of a couple of pool halls and a swimming pool that was open only during the summer, there was literally nowhere to go and nothing to do. If you wanted to see a movie, you had to pester someone with a driver's license into driving you to either Dumas (twenty miles away), Monticello (thirty miles away), Pine Bluff (fifty miles away) or Greenville, Mississippi (across the state line). Once you learned to drive, this became less of an ordeal, but not by much.

Delinquency, teen pregnancy, and alcoholism became more and more of a problem. Unlike others my same age, I turned to books and comics for my entertainment instead of beer and sex. (Those would come later.)

In 1979 there was an attempt to revitalize the old Malco by turning it into a second-run venue, but the doors had closed again by 1981, and they have yet to reopen. The chances of the Malco ever reclaiming its audience are not good. In 1990 a fire began in the abandoned five-and-dime two doors down from the theater. The blaze halted at the Malco's firewall, leaving it unscathed, but the rest of the block was totaled. The rubble from the fire is still there, since the city is too poor to pay to have the detritus carted away.

Now I'm thirty-one years old and live in a major metropolitan area with at least twelve first-run theaters within a half hour's drive, not to mention several second-run "bargain" movie houses. So why am I not making up for those squandered years of enforced boredom?

Because I *detest* modern-day movie theaters.

With a few exceptions, independently owned, family-operated, neighborhood theaters are things of the past. They have been replaced by soulless multiscreen shoeboxes, much as the old-fashioned commercial districts have been replaced by faceless malls.

The local chain theaters carry what their disembodied owners *tell* them to carry. Some insist that multiscreen cinemas provide theater goers with greater variety. But if you look in the newspaper, you can find up to six multiscreen "cineplexes" playing the exact same programs in the same town. The illusion of variety is just that: illusion.

Today's theater is an impersonal place, a setting that would seem alien to the concept of dreaming with your eyes open. Don't get me wrong; I don't need plush wall coverings and art nouveau nymphs holding up speakers for me to enjoy a film. But sitting in a cramped, uncomfortable seat, surrounded by people who talk like they're in their living rooms decidedly detracts from the experience. And with the inflated prices at the concession stand (more often than not for prepopped popcorn that is trucked into the theater in plastic garbage bags), I've found it easier on my nerves and pocketbook simply to wait until the newest releases make it onto video.

I doubt my personal preferences will make much difference to the megaliths running the motion-picture industry. To a great extent, I'm something of a dinosaur. More and more Americans are growing up knowing nothing but the sterile "Hellplaza Octoplex" as the sole venue for films. Many would, no doubt, feel overwhelmed—if not intimidated— by a screen larger than that of a wide-screen TV.

Still, I don't want to close this on a depressing note. While few citizens of McGehee under the age of thirty can remember a time when the Malco was something besides a big, empty building with chains on the doors, C. B. King's legacy lives on, but in a different area.

In my hometown there exists the C. B. King School for Mentally Retarded and Physically Handicapped Children. It has been in operation since the seventies and was originally funded from a charitable bequest in Mr. King's will. It provides daycare for special children between the ages of three and nine, regardless of race, creed, or financial status.

Like the countless heroes, heroines, sidekicks, and villains who flicker across the screen, C. B. King has attained a form of immortality. What could be better for a man whose business was dreams?

Chapter

6

John Farris

His first novel was published in 1956 and thirty-odd follow-ups have made him one of the premiere writers of horror and suspense. His influence has extended over a generation of his fellows, and no less than Stephen King has stated that as a young man, he "adopted" John's career as "a goal to be reached and an example to be emulated."

As horror writers go, John is among the most devoted to the silver screen. He has optioned and/or written screenplays for the majority of his novels, including Brian De Palma's successful 1978 version of his novel *The Fury*. He also wrote and directed an earlier film, *Dear Dead Delilah*.

These days, John is almost always on the run, working tirelessly to bring his work to the screen, and he is perched atop what may be his second big roll. The first began with *The Fury,* and now thirteen years later, he's a frequent flier to L.A. While Richard (*Lethal Weapon*) Donner steps up to the plate with a film version of John's novel *Fiends*, there are a half-dozen other Farris-penned screenplays on deck and waiting in the dugout, including *The Axman Cometh*, *Sharp Practice*, *The Uninvited*, and *Nightfall*.

In the following piece, presented by Kelley Wilde, Farris speaks quietly and, according to Kelley, "with the controlled intensity of a large jungle cat," about Hollywood's horrors . . . and also its spoils.

Kelley Wilde

Born and bred in Buffalo, New York, he is quietly unassuming in the manner of the logically confident. Polite. A gentleman. Kelley spent quite a bit of postcollege time pursuing a journalistic career and skipped around North America for a number of years . . . Toronto . . . San Francisco . . . Montreal . . . New York. His first novel, *The Suiting*, was penned on both coasts, and in 1989 he was awarded the Bram Stoker Award for Best First Novel for his efforts. The paperback of his second novel, *Makoto*, has just hit stores as I write this and he has two more (the first of which is *Mastery*) already scheduled for release by the end of 1992. VanDerKloot Film and Television Productions has optioned *The Suiting* and will begin shooting from Kelley's own screenplay sometime in 1992.

A User's Guide to Hollywood Horror

John Farris as told to Kelley Wilde

Breaking In: When Michael Calls *(1971) and* Dear Dead Delilah *(1972)*

In 1968, a friend in the record business, who had a lot of money, said he was thinking of making an inexpensive horror film. They were just coming back in at that time—stuff like *Blood Feast* and *Two Thousand Maniacs*—and he wanted to do something along that line for a hundred thousand dollars, a hundred fifty thousand.

The only previous experience I had was on *When Michael Calls*. James Bridges was assigned by Larry Turman, when Fox bought it, to do the screenplay. Turman sent it to me and I thought it was lousy and told him so. I did a hundred-and-thirty or -forty-page treatment of what I thought it should be. Turman said, "This is great," and took it to Zanuck and Brown. Well . . . They said, "We've spent enough money on this and we're not gonna make it." So, the project languished. Eventually, there was a TV movie made from the Bridges script. It had a good cast: Ben Gazzarra, Michael Douglas, Elizabeth Ashley . . . A lot of people liked it, but it wasn't a very good film.

Then Jack Clement came in with his plans for a movie, and I ended up writing two screenplays. We decided to do both of them, back-to-back, for a hundred fifty each. I thought *Dear Dead Delilah* was a little classier, so we put most of the budget in that. A good thing. We couldn't have done two of them. It was hard enough directing and shooting one in thirty days. But the movie that we didn't shoot—a little vampire number—eventually became *Fiends*.

The Fury *(1978)*

The next thing that was turned into a movie was *The Fury,* which I did the screenplay for. Fox didn't particularly want me to write it, but that was too bad—I insisted.

The usual amount of time lapsed while they dickered for a director. They gave it to Norman Jewison and a couple of others I thought were inappropriate.

In the meantime, I'd gotten a job with Brian De Palma on a thing called *Where Are the Children,* a Mary Higgins Clark book that had big problems as far as translating it into a film. I mean, it was a dead giveaway who the guilty party was.

About that time, Brian's option on the whole thing was up. *Carrie* had come out and suddenly he was a really hot item. One night we were up at his place in New York and I said, "This is the way we can work it. . . ." He said, "That's great, but I've lost interest. What are you working on—anything else?" So I gave him the script for *The Fury.* Two or three days later, he called Frank Yablans and said, "I want to do this."

Hollywood's Long, Winding Road

See, that's nothing new in Hollywood. Screenplays are all over the place. They're just awash in screenplays that somebody thinks they should do. The Writers Guild of America West registers, like, twenty-five thousand scripts a year. All the movies in production last year in the U.S., including independent features: about one hundred seventy films. So, you figure the difficulties! Everybody's writing movie scripts. Everybody thinks, Wow, a hundred and twenty pages—and all it is is dialogue!

The problem is, there are very few directors who can get a project moving. I think the key right now is first to get the director. If you've got a director, you can get the actors. You've got to have the director. Say you've got Tony Scott directing and you've got a good screenplay, they will let you cast somebody who's on the verge, like Andy Garcia or Ray Liotta. Even if you can't get Tom Cruise, they'll still make the movie. If you don't have the director, and you've got Ray Liotta . . . it's tough.

The guy that wrote *Dances with Wolves* would still be washing dishes in a Chinese restaurant if it hadn't been for Kevin Costner. At the time he was working on it, first as a novel and then as a screenplay, Costner was slowly rising in the world and becoming a hot commodity. And only because of that could they even get to see anybody to get the thing going. And then they couldn't find a director!

So, getting anything done in Hollywood depends on the attention of a viable director, "viable" meaning somebody who's got a fairly decent track record, or a star who's attached to the project. Better yet, these days, they like to have both.

After *Carrie,* Brian De Palma was hot.

With *Fiends,* you've got Richard Donner, who's an A-list director. A-list is really twelve or fifteen names, as far as directors go, who are busy all the time.

When I was writing *Fiends,* I never anticipated it as a movie. But my agent happened to know, since he's very good friends with Donner, that Dick had wanted to do another horror movie. Of course, *The Omen* was his big breakthrough. He'd been wanting to do another one for years and years, and had been looking for material. But it was all the same shit. He read *Fiends* over a weekend. And things happened pretty quickly. My agent called me up and said, "You want to do the screenplay?" I said, "Sure! If he's interested, I'm interested."

The Fury *vs.* Fiends

When *The Fury* was shot, in 1977, it came in for an average budget at that time, about $7 million.

This one will come in at twenty-five or thirty and then they'll spend another $15 million on top of that to promote it.

Fiends will not be treated as a horror film. That was the first thing I heard from Richard Donner's lips. He was interested in the scary parts, and there's a lot of scary stuff in there. I was cautioned, though, before I started writing. . . . I said, "How violent and gruesome and so forth do you want this? Do you want these elements?" He said no.

Except for some scenes not in the book that I put in the movie, it's not really bloody or gruesome. We prey on the viewer's imagination.

What we're really highlighting is the fantastic element. There'll be an almost Kabuki-like atmosphere to it with the Fiends' robes and wings, they way they look. Donner will spend the big money on great set designs and the caves, an element he especially liked.

The Fiends themselves . . . Well, they're different. Like a family from Mars. In the screenplay, I wanted to emphasize the family aspect of them. Give them human qualities. They're not that far removed from being human. . . . Fiends, yeah, but not monsters. There's a difference. I wanted to emphasize that aspect of community.

I don't know how they'll sell it . . . but it won't be as straight horror.

On the Horror Market

I prefer suspense. I think that's the only way to go today. This little corner of the horror world that Douglas Winter thinks so much of—splatterpunk?—is a dead end if ever there was one. I think you have to scare people . . . but viewers are too sophisticated in all the state-of-the-art gore and there's a limited market for that. Nobody in his right mind at a major studio wants to make that kind of picture. You can, if you have the talent, write about people who are down and out, but still at the same time there's something human that comes through that makes you empathize with them. Why else are we watching this movie?

Straight horror's kind of a worn-out market now, although I read that there are seven or eight vampire films in the works. Including some old-timers like *Interview with the Vampire,* which has been around for years. And they've revised *Dracula* for Columbia with Francis Ford Coppola directing.

But, also, eighteen months ago, there were three Robin Hood films in the works—and, of course, the one that got made is the one Costner agreed to do. See, people think alike out there. Everything goes in cycles. And, for a pure horror movie, I can't think of anything that's been a big grosser.

I guess *Arachnophobia* would fit into the category, but they tried to market it as something else.

Pet Sematary was an out-and-out horror movie. There's no other way to describe it. That did about $56 million, the biggest grosser I can think of. And that's the only movie my kid ever walked out on. Someone getting their head cut off doesn't upset him, he knows that's just fantasy. But the flashback to somebody dying of some terminal, awful disease. . . . That was too close to home.

I'm afraid that horror may be going the way of the western, except for the cheap stuff that they grind out for foreign markets. Depends on what you call a horror film. If you call *The Silence of the Lambs* horror . . . I don't. I think it's a good thriller and extremely well made. Some people think *Psycho* is horror. I don't.

And I'm not out to do straight horror. There is a Stephen King type of book. I mean, that's pretty well established. Like *Summer of Night*—Dan Simmons wrote it, but it's a Stephen King book. That's a whole genre that King actually perfected. I can't think of anything I've written that's remotely like anything that he would even think about.

I'm more interested in my own genre . . . and I get harder to please as I go along.

On Past Horror Favorites

Oh, *Frankenstein*—the original . . . The Howard Hawks version of *The Thing*, which I thought was a ground-breaking movie . . . *Alien*, that would be really close to the top of the list . . . I liked *Rosemary's Baby,* but I thought it was—once you'd read the book, what was the point of the movie? . . . *The Exorcist* was certainly eye popping at the time, but I didn't react well to it. . . . The Hammer Films version of *Dracula* with Christopher Lee—I thought it was sensational, the best they ever made. . . . Nothing else really pops into my mind.

On Writing Screenplays

Learning wasn't tough at all. I just did it, it was in my head. I have an extremely precise and accurate visual sense, and a sense about things—just from watching movies, I assume. I never read a book about how things should work or took any courses. I had a couple of tips along the way from people who knew what they were doing. Like William Goldman, who said, "If it's more than three straight pages of dialogue, it's too much." The rest of it, the visual sense, just translates into script terms, so I had never had any problems.

Most novelists who write screenplays don't understand suspense. Basically, if you can make it believable in a book, it's a cinch in a movie. Because people grasp so much more quickly and want to move on, impatiently. You provide them with a coincidence, and if it's not totally outrageous, you don't dwell on it, you just do it, and they say, "All right, let's get on with it." As Alfred Hitchcock said, "Is it a coincidence? Very well, it's a coincidence." Movie audiences are quick and really ahead of you most of the time. You don't have to belabor the point. It's all visual.

On Surviving the Hollywood Jungle

Gore Vidal goes out there, they pay him three or four hundred thousand for a screenplay. It's relaxation for him. He enjoys the ambience . . . you know, once in a while. He goes out there, does his job, collects his money, and goes back to Italy to work on a book.

You have to have that attitude. As far as being corrupted goes, there's an awful lot of mediocre and bad movies made. And the reason is, basically, that good screenplays are hard to find. I've made some catty remarks myself about the ability that goes into them, and that's true up to a point. In a sense, *Rain Man* was made by the performances and the direction, but the screenplay had to add up before they had anything to work with. All the good performances and direction in the world can't save a bad script.

Post-Fiends *Movie Plans*

I've got another project, an original screenplay that I would direct on a shoestring budget. The suspense genre really lends itself to inexpensive movies. A picture like *Blood Simple* . . . They made that on a shoestring—about five hundred thousand—but they knew exactly what they were doing and they had a good script.

I'm collaborating with a friend of mine who is a cinematographer. He's dying to make a movie because he's bored with what he's doing—directing Brooke Shields and people in lettuce commercials. He's one of the highest-paid fashion photographers in the world and he has about $3 or $4 million a year in income.

I said, "Look, why don't we do this? I'd like to have a movie that I direct which I can show. You need a movie that you photograph, which you can show. We need it as a demo, really. But, hopefully, since I'm good at this and you're good at what you do, we can make a movie that would be releasable and make some money for us. And we can do it for about three hundred and fifty thousand dollars—avoiding the unions totally. No unions, no nothing. I'll donate my time for expenses, you donate your time and equipment. And you know everybody in the world: we need a penthouse apartment, you can call somebody and get the use of it for a day in New York. You know all the ins and outs of doing this kind of thing anyway, let's get together and do it."

He said, "Fabulous! Got any ideas?"

I said, "Well . . . Not at the moment!"

Then I thought of something that just may work out. *(Pause . . . Quiet, wicked laugh.)* Yeah: The dark side of *Pretty Woman* meets *Rebecca*!

Chapter
7

Craig Shaw Gardner

Horror writer? That guy who writes those funny-fantasy books? The Batman guy?

Yeah, that's him.

Craig doesn't like to be pigeonholed, yet he seems to have resigned himself to its inevitability. With a very successful string of fantasy trilogies and a lucrative turn at film novelizations including *Batman* (which mutated him for all eternity into '*New York Times* best-selling author Craig Shaw Gardner,' not bad work if you can get it), most readers tend to see him as a "funny fantasy" writer.

This is unfortunate, not because his *Revenge of the Fluffy Bunnies* and *A Difficulty with Dwarves* and *The Other Sinbad* aren't great, but because his horror is just as good. Though he continues to insist that there is an epic horror novel in the works, to date all of his work in the field has been in short form. He doesn't get too many complaints. Numerous anthologies, including those of Charles L. Grant, have been home to Craig's twisted tales.

At first glance, it may seem odd that someone with such a wonderful command of humor would be able to be equally effective with terror as a tool. But, as Craig explains herein, there's a fine line between humor and horror, an intangible and easily crossed line between slipping on a banana peel and cracking open your head. It is precisely because he sees that line so clearly that he crosses it so easily. Now he focuses that light of clarity on the silver screen. Silver turning crimson as we speak.

Blood and Laughter:
The Humor in Horror Film

by Craig Shaw Gardner

It's so funny I could scream.

At first glance, humor and horror might seem like opposites. It's certainly very difficult to balance the two of them in fiction, and humorous horror, especially at novel length, is virtually nonexistent.

The movies, though, are a far different place from books. There have been many horror films with humorous subtexts, as well as funny movies with scary moments. Combining humor and horror, when it is done properly and in proportion, can actually heighten the cumulative effect of a film.

Why should this be so? Well, there's a couple of reasons. Let's start with the basics. Those of you familiar with my work know that I've written both humorous novels and horror short stories, and I believe that the basis of both of these forms rests on the same simple assumption: Something is wrong with everyday life.

In other words, both start from something we know well, but that something has changed. In humor, that change will often take the form of a caricature, a reasonably benign exaggeration of something we know to be true, like a windbag politician who is incapable of shutting his mouth.

Of course, the "wrong" can take other forms as well. It may be a sequence of events or misunderstandings, played against each other so that the normal meanings and results become totally twisted and comically complex, and a single missed word or misinterpreted gesture can take on great social importance. Screwball comedies of the 1930s and 1940s were especially good at this sort of thing. Fred Astaire is sure Ginger Rogers is married to Edward Everett Horton because he spotted Ginger wearing Horton's wife's hat—that sort of thing. Or it could be the comedy of surprise and sudden reversals; anything from the clever verbal comebacks in a film like *His Girl Friday* to the blunt shock of seeing someone fall because they stepped on a banana peel. We find all of these things funny because, since we recognize and relate to these characters and situations, a change in those familiar, everyday things startles us into laughter.

Effective horror begins in the everyday as well, in that house down the street, or on a summer vacation, getting away from it all, or in the relationships between lovers, friends, or parents and children. But in this case the world we know twists a different way, and our home, our street, our lives are in danger from something just out of our sight. Maybe it's our childhood fears come back to haunt us, as in *Poltergeist,* or maybe we've taken one step too far away from the world we know, as in *Alien* or *The Texas Chainsaw Massacre*. But chaos is waiting for us with a knife or a ghost or a dream or some unspeakable thing sporting claws or a chain saw, and as we know all too well, that thing is going to get us.

Wait a minute! I hear you say. I don't know about your everyday life, but I don't see many unspeakable things (even without claws and chain saws) down at my local 7-Eleven! Well, yeah, it's not the monster, but the people the monster confronts that must be drawn from the everyday. As an example, let's look at the previously mentioned *Alien,* a movie that on its surface seems to be as un-everyday as any movie can be. Here's a film that takes place on a spaceship that encounters the ruins of an alien culture sometime in the far future. Not a 7-Eleven in sight.

But let's look at what is generally considered to be the film's most successful scene, the "chestburster" sequence. Notice how the scene is set up. A crew member, who has recently had an alien "thing" attached to his face, seems miraculously recovered. He joins in a meal with the other crew members. They all talk and joke, like any group of old friends that have worked together for a long time, not unlike somebody might talk and joke with fellow shift workers, or an after-hours softball team. For a moment, even though we are in a spaceship somewhere in the far future, we are plunked down in the middle of an everyday situation.

Then—*wham*—out of this familiarity comes the chestburster. When this horror does occur, it is that much more effective because, within this context, the audience has gained a strong identification with the universal humanity of the characters on the screen. *Alien* never achieves this close identification again, and the rest of the movie is weaker for this.

The real star of *Alien* is, of course, H. R. Giger's design for the alien civilization and the various forms the monster takes as it grows larger and ever more deadly. And Giger's brilliance is also based on the familiar. His spaceships and aliens are strangely organic, as if they were made out of human body parts—the creature that bursts out of the crewman's chest looks like nothing so much as a penis with teeth, an object simultaneously familiar and culturally forbidden. This tension between the everyday and the taboo is what gives Giger's designs their power, and increases the feeling of unease in the audience. Any design based upon the truly unknown would not be horrible. It would only be incomprehensible.

Both humor and horror, then, are based on change; usually unexpected change. But how does humor work in the context of the horror film? The most common answer is as a release mechanism.

For example, in the original version of *The Cat People,* there is a very effective scene that takes place in a park. The heroine is walking as quickly as she can from the brilliance of one streetlight to the next, and both she and the audience are convinced she is being followed by something, perhaps a large black panther that will tear her to shreds. Every time she leaves the relative safety of the streetlight's glare and rushes through the dark for the next streetlight, the audience waits for an attack from that dark. Suddenly there is a great noise offscreen, a roaring sound followed by a loud screech. The audience is convinced the huge cat has come for her at last. And then a bus pulls into the frame. The roar was the bus's engine, the screech the sound of its door opening. The bus driver demands that the startled heroine make a decision. Is she going to get on the bus or not? The heroine gets on the bus.

And the audience laughs. They were expecting a supernatural black panther, a change from the everyday, but instead received a second change, and were pushed across the border again, back to the familiar, with the arrival of the bus.

Humor is present in all film genres and, historically, has increased within individual films as the genre becomes more familiar to the audience. Thus, the monsters that were played more or less straight in Universal horror films like *Frankenstein, Dracula,* and *The Wolf Man* are played for laughs a few years later in *Abbott and Costello Meet Frankenstein.*

But film genres have a way of reinventing themselves. Thus the tired monsters of the *Frankenstein* era gave way to the atomic monsters of the fifties cold war, and those monsters fell before the rebirth of the traditional monsters by England's Hammer studios and Roger Corman's adaptations of Edgar Allan Poe, movies set safely in the past, but featuring much more explicit sex and violence than films had shown before. Hitchcock's *Psycho* showed up soon thereafter, and ushered in a whole subgenre of psychotic slasher films. Big-budget films like

Rosemary's Baby and *The Exorcist* followed, but perhaps more important to the genre as a whole was an independent production out of Pittsburgh, *Night of the Living Dead*. There was a new generation of filmmakers showing up in the seventies, including Steven Spielberg, Joe Dante, and John Sayles, who mixed horror with hip characterization in films like *Jaws* and *The Howling*. But it was back to more sex and violence, more explicit and in the present day now, in the new breed of slasher films, led by the phenomenal success of the *Friday the 13th* and *Nightmare on Elm Street* films.

Humor has played an important role in all of these cycles, reflecting the changing nature of the horror film.

To examine those changes, let's start with the greatest example of the Universal horror boom of the 1930s, *The Bride of Frankenstein*. The humor in this film is very dark. After a slightly overwrought (and not unfunny) framing piece, the true action of the movie begins where *Frankenstein* left off, with the supposed destruction of the monster in the fire at the mill. But the first character with any notable lines is a comic one, one of the Baron Frankenstein's maids (played very broadly by Una O'Connor), who announces that the monster must be burning because the fire flared up there, and everyone knows that innards make the fire burn brighter.

This outrageous statement is a sign that not everything is to be taken seriously here, although the horror shows up soon thereafter, as the monster quickly kills a pair of peasants. But the movie strikes a precarious balance, between horror and humorous relief, and between humanity (especially that of the monster in his relationship with the blind hermit) and exaggeration (in the character of Dr. Pretorius and the later creation of the bride) that is so over the top that in a later film it might be referred to as high camp. It's as if, by juxtaposing these different elements in a seventy-five-minute film, director James Whale and his screenwriters were striving for Shakespearean rhythms, rather like having comic gravediggers lighten the tone around a Hamlet soliloquy. And, while it might not quite be Shakespeare, *Bride of Frankenstein* works well even today.

There are parts of this film, such as the revelation of Pretorius's miniature humans, that are played strictly for comedy. Yet the movie's horror still retains much of its potency over fifty years after it was made. The final scene, when the humanized monster pulls the switch that will kill them all and intones "We belong dead," is still chilling. We care about the monster (actually far more than about Dr. Frankenstein) precisely because he has been presented with humanity and humor.

The integration of humor and horror was less successful in the cold-war cycle of the fifties. Humor did lend some redeeming value to Roger Corman's cheaply made quickies, especially *Little Shop of Horrors* and *Bucket of Blood*, but these films were really comedies with horror trappings, closer to *The Cat and the Canary* and *The Old Dark House* than to *Frankenstein*.

A subtler form of humor, that of social satire, did inform some of the more successful science-fiction/horror blends based on novels from the period. *Invasion of the Body Snatchers* (based on a novel by Jack Finney), where people are replaced by their vegetable look-alikes, and very few of their neighbors notice the change until they, too, are vegetables, criticized conformity in fifties society. *The Incredible Shrinking Man*, from the book by Richard Matheson, took the story of a man who inexplicably shrinks from a full adult down to microscopic size to examine the social and physical trappings of society. This form of social humor would become even more important in later horror films.

The late fifties brought the British horror boom. These films, quite serious at first, attempted to add humor, often through the use of comic British character actors (along with ever-more-explicit sex and violence), as the cycle continued. While Hammer, the main producer of this sort of film, never had a commercial success with a humor/horror hybrid, another British film company, Amicus, had a successful series of anthology films, which would often contain humorous segments with twist endings, rather like stories in the old EC comics, which actually formed the basis for a pair of Amicus productions. Robert Bloch became the house screenwriter for a number of these films, and his macabre wit informs most of the best of them, such as *Asylum* and *Torture Garden*.

Meanwhile, back in the U.S.A., Roger Corman brought back the same sort of dramatic overstatement that Whale gave us in *Bride of Frankenstein*, only this time in living color (!) with a series of Poe adaptations. These films, such as *The Pit and the Pendulum* and *The Masque of the Red Death*, all featured Vincent Price at his scenery-chewing best, and are enjoyable in large part because of his dramatic overstatement. Corman also made a humorous film in his Poe cycle, *The Raven*, which featured a much drier wit than earlier spoofs. (When Vincent Price mentions that his wife's crypt is located in the living room, Peter Lorre replies, "Of course." The script was written by Richard Matheson.)

So by the late 1960s, humorous horror films had met with some success, although as in the case of *The Raven,* they would always appear in the later stages of that particular horror cycle, making fun of what had gone before. But the sixties and seventies brought two distinct new trends to the mix which would change all that.

The first change was brought about by George Romero and *Night of the Living Dead.* A low-budget, and somewhat crudely produced movie filmed entirely in Pittsburgh, PA, *Night* became a hit on the newly created midnight-movie circuit and paved the way for the production of independent horror films. And what a movie it was.

I remember quite vividly the first time I saw *Night.* It was the third part of a triple feature, the first two parts being a reissue of the breakthrough Hammer horror films, *Curse of Frankenstein* and *Horror of Dracula.* A couple of my dorm mates and I ventured to the Loews Central in Boston's Combat Zone (right next to the famous Two O'Clock Lounge) and we had watched both the Hammer films. It was getting late. At that time, the Combat Zone was not a particularly safe place to be late at night. And this *Night of the Living Dead* thing came on, and it was in black-and-white for chrissakes! Well, we decided we'd give it five minutes.

In five minutes, we were hooked. By the end of the movie, we were devastated. Hey, *Horror of Dracula* is a great movie, but *Night of the Living Dead* is the *Truth*! Humanity versus zombies, and humanity falls apart. The social satire in movies like *Invasion of the Body Snatchers* was right on the surface here in the television broadcasts and the group of locals Romero recruited as zombie fighters, so deadpan that they make the living dead look lively.

And there was a lot more going on here than humor. The movie was downright disgusting. Zombies eating the intestines of the recently fried young lovers? How gross—and how neat—could you get? And then, when the only decent human being in the entire film, who also happened to be black, gets gunned down at the end—wow! Like I said, in 1967, this was the *Truth*.

Night of the Living Dead did more than open the floodgates for independent horror films. It created a whole new breed of irreverent horror. Think back to *Frankenstein,* when the mob burns the monster, on to all those fifties films like *Tarantula* where they call in the army and the air force and all the might of society to kill off a giant spider.

In all these movies, the hero and society triumph, even if it might occasionally be implied that society was wrong. (The end of *Invasion of the Body Snatchers* was changed before release because the original ending, in which it was implied that the vegetable people could be winning, was considered too upsetting.) But in *Night,* the hero dies!

Well, the floodgates were open. Heroes and protagonists started to die right and left in horror films, and the monsters were even sometimes created or brought into the picture thanks to evil government plots! It got so you couldn't trust anybody. Thanks not only to *Night,* but the general atmosphere of the counterculture film, with hits like *Easy Rider* and *Bonnie and Clyde,* horror was breaking loose of its formalized boundaries.

Meanwhile, a new generation of hip horror screenwriters and directors had shown up in Hollywood. And a new breed of horror film came along, one that acknowledged the past history of the genre and even asked you to laugh at some of the associations with older monster movies, just before that new film scared the bloody wits out of you. One of the most successful mixes of this transitional period is 1980's *The Howling,* directed by Dante from a script by Sayles.

The Howling begins with a very effective scene of a TV anchorwoman, played by Dee Wallace, who has volunteered to act as bait to catch a man the police think may have committed a series of grisly murders. She wanders through an inner city filled with strip joints and sex shots as the police realize the wire they've placed on her is defective. The audience realizes the heroine is on her own when she finally meets the killer in a booth in one of the sex shops. The killer starts showing a film, in which a woman appears to be having violent sex, as the police burst into the shop. The cops gun down the killer after they hear the woman scream, but not before the heroine sees something horrible.

This opening scene, which is edited with a razor efficiency, is down, dirty, a trifle sarcastic about the ineptitude of the police, and very effective. It is immediately followed by a scene at the anchorwoman's TV station, where we see a pompous TV anchorman practicing his lines in front of the men's-room mirror. This hyperrealism played against buffoonery continues throughout the film, and gives the proceedings a surreal quality, which, in an odd sort of way, make the supernatural events that occur later all the more acceptable. Both the oddball humor and the horror accelerate as the film progresses, until the same werewolf the protagonist had shot early in the film shows up to pull a bullet from his scalp as he says "Let me give you a piece of my mind," a moment that manages to be frightening and perversely humorous at the same time.

That the kind of balance present in *The Howling* is difficult to achieve can be shown in another werewolf film from the following year, *An American Werewolf in London*. This film, directed by John Landis, boasts some fine comic moments, especially when Griffin Dunne, who is killed early in the film, keeps returning as an ever-more-rotting corpse to advise the hero, and one tremendous horror setpiece, when the werewolf stalks an unfortunate commuter through the London under-ground. But the total effect of the film is wildly uneven, and moments like the ill-thought-out fantasy sequence when lovable muppets turn into gun-wielding terrorists are more jarring than effective and undermine the mood of the film. Even more damaging is the film's conclusion, which is taken up largely with a never-ending car-crash scene, the sort of thing Landis likes to do in his comedies (just watch *The Blues Brothers*). The net result is a lot of slam-bang action and no thought, as if they really didn't know how they could end the picture.

As the eighties progressed the horror film became faster and bloodier, dominated for a time by the slasher film, inspired by the success of John Carpenter's *Halloween* (and the earlier Hitchcock classic *Psycho*). Unfortunately, most of these movies fell far short of their models, especially the phenomenally successful and every-bit-as-formulaic (Let's have sex. Let's get killed by a pitchfork.) *Friday the 13th* series. The somewhat more adventuresome *Nightmare on Elm Street* series did bring humor in the mix, with the supernatural slasher Freddy dispensing with pun-filled quips as he annihilated his victims.

In fact, by number four in the series, Freddy's humor seemed to dominate the series, and when they tried to downplay the humor and reinstate the horror of the first installment in *Nightmare* five, the movie failed at the box office.

There were a couple other remarkable movies in the eighties as well, brought by a pair of new directors.

What can you say about *Re-Animator*? No film had affected me in the same way since *Night of the Living Dead*. I entered the theater (this time the film was playing at an art house in trendy Cambridge), not knowing what to expect, but tired of the blood-for-blood's-sake of recent slasher films, I sat toward the back. There were about a dozen other people in the theater (a matinee) when the film began. A half hour into the movie, everybody else had fled the theater, and I had gone down to sit in the front row.

Directed by Stuart Gordon, this movie assaulted the senses from the beginning, and the moment the film had reached the zombie cat sequence (Zombie *cat*? Hey, horror movies do terrible things to people, not animals!) I knew we were dealing with a wonderfully demented concept. The movie is in the best Grand Guignol, mad scientist tradition, with gallons of blood and huge hypodermics filled with glowing green liquid. Yet, for all the over-the-top grue, whole segments of the film are played for laughs, including a pratfall scene involving a headless corpse and an off-color pun involving a severed head. We're talking *no limits* here, yet while you couldn't call the end result exactly tasteful, it is very—ahem—satisfying.

Another fascinatingly over-the-top film is Sam Raimi's *Evil Dead II,* a sequel that takes Raimi's original *Evil Dead* and remakes it as a Three Stooges comedy. It's bloody and hilarious at the same time, a combination of horror and assault comedy.

And the horror/comedy mix showed up in products from the major studios, too, with a successful run of films including Tom Holland's *Fright Night* and *Child's Play,* the even more mainstream *The Lost Boys,* and a new sequel of sorts to *Night of the Living Dead,* cowritten by John Russo, co-author of the original, called *Return of the Living Dead,* which emphasized the comedy over the horror. Yet all these movies, even *Return of the Living Dead,* have wonderfully frightening moments.

The combination of humor and horror, so tentative only a few years before, had come to stay. In fact, the mix had become so popular that Troma, a small, independent studio, based its entire output on the formula, with titles like *The Toxic Avenger* (the only somewhat-worthwhile film in the bunch), *Rabid Grannies,* and *The Class of Nuke-em High.* Burlesque, slapstick, satire, visual puns all added their own kind of shocks to the ever-more-sophisticated horror on the screen. They have helped to keep the horror movie fresh and alive, while other traditional genres such as the western and the musical seem ready to die.

So be ready to laugh the next time you see a horror movie. And be ready to scream for years to come.

Chapter
8

Ray Garton

Ray has built up quite a reputation over the past few years, part of which revolves around certain portions of his work that have been expurgated previous to American consumption. Silly, really. Though the scenes taken out were graphic, it was the brutality of their depiction that made them so disturbing. Fortunately, the rest of the book *Crucifax Autumn* (*Crucifax* in the United States) is just as brutal.

Throughout Ray's work, including the books *Live Girls* and *Trade Secrets,* there is an unflinching sense of honesty, a close-up look at sex and death and a real feeling of terror. What is most impressive about his work is the same thing that causes the MPAA to give the film *Henry: Portrait of a Serial Killer* an X rating: tone. It is the tone of Ray's writing that evokes the highest intensity, the deepest horror, the ultimate revulsion.

At the movies, Ray is a discriminating viewer. In the following piece he talks quite a bit about how different are the tastes of his adult self from those of his childhood self. To refer back to Ramsey, he now prefers the quality of terror rather than the nudity and gore that brings out the "kid" in him. It seems that at the movies, he must separate the desires of his current and former selves. But, as author, he is able to meld them perfectly, creating a visual, visceral, often erotic terror, with all the horrifying subtleties of a black-and-white classic.

On Kids and Cat People

by Ray Garton

When I was a kid, a show called *Creature Features* showed a horror-movie double feature every Saturday night and one of the double features that stands out most vividly in my mind is *Blood and Lace* followed by *Cat People*.

Blood and Lace had something to do with murders taking place at a creepy orphanage, but all that was unimportant to me. What really mattered was that this movie was packed with *great stuff*! There were scantily clad women, grisly murders, incest, and—my personal favorite that Saturday night—plastic-bagged corpses hanging in a meat locker. I was in kid heaven!

Then *Cat People* came on. Boring. Black-and-white, no skin, no scares, just a lot of people whispering in shadowy rooms and, now and then, a couple of big cats roaring at the camera. It was, of course, dwarfed by the high-quality horror of *Blood and Lace*.

A few months ago, I spotted *Blood and Lace* in the television listings and, recalling the fond memories I had of that movie, stayed up late to watch it. It was awful. It was abysmal. It starred Vic Tayback, for crying out loud! (Remember him? The owner of Mel's Diner in TV's *Alice*?) Terribly embarrassed, I went to bed after thirty minutes, maybe less.

However, as an adult, *Cat People* has become one of my favorite horror films and I own a copy so I can watch it at my leisure.

On the other hand, while there's not enough of that kid left in me to enjoy *Blood and Lace,* there's still enough of him left for me to have a copy of Paul Schrader's remake of *Cat People* as well, because it has much of the same "great stuff" that kid enjoyed in that earlier barker.

The two versions of *Cat People,* while trying to tell—sort of—the same story, are at opposite ends of the horror spectrum. The 1942 version tells its story in whispers, while the 1982 version uses, more often than not, a club. Together, they form a good example of the tastes of the two horror-movie fans—the adult and the kid—who coexist in me.

Some film critics (Leonard Maltin, for example) have said that the original *Cat People* (the first teaming of producer Val Lewton and director Jacques Tourneur) is outdated, that characters and plot elements don't hold up. I disagree entirely . . . well, *almost* entirely. In fact, I think that the central relationship(s) might have been ahead of its time.

Oliver (played by Kent Smith), a nice, ordinary fellow, meets and is smitten by Irena (Simone Simon), an exotic Serbian woman who is shy and, somehow, sad. He takes her out and gives her gifts—one is a kitten, which only hisses and spits at her and gives us our first clue that something's not right—and seems to be breaking through her shell. But

jerk (a distinction that is usually unnecessary). He is the only
ter in the movie who's idiot enough to avoid the truth right up
is clinical stubbornness (not to mention his sliminess) gets him

a staggers to the only real lover she's had since we met her, the
e's returned to again and again: the black leopard in the zoo. She
out, it pounces on her, and she is killed.
last line is Oliver's. As he hunkers over Irena's dead body he says
ce, "She never lied to us," and we know that that's important to
Yes, she was weird and dangerous; yes, she turned into a big
. . but she never lied to them. Even in the worst of situations,
remains true to character and salvages something good, some-
comforting.
n think of very few movies in the horror genre that are this rich,
n fill an hour and thirteen minutes to bursting the way the original
eople does using a simple, subtle style that maintains respect for
dience's intelligence.
course, the kid in me—the one who, if he could, would jump out
right now, brush off his jeans, and try his damnedest to convince
at Blood and Lace is one of the finest horror movies ever made,
ps one of the finest movies period—is bored silly by all this talk
aracters and relationships.
wants to know, But did we see any tits?

bitchin' special effects? Any gore? Any slime?

ool soundtrack?

ybody in the movie who looks even a little like Nastassia Kinski or
te O'Toole, even if they are wearing clothes?
afraid not.
n what're we wasting our time for? This other Cat People
—which was made after they invented color—is excellent, it's the
st. Nastassia Kinski plays this weird woman who talks with an
t sometimes and she comes from . . . well, I'm not sure where
omes from, but it doesn't matter. Anyway, she comes to see her
brother, Malcolm McDowell, who creeps into her room at night
umps up on the foot of her bed like a cat and watches her while she
s and who wants to do the bone dance with her—his own
—'cause he's a real pervo! And there's this cool scene where this

even after confessing her love for him, Irena withholds any physical
affection and won't give in to so much as a kiss. Her reason is that she
believes there is something evil in her waiting to be triggered. Long
ago, Irena explains, when King John freed the Serbians from slavery
under the Marmadukes, he found that many of the Serbians had become
wicked, Satan-worshiping savages. Some were executed, but others
escaped to the hills, where, we are vaguely led to believe, they coupled
with cats and began a line of people who, when their physical or
emotional passions are ignited, turn into great, bloodthirsty cats. Oliver
decides that Irena only needs to forget these fairy tales from her
childhood and she'll be happy; he also decides they could get married.

Now, when I said earlier that I disagreed *almost* entirely with those
critics who said some elements of the plot didn't hold up, I was referring
to this. I can understand a nineties kinda guy *dating* a girl who won't
make love with him because she's afraid of turning into a big cat, but
deciding impulsively to *marry* one? I don't think so.

Anyway, after the wedding, things don't get better between Irena and
Oliver. She spends most of her time at the zoo staring at a black leopard
while he grows closer and closer to Alice (Jane Randolph), his
coworker and friend, whom he begins to see in a different light. At
Alice's suggestion, he sends Irena to a psychiatrist, Dr. Judd (Tom
Conway). Judd looks a bit like a lizard and laughs smugly about her
problem, telling her he knows exactly what's wrong and can fix it. (I
think this rings remarkably true today. I mean, don't you think that if it
had been up to the psychiatric community, a gaggle of therapists would
have been sent to Iraq in August of 1990 to nurse Saddam Hussein back
to health with group therapy, positive imagery, and Prozac?) She only
goes once, but Judd is intrigued. As Oliver and Irena grow farther apart
he and Alice grow closer together. But Oliver is a stand-up guy. He
wants to do everything he possibly can to help Irena and he continues
to be patient with her, all with the support of his friend (nothing has
happened between them yet) Alice. Meanwhile, Irena is becoming very
jealous.

I think these two relationships are the strength of the movie and help
to disprove the claim that it's outdated. I know I'm not the *only* guy to
get involved with a neurotic woman. There seems to be a lot of that
going around; in fact, there are so many neurotic people out there that
they have their own television shows. Haven't you seen Phil or Oprah?
I think a lot of people would give nods of recognition during this movie,

so it can hardly be called outdated. (And I refer to both men *and* women, so, please, no angry letters.)

There's something else here that you don't see often in movies today, horror or otherwise, and that's certainly not because it's outdated. Oliver is a *nice guy*! He's genuinely concerned for Irena's welfare. He really loves her. He isn't annoyed by her fear of sex. As anyone would, he gets frustrated, and *that* is what turns him to Alice, not simple horniness. He does everything he can to save his relationship with Irena before deciding he made a mistake and should be with Alice—and even *then*, he waits until the movie's almost over.

At the same time, it's easy to understand Irena's jealousy and pain, her feeling of being excluded from her husband's life, because she genuinely loves *him* in spite of her condition. Early in the movie, she tells him, "I didn't *want* to love you," presumably because she knew how her fear of turning into a cat between the sheets would interfere with their relationship. But she gives in to her feelings, apparently hoping that Oliver, in his enthusiastic optimism, is right about their future happiness.

In the midst of all this, Alice stands quietly, patiently, and yet with great strength. She shows a good deal of affection for Oliver from the very beginning—we can tell she cares very much for him from the way she looks at him, talks to him—and one finds oneself wondering why Oliver is paying attention to anyone *else*. Yet she wants Oliver to be happy, even if it's with someone else.

Character strengths like these are not often found in horror movies of *any* year. Relationships this strong and compelling seldom show their faces in a genre that rarely goes beyond scratching the surface of its characters' interactions with one another. That's one of the foremost reasons why there are so many bad horror movies. All the eerie atmosphere and nail-biting tension in the world isn't worth a damn if we, the viewers, don't want—*need*—to follow the movie's characters through all of it and see what happens to them.

When Oliver finally tells Irena that he realizes he's made a mistake and that he loves Alice, he blames *himself*, says he'll do the best thing for her and give her a divorce. This is perfectly congruent with Oliver's behavior through the whole movie and makes him even more endearing. It also makes us fear for him, when Irena's jealousy comes to the surface and we begin to suspect that what she's said about herself all along—all that cat business—is true (for the greater part of the movie, it could go either way—she could be telling the truth, or she could be loopy).

When *Cat People* gets scary, it still packs a surp[rise] movie its age. In one scene, Irena is following Alice at night. Both are wearing high heels. Alice's hee[ls] normal on the sidewalk, but Irena's sound a little lik[e] driven into the concrete, and with almost no change started out as a jealous wife following (she thinks) turns into a monster chasing the woman in distress th[at] cast by street lamp after street lamp. No music here their heels on the concrete in the night. Then, the d[...] pursuing pair of heels stops and Alice is alone . . . on, still no sounds behind her. Has Irena transform[ed] silent? Something that doesn't wear high heels? approach of a throaty, catlike roar . . . but it's o[nly] to its stop.

I'm sure there are film experts out there who can write long papers on exactly why that scene work[ed] Tourneur did to *make* it work. All *I* know is that feeling as Alice while walking down dark streets a[ll] my life and I felt it just as vividly while watching th[at] is that, simple as it is—perhaps *because* of its simpl[...] it's still chilling today after numerous viewings.

Another equally simple, and equally frightening trapped in a darkened indoor swimming pool while a[...] darkness around the pool's edge, snarling, roarin[g] rippling reflections of water on darkened walls and ominous. When Alice finally screams, we see a da[rk] the darkness and the lights are flicked on. It's Iren[a] little smile. Others arrive then, too, but she keeps sm[iling] happened is not mentioned, but it's obvious that Ire[na] knows that Irena knows that Alice knows w[...] and . . . well, you get the idea. The effect of the[...] bring the threat to the forefront and raise the tensio[n] it remains until the end of the movie, when Irena Dr. Judd, who explains that unlike Oliver and Alice her story and intends to prove it false by kissing her back. In a close-up, Irena's face darkens slightly frame, and next thing we know, she's a big, angry she thrashes Dr. Judd, but not before he stabs her

I say "naturally" because, yes, it's predictable, All through the movie, Judd has been a manipul[...]

hooker goes into a room and she thinks the guy she's supposed to meet—I think it's the pervo brother—is in the bathroom and she takes her clothes off and sits on the bed and puts her hand in this puddle of slimy sticky goo that's sooo gross. Then she sees this long black cat's tail sticking out from under the bed and a claw rips a chunk of meat off her ankle and she runs out screaming and falls down these stairs and her bra pops open. Some people from the zoo come and catch the cat and take it to the zoo, where it rips the arm off one of the guys who works there and you can see the bone sticking out from his shoulder and blood gushes all over Nastassia Kinski's shoes. Then the big cat disappears and it turns out it was the pervo brother! Later, Annette O'Toole is getting ready to go swimming in this indoor pool and she takes off her clothes and . . . well, she's got the best tits and . . . well, there they are, right there, out in the open with nothing on 'em and . . . it's sooo cool! And Nastassia Kinski gets naked and walks around in the woods, where she eats a rabbit. She gets naked a lot and—

Okay, that's enough! Sorry, but I just can't take it anymore.

That happens more often the older I get; when I let that kid in me out, when I let him have his way, it takes less and less time for me to get fed up with him . . . at least, with his *tastes*. But Paul Schrader's *Cat People* is far more suited to his tastes than mine.

In this version, we have another Irena (Kinski), another Oliver (John Heard), and another Alice (Annette O'Toole). But instead of a slimy therapist, we have a slimy religious fanatic (or so we're told, although we're shown nothing to convince us of that fact), Irena's older brother Paul (McDowell). What we don't have, I'm sad to say, is a good reason to want to follow these people through the events that make up this story . . . excuse me, this *movie*.

The movie begins in a desert that looks almost alien; everything has a dry, parched orange tint. A young native girl is tied to a tree and a black cat comes to her, rears up on its hind legs, and licks her neck. A bit later, another girl is taken, apparently by her mother, to a cave, where she enters and has a stare-down with another black cat (or perhaps the same one). We close in on her face, then dissolve slowly to Irena's. Now, I don't know about you, but I thought for the longest time that Irena was supposed to be that young girl as an adult. But *nooo*! I think that girl was one of her ancestors. Or perhaps she was dreaming while standing in a busy airport. I just don't know.

Irena and Paul were orphaned as small children and haven't seen one another since. One would expect their reunion to be awkward but happy, bittersweet. Instead, the reunion sets the tone for the entire movie; it's stilted, artificial, and seems to have been given no thought. Late on the night Irena arrives, a prostitute is mauled by a black leopard in a hotel and the cat is captured and caged at the zoo, where Oliver is the curator. We see Oliver kissing Alice, one of his coworkers, so we know they have some sort of romantic relationship. But that kissing is about all we *ever* know.

Paul is gone when Irena awakes the following morning and she has to show herself the sights of New Orleans (in one of those long traveloguelike music videos that makes us want to reach for the remote control, even in a movie theater) which leads her to the zoo, where she is strangely attracted to the captured leopard. There, she meets Oliver and he is, once again, smitten. But what, we ask, about Alice? There was *something* going on there, wasn't there? Apparently Oliver doesn't think so because he immediately becomes an asshole and starts treating Alice with something approaching contempt. Oliver hires Irena to work in the gift shop, where she and Alice meet and get chummy. They have a drink together, talk about sex, and we learn that Nastassia Kinski is a virgin. Okay, now, this development isn't all *that* bad, but where are those critics who say the old *Cat People* doesn't hold up? As necessary as this virgin thing turns out to be, I think it was outdated half a second after it was written. It becomes even harder to believe later when, after years of virginity (because, she says, she just never found a guy she liked enough to do it with), she decides to have sex with Oliver right *after* she finds out precisely why she *shouldn't*: it'll turn her into a cat.

We get to see the captured leopard rip off Ed Begley, Jr.'s, arm while Begley (one of Oliver's assistants) is trying to calm the cat down. Now this might *sound* entertaining (unless, of course, you're a Begley fan), but it's one of the more horrifying and unnecessarily unpleasant bloodlettings I've seen in a horror movie and is ultimately pointless because Begley's character (notice I can't even remember his name?) is nobody to us, just some lumbering flunky who cracks jokes and watches soap operas with an orangutan. Later, when everyone returns to the cage, the leopard is gone.

And, of course, Paul has returned. He explains to Irena that she must make love with him, that they can make love to no one but each other. Irena jumps off a balcony with unhuman—but very feline—agility.

Irena and Oliver go into the country together, where she gently declines his sexual advances. Instead, she crawls around in the woods, naked, and eats a rabbit. She doesn't turn into a cat, just crawls around and eats a rabbit.

And what's become of Alice? Not much. At one point she asks Oliver what's wrong and he snaps at her. She remarks that she's seen him obsessed before, but not *this* bad. Oohhh, is *that* it? He's obsessed? I thought he was just a jerk. Actually, the jerk explanation is more believable. To me, dragging a riverboat over a mountain is obsession. Jimmy Stewart's feelings for Kim Novak in *Vertigo* are obsession. But a zoo curator snapping at people and punching out a friend because some weird girl won't go to bed with him? Sorry. I don't buy it.

Oliver accidentally catches Paul in midtransformation one night, and once the Paul-cat is killed, Oliver takes him back to the zoo and cuts him open. A human arm pops up out of the inside like a jack-in-the-box, and the cat's body melts. Now Oliver seems to know what's going on. I *guess*, anyway.

Irena, meanwhile, is on a train headed for Richmond, Virginia, ostensibly to get away from it all. While traveling, she has a dream in which we return to the orange-tinted desert. Paul is there, and he explains everything to Irena, and to us. Their ancestors, he says, sacrificed their children to leopards, and after the children's souls had grown inside them, the leopards became human. An incestuous race, they must only make love with their own or they will turn into cats, and they won't become human again until they kill. After the dream, she goes back to Oliver. In the end, once Oliver knows what will happen if they make love, she begs him to take her, to free her. He does. Later, we see him at the zoo, lingering at the cage of a particular black leopard. . . .

Schrader, a talented director, has given this movie a very slick and sexy look. To that were added the talents of David Bowie and Giorgio Moroder, who gave it a haunting sound in places that blends well with the appearance and feel of the movie (except when there's too *much* of that sound, which happens). Albert Whitlock provides some remarkable special effects; Irena's transformation into a leopard is stunning. A capable and respected cast has been assembled, not to mention some breathtaking leopards. But there are a couple of very important things missing here. It's as if Schrader thought that elements like logic and character development would only muddy up the glossy look of his movie, so he chucked them.

The nighttime walking scene and pool scene from the original movie are resurrected here, but there's a crucial difference. The legend in the original movie says that Irena will change into a cat if any of her passions are ignited—not only sexual passion, but also anger or jealousy or hatred—so it makes sense when we hear the growl of the cat in the darkness around the pool; Irena is jealous of Alice's relationship with Irena's husband, Oliver, she's angry at Alice, maybe even hates her for being able to give Oliver what she can't. But in the remake, we're told that the cat people must first make love with someone other than a sibling in order to transform, then must kill in order to become human again. And yet, without any of this taking place, Irena, as a cat, stalks Alice while she's jogging to a health club, then, in the club, she creeps through the darkness around the pool and growls. Then Irena suddenly becomes human again. With whom did Irena have sex? And whom did she kill to change back? We don't know because, it seems, it simply doesn't matter to Schrader. After all, this is a horror movie, right? It's supposed to be scary, right? It's not like this is a documentary, or anything; there are already people who change into cats here, for crying out loud, so what if a few *other* things don't make any sense, right?

Wrong. I think there are way too many people out there making horror movies who, first of all, have no respect for the genre, and who wouldn't know a solid story from a bowl of pudding. Some of them *say* they love horror, but what they really love are the special effects, the mechanics of *making* the horrors. Or maybe they just want to make a buck. They don't seem to realize that a horror story, just like any other kind of story, has to make sense. Once the story's own little universe is pieced together (the explanation behind Irena's cat condition, for example, was a *very* important piece) it *must* be followed. Every story has rules that are made up during the story's evolution that, once that evolution is complete, must be followed. If they are done well, they will fit together neatly to form an unbendable logic by which the story's characters must live. A horror movie that doesn't follow its own rules—or has poorly thought out rules to begin with—is displaying a contempt for its viewer, a disrespect for the viewer's intelligence. And speaking of disrespect for viewers' intelligence . . .

While watching the original *Cat People,* we recognized the feelings that were passing back and forth between the characters. We felt for them, understood why they were doing what they were doing, and believed in them, even if, for whatever reason, we didn't like them. We believed in them so much that we believed in the things that happened to them, too, no matter how extraordinary, how impossible.

Would you want to spend two hours locked in a room with three or four people who have nothing interesting to say? Who have no discernible personalities? Who don't seem to know *themselves* what kind of people they are? Who might take their clothes off for you, but in the meantime are jerks? If so, the characters that populate Schrader's *Cat People* will hold you spellbound. If not, and you're in a cat kinda mood, you might want to rent the old one. Or you could just read a Garfield book.

Of course, that noisy little kid in me still has some affection for that bloody, sexy remake. But his voice is getting quieter all the time. I prefer to have my mind upset rather than my stomach.

However, there are other kids like him. They *aren't* growing quiet, they're getting louder by the minute. They buy movie tickets and rent videos and, unfortunately, are sending filmmakers a message. It doesn't have to make sense, it doesn't have to have people we like in it, just make sure it's got plenty of skin and plenty of loud music and lots and *lots* of dismembered and leaking bodies!

I wish more people—consumers and filmmakers alike—would show their kids more discipline.

Chapter
9
***

Ed Gorman

Ed is that rare fellow who gives advice that is nearly always good. Read this, watch that. I suspect that most of the people in this book, and a majority of you reading it, are among the incredulous: "You never saw *that*? I can't *believe* you never saw that." You can easily substitute "read" for "saw." Not that Ed is entirely innocent of these sentiments; rather, he will say "It might be helpful for you to read this," and then he'll tell you why. That's the key to good advice—why.

A well-known mystery writer whose many novels include *A Cry of Shadows* and *The Night Remembers*, Ed is also the editor of *Mystery Scene* magazine. His short horror and mystery stories are widely acclaimed, and as an editor, he has produced such successful anthologies as *Stalkers* and *The Black Lizard Anthology of Crime Fiction*. In addition, he has built a reputation in the field of historical fiction.

And movies? He's seen 'em all.

Several Hundred Words About Wes Craven

by Ed Gorman

In some ways, Wes Craven's *The Hills Have Eyes* is an existentialist's notion of a Saturday matinee, one of those films that is structured to be peak on peak, without much time for human values or even logic, but with the kind of relentlessness that makes these films fun to watch.

As an extremely linear entertainment, *Hills* works well enough, even if it does depend on everybody in the cast doing some very stupid things. Five or six times I felt my pulse literally begin to race and my backside to shift anxiously in my seat. Craven knows how to handle cliff-hangers.

You probably know the story by now: the all-American Carter family from Cleveland heads for California only to take a detour that eventually puts them in the hands of another family, a pack of desert rats spawned by a mutated child who eventually "stole" the town whore and began having mutant kids of his own. The latter family is anything but all-American—they mean not only to kidnap the Carter infant, they mean to eat him. Pluto, Mercury, Mars, and Ruby (the grown children of the mutants) are cannibals. Craven hints that all this degeneracy is the result of the nearby atomic test site doing genetic damage, a point that may be sly homage to the Corman films of the fifties.

I mentioned that the film reminds me of an existentialist's notion of a Saturday matinee. I say this because despite the breathlessness of the presentation—dialogue is spare, action is everything—there is an undertow of grief here common to most of Craven's films.

The all-American Carters strike me as unfailingly neurotic—Papa Carter, a retired cop, gives big booming speeches that make him look foolish; Mama Carter is so long-suffering, she seems to have wandered over from a Tennessee Williams play in rehearsal down the hall. Daughter Dee Wallace and son-in-law Martin Speer are TV-commercial perfect (right down to their lovemaking, humping away in the trailer attached to the Carter car, with none of the family members seeming to take any note of it). Susan Lanier, the other daughter, whines a lot, especially when brother Robert Houston is around. Lanier is a babe given some depth by her poutiness: you get curious about what it would take to make this girl happy. Then there are the two family dogs, Beauty and Beast. Put them all together and you have a TV family not much different in appearance from the Archie Bunkers (popular at the time the film was made), appealing in the cartoonish way of most sitcom families, yet with the melancholy resonance found in most Craven depictions of "nice normal people."

I wish Craven would have given us a few glimpses of these folks as people and not just spear carriers for the plot. In a peculiar, sad way, the mutant family is more convincing—as usual, Craven lends his villains a shabby sorrow that makes them understandable if not admirable (with the exception of Freddy Krueger, whom I find both silly and despicable). The girl Ruby is certainly sympathetic (she doesn't want the baby snatched) and even odd Michael Berryman has a certain sorrowful dignity; he should be killed, not out of anger but mercy. He did not ask to be thus born.

Craven makes good use of the desert, perhaps the best use since Jack Arnold hauled his cameras out there for the Universal pictures of the mid-fifties. Craven captures the eeriness of vast emptiness and the frantic, furtive way one must live in such conditions to survive. The old-timer who sets up the movie for us is an especially good creation, a man of small dreams and big fears, a perfectly rendered creature of the desert.

Craven is also good at action scenes. While the film is occasionally infested with the film language of the time—zippy zoom-ins and pullbacks; pans so wide they fail to set mood *or* render information—Craven is never showy, and knows how to shoot, cut, and pace action. *Hills* is a very exciting movie.

In a recent interview, Craven said, "The film business is just so tied in with money that not only do you want to do something that in some way is artistically pleasing, you'd like to think that it's going to survive in the marketplace so that you can do another one."

Despite these words, I think Wes Craven is a real if not always successful artist. One could argue that *Shocker* lacked a thematic center and therefore got lost in its special effects; and that *The Serpent and the Rainbow* was more documentary than drama, and therefore failed to hold any emotional appeal for the audience; and that *Deadly Friend* needed better writing to achieve what Craven had in mind—but again, these arguments aside, Craven is a vital, intelligent, and resourceful director who has continued to grow and get better.

He may need a good screenwriting collaborator, the way Billy Wilder needed collaborators I. A. L. Diamond and Charles Brackett to produce his best films.

Craven's masterpiece awaits; and I for one am eager to see it.

Chapter
10

Charles L. Grant

His books carry the tag line "One of the premier horror writers of his or any generation." It's a quote from Stephen King, and it's quite true. Charles L. Grant writes with sophistication, with class, and better still, he writes a lot. Prolific by any standards, he has branched out into romance, science fiction, and fantasy, albeit under pseudonyms so that he doesn't overwhelm his fans. He has published nearly fifty novels (including *The Pet* and *For Fear of the Night*) and half that many anthologies and collections (including the *Shadows* series). His own short stories now number well over one hundred.

As an editor, he has introduced the audience to dozens of new talents and, in fact, gave several of the writers in this book their first major exposure in the field.

Charlie's reputation portrays him as the spearhead of an atmospheric horror, usually called dark fantasy. When it comes to the movies, then, it should be no surprise that he is attracted to films that offer their fright up quietly, subtly, not to mention fond memories of black-and-white.

Black-and-White, in Color

by Charles L. Grant

Most professional photographers, either of the cinematic or still variety, will tell you that there's something of the cheat about using color for every occasion. While it's great for sunsets and vivid portraits of flowers and contrasting the differences between land and sky, color often robs a scene of intended drama simply by being there.

For example, a photograph of a ghetto stoop and the people who sit there is almost "pretty" when it's taken in color, no matter how squalid the surroundings; use black-and-white, however, and the scene achieves a certain depth, an overlay of despair, a depiction of something that isn't "pretty" at all. There is a reality in black-and-white that is impossible to see when color is used because that same color masks what's actually present—grit, garbage, age, decay.

Ruins taken against a beautiful sunset are beautiful ruins; ruins in black-and-white are . . . ruins. It all depends on the effect you want to achieve, the emotions you want to stir, the depths you wish to reveal, or conceal.

A photographic portrait of a man or woman in colorful costume, or in simple dress, draws the eye not only to the face, but to the surroundings as well, to the colors of the headgear, the gown, the suit. Without color, the eye, and the emotions, are drawn to the person. To the lines in the face, to the eyes, to the features often concealed, or camouflaged, by makeup and the set of the head or the lips.

Color will reveal personality; black-and-white will reveal the personality's layers.

In film, black-and-white has long since fallen into disrepute because audiences prefer to see color. Why? I suspect because it's there. In the beginning, it was a novelty, just like sound. Now it's pretty. It's more "true to life." It makes explosions gaudy, and eviscerations garish; it provides a seeming vivid contrast between day and night.

And these days, of course, it's also a lot cheaper to make a film in color, not simply because of the stock, but also because there are very few industry technicians left who know how to light a scene for black-and-white and who know how to film it effectively. The skills and techniques involved are most definitely not the same for color, which is why the recent trend toward colorization is such a vile offense: the movies, aside from the very fact of color being present, aren't the same when color is added because those skills are different.

And aside from technique and skill, there is also the matter of imagination.

The most powerful tool any writer, or director, or photographer, has at his disposal is the utilization and cooperation of the viewer's (or reader's) imagination. With imagination comes individual emotion; and with individual emotion comes power.

There is, I have maintained for what seems like forever, more strength (and thus potent emotion) in suggestion than in depiction; there is a difference between being scared and being shocked or repulsed; and there is a vast difference in the reaction of the mind to images bright and colorful, and to images where color must be supplied.

This is the major distinction between black-and-white and color.

While obviously neither suspense nor terror, apprehension or fear and the tensions thus created because of their interaction are dependent solely upon the use of one film stock or another, scenes created in black-and-white, with the audience providing the *necessary* color, tend to dramatically heighten anxiety and deepen revulsion more so than those presented in the full spectrum. With black-and-white, it is the filmmaker and the audience working together, with the filmmaker providing the visual cues and the audience providing the reaction.

Perhaps one of the most famous scenes in cinematic horror appears in *The Leopard Man.* An unwilling child is sent on an errand by her mother. When the child returns sometime later, screaming that something is trying to kill her, the mother has locked the door because of an earlier argument. Screaming. Pounding. And finally, a pool of blood seeps under the door into the room.

There is no need to tell the audience the blood is red.

The cues are there; the audience has supplied most of the offscreen action, and all of the reaction.

By the same token, there is no need to provide the color details in something like *The Cat People.* The 1942 version, I hasten to add.

Here, the use of light, of shadow, of light-and-shadow imagery is far more important than the color of a dress, the color of a house's interior, the color of a zoo cage where a panther prowls.

Light.

Shadow.

More stark in black-in-white. More expressive, and therefore more loaded with emotional power. Bands of sharp-edged shadow that suggest cages, and therefore entrapment; pools of shadow that suggest a slow, inexorable gathering of supernatural forces not quite explained; swift-moving shadows thrown against the wall, as when Tom Conway discovers that his knowledge of psychiatry doesn't provide the answers.

There are no distractions here.

When Jane Randolph walks along the Central Park wall that night, there is nothing to catch the audience's eye but the uneasiness on her face and the movement of the leaves above and just behind her. We don't see what's up there. It doesn't matter. We already know.

For that reason, the footsteps that follow her through half the scene are just the slightest bit louder, a shade more menacing.

Especially when they stop.

And those leaves begin to tremble.

When she swims alone in the pool and the lights go out, it's dark. Period. The rippling shadows on the tiled walls match the ripples on the dark water, and the fleeting shadow of the panther stalking along the pool's edge is more disturbing for it because it is a part of that dark. A part that merges and separates, and merges again. The same scene in the 1982 remake is rather puny by comparison because the intrusion of color, however slight, pulls much of the emotion from that encounter. It's . . . distracting, whether the audience is conscious of it or not. It's certainly unnecessary.

Yet, having said all that, there are a handful of relatively recent films that have managed to approach a black-and-white sensibility without actually using it.

Again, obviously, night scenes work better than those in broad daylight when you're working for a sense of black-and-white. But once in a while a film creates an *illusion* of black-and-white throughout its length, an illusion of color absence, whether by design or accident, and thus is able to tap into those audience reactions missing in other films.

Halloween is a black-and-white film, in color. And believe it or not, *Halloween 4* is, to a lesser degree, much like that. Both could easily have done without color stock because nothing in the stories, or in the design of the film, is color dependent. Not even the blood. Most effective, then, is the featureless mask that Michael Meyers wears—it's as visible at night as it is at noon, and just as blank, just as menacing. Just as colorless.

And I have a feeling, and it's nothing more than that, that John Carpenter often deliberately thinks in black-and-white when developing his sense of menace, his sense of light and shadow. Of all his films (*Halloween* excepted), *The Fog*, with one glaring (and rather silly) glowing-eye exception, is the most true in that respect to something by, say, Jacques Tourneur or James Whale. Again, and again with that one (really silly) exception, there is nothing here that requires color. Nothing at all. The contrast between the "light" of the fog and the "dark" of the community it invades is sufficient in and of itself to create the tensions that exist between the characters, the characters and their respective fates, and the town and its history. Try watching it with the color turned off your set; and keep in mind the physical requirements for lighting and such.

It almost works.

Now try adding color to *Frankenstein* or the 1935 *Dracula*.

It doesn't work at all.

Not because of the lighting, but because the addition of color simply is not necessary. Not necessary because you, the viewer, have already added what color you want to the things you want colored. And if you don't want the monster's face a pale green or mottled gray, it won't be. Unless you watch the colorized version. As a result, there's no true audience participation here; only audience disappointment. It's like the monster behind the door that's been knocking off the actors one by one—you *know* what it looks like, you've created it in your head, and it *never* looks anywhere near as stupid, or as rubbery, or as tame as the one they might show you on the screen.

There are, of course, a dozen different types of horror film, each with a different goal. The best ones work, in color or not; the worst ones are god-awful, in color or not.

What it all boils down to, I believe, is light. And shadow. And the power of their emotion.

The Haunting vs. *A Nightmare on Elm Street*.

The Body Snatcher vs. *Friday the 13th*.

To cast light upon something as fundamental as our most basic fears results, too often, not in illumination but in a bleaching, a washing-out of all that's necessary to react to those fears; i.e., the conscious or unconscious participation of those who sit down to watch what that light does.

To juxtapose, however, light and shadow without the distraction of color, and to use them the way one uses both script and actor, results not in a flat and boring surface, but in an almost palpable texture, and in a palette of the imagination no actual color could ever hope to duplicate.

Watch, then, for those films that are black-and-white, in color. They are the dark fantasies, literally, that will restore your faith in the horror film. The exceptions, like *Paperhouse*, are all too few and far between.

The rule, of course, is black-and-white.

Chapter

11

Melissa Mia Hall

This native Texan is a journalist by education, a writer by trade, and a filmmaker, poet, photographer, and teacher by inclination. Her first major horror credits were in the now defunct *Twilight Zone* magazine and, of course, Charles L. Grant's *Shadows* series. Melissa's work has appeared in dozens of major genre anthologies over the last ten years, including *Women of Darkness*, *Whisper of Blood*, and *Dead End: City Limits*.

Melissa is also a practitioner of what is referred to as "literary" fiction, and living proof that this form and horror are not mutually exclusive.

Her experience in cinema includes some free-lance screenwriting, her film *Manikin* was exhibited at the Fort Worth Museum of Modern Art, and she has acted in a number of short films.

Her fiction and her journalism are intelligent and incisive, as is the following reevaluation and analysis of *Fatal Attraction* and gender roles in films of the same order.

She is currently at work on her second novel.

Love Kills: Another Look at Fatal Attraction

by Melissa Mia Hall

Fatal attraction, scary sex, obvious obsession, dangerous liaisons, how those words roll off the tongue with sensuous glee. But *fatal attraction*, good old FA—that particular pairing of love and death permeated the latter part of the eighties thanks largely in part to that most dangerous movie of the same name, a catch phrase of American

123

insecurities regarding love and sex. The film was directed by Adrian (*9½ Weeks*) Lyne, based on a script by James Dearden, adapted from the script of his own British short subject *Diversion*. Howard Atherton supplied excellent photography, Maurice Jarre supplied the great music, and Stanley R. Jaffe and Sherry Lansing produced it. Peter Berger cut the film, slicing the original, subtler ending (I also read the final shooting script wherein the temptress kills herself and frames it to look like a murder, although you have to admit it's not likely that someone committing suicide would be that clever) and adding the controversial and garish ending reminiscent of *Carrie* and *Friday the 13th*.

A singularly unhealthy movie, creepy, well acted, well crafted, and sensational. If it had been a newspaper article, it would've been labeled yellow journalism but been written by Pulitzer Prize–winning journalists.

At the time of its 1987 release, critics and audiences flocked to see it. Theaters were consistently jammed. Critics raved and panned it with equal abandon. My favorite quote had to be this from Roger Ebert: "*Fatal Attraction* clearly had the potential to be a great movie. I walked out feeling cheated and betrayed." (Tell 'em, Rog.)

Ebert's strong reaction echoed my first reaction to the movie, an experience I have yet to forget, which says something about how successful the film was as a theater experience. When I saw the movie, I felt like I did when I saw *Wait Until Dark* when I was small and the whole audience scared me when we leaped in unison and screamed when the bad guy jumped out at poor blind Audrey. The same collective sighs and chills leaped out from *FA*'s late-eighties audience. At *FA*, these knee-jerk reactions were also accompanied by nervous laughter and chatter, adults muttering and shuffling about like trembling children. "That would never happen to my marriage—"; "She reminds me of his secretary"; "Oh God, what if he finds out about—"; "What if he knows about—"; "I wonder if—"; "Don't you get any ideas, stud—" How they slid their eyes down and around, the emotions tumbling beneath the surface and able to spill out. "I wonder if I'll catch AIDS. I wonder if she's really faithful. Should I get married? Do I really want a child?" This movie pushed all of the right buttons with Lyne's rapt and efficient direction, the excellent cast, the on-target dialogue.

The film fastened on the very real fear most of us have regarding love and its darker side, obsession/possession, which is also another word for hatred. *FA* is the film we love to hate and hate to love. The cost of playing around in the eighties had surfaced, the fear of AIDS had begun to make us all sit up and take notice. Pair it with the fact that most people have come into contact with jealousy in their lives, in one form or another, and this film exposed that nerve with a violent exuberance that moviegoers responded to even though many knew, like Ebert, that they were being manipulated.

But it was such an uncomfortable catharsis. At what price were the thrills made and what do they say about the American moviegoing public? Even detractors should applaud the movie's accurate and disturbing portrait of middle to upper-class yuppies in sexual angst just as the specter of AIDS began to sink into that thirtysomething consciousness, the warning that a good job, a good marriage might not protect one from death, that all of that sexual freedom of the sixties and seventies might have a price tag attached. *FA* never mentions AIDS, but it never had to because the audience could. ("If I make love, will I die? Honey, be faithful to me—I think you are safe—are you safe?") The movie stressed the importance of honesty in relationships, that things can go wrong not only when you are unfaithful, but when you are dishonest. No wonder the response to this movie was so $$$$$$.

I attended the movie with my sister, at the time married, but about to separate and eventually divorce, and her teenage daughter. The theater, as mentioned earlier, was packed and I had no idea what I was going to see. All I had heard was that it was scary and about a love triangle. We were all willing to be taken for a ride and *FA* gave us one, bumpy, thrilling, but dangerous.

And at first, I felt cheapened after the lights came up. I thought it was repulsive in what I thought it said about single career women. I'm still repulsed, even though I know Alex Forrest is an abuser of power and an exception to the rule. As time has elapsed I can now applaud the historical significance and the gloriously garish horrific aspects of the film, its roller-coaster theatrics, its absurd, last-second happy ending inspired by audience preview-card dissatisfaction with the original ending (frustrating Dearden and Nicholas Meyer, whose name was on the final shooting script, but not on the screen). At the same time, I'm still disgusted by my own enjoyment of a film that so accurately portrayed how most Americans were feeling at that point in their lives about love and sex. Terrified.

The casting was terrific. Michael Douglas played Dan Gallagher, the bored lawyer with that boyish "hey, why me, I just fucked her" charm the audience responded to with irritating conspiratorial sympathy. Maybe we still hadn't recovered from *Romancing the Stone* '84 and

Jewel of the Nile '85. Ironically, not much later, he gave us yet another excellent husband-gone-wrong portrayal in the darkly humorous *War of the Roses* '89.

Then there was the beautiful Anne Archer, who played Dan's sweet, put-upon wife and mother to Ellen, played by the adorable Ellen Hamilton Latzen. Archer turned in an underrated performance that made all women in the audience go home and check their panty drawers and wonder why they don't have flat stomachs like hers despite weekly aerobic classes. Note that she was a brunette and the villainess, in a role that changed a career dramatically, was blond Glenn Close.

The wild and wonderful Alex Forrest leaped across the screen with a high-voltage intensity that was unforgettable. Anyone who has seen *FA* can recall Alex switching the light off and on in tormented loneliness while Dan's off with Beth playing perfect husband. It wasn't scripted and I've no idea whose inspirational impulse brought that to the screen, but it's that one scene that to my mind lifted *FA* into reluctant greatness. Alex echoed the fears of a million women ("I'm thirty-six years old. . . . This may be my last chance to have a child"). Why didn't she get an Oscar for this performance? Somehow I could never picture Meryl Streep pulling this off.

A quick reminder of the plot, if for some reason you have not seen *FA*—Gallagher is a married lawyer and Forrest is a single editor whose paths cross in their interconnecting business worlds. Gallagher's wife goes out of town and they fall into a brief, extremely (if a tad silly) passionate love affair. The problem occurs when the emotionally unstable Forrest wants more than an affair, especially when she turns up pregnant. Forrest becomes obsessed with Gallagher and Gallagher becomes obsessed with getting rid of her. The affair puts his family at risk and eventually ends up almost destroying it. An unpleasant twist that makes *FA* unhealthy at the same time it satisfies, includes Gallagher apparently uncaring about the unborn child Forrest is carrying. His manic murder of the demonically crazed (pathetic and tragic at the same time, thanks to Close's acting brilliance) Forrest includes, after all, the murder of *his* unborn child.

There are so many questions that bubble to the surface when you contemplate it. Responsible for a resurgence of this film genre, *FA* has its roots in the film noir of the forties. Film buffs might want to check out its ancestors, which include *The Locket* '46, starring Larraine Day; *Sign of the Ram* '48, starring Susan Peters; *Ivy* '47, starring Joan Fontaine; *The Dark Mirror* '46, starring Olivia De Havilland (remade for TV in '84 starring Jane Seymour); and *The Female on the Beach* '55, starring the redoubtable Joan Crawford. The bad girl is always such an excellent topic, coupled with sex and violence—audiences thrill to complications of love gone wrong.

The fascinations we have with love stories when mated with the horror genre spells out thriller par excellence when done right. What makes *FA* so important is what makes it so horrific on levels beyond the mundane. The dark mirror it holds up to our culture in its most manipulative moves shines with such light that Alex Forrest's death haunts us still. There's a sticky thread of jealousy there, too. It's the jealousy our society displays toward unattached successful women and the jealousy unattached successful women display toward the attached couples with children, i.e., the happy family we are told we must have to be whole people, male or female.

FA is glossy and glorious. The family life the Gallaghers share is readily accessible—the child pulling off her dad's earphones, the sloppy dog, the wife playing supermom and plaintively talking about going back to school—the audience can't help but love the Gallaghers. It's the comfortable rightness of the old shoe vs. the new shoe. Alex Forrest is a stiletto shoe vs. Beth's athletic shoe. Witness the Gallaghers' comfy home vs. the bad woman's artsy loft apartment. It's the alien allure of the forbidden fruit Dan longs for, but the film fails to explore why Dan wants Alex; it fails to explore why Dan "does Alex" and it also fails to explore why Alex goes over the edge. There's a brief allusion to the tragic death of her father when she was a child, a death she has witnessed. But it's not enough. Close's portrayal of Alex is so great that she suggests so much more (incest?)—and the audience would love for the mystery of Alex's motivations to be further explained. The film just shows us what happens when a psychotic is part of a love triangle and the audience walks away, emotionally satisfied but intellectually and spiritually impoverished.

The catharsis and emotional explosion the audience feels when the good guys (the family) kill the bad guy (the single person) is incredible—a gut release of pent-up fears: married people are good and single people are bad? Primal fears. Paranoias—protect the family, but what if you don't have a family—coupled with the fear of love/sex. Ironically, this is perhaps why *FA* may, in the long run, be viewed and respected historically, as one of the most important films made in the eighties. It says so much about us. And it continues to inspire imitations and derivative films.

One of the most interesting, if terribly flawed relatives, is *Sleeping with the Enemy* '91, based on the suspense novel by Nancy Price. Also the story of a love triangle, this one pits the good girl against the bad boy and the "put-upon wife" role becomes masculine. Kevin Anderson plays the poor innocent bystander/lover of the errant wife—who happens to be trying to save her own life. Julia Roberts, the young and very talented actress who catapulted to early fame in *Mystic Pizza* '88 and *Steel Magnolias* '90, then rocketed to celebrity with *Pretty Woman* '90, plays the abused wife. She fakes her own death instead of getting a divorce in order to get away from a psychotic husband. She knows her husband would never accept a divorce. Many critics found this aspect of Price's novel unbelievable, but Price knows that there are women out there who know lawyers and police can sometimes fail to stop abuse. Witness *The Burning Bed* and you know there are lots of women who can accept the plausibility of a woman running for her life. At any rate, Roberts delivers a glowing portrayal that turns this film into an acceptable *FA*, although the Ronald Bass adaptation is, at times, clunky and limp. Joseph (*Dreamscape*, *True Believer*) Ruben supplies story-book direction that is at turns manipulative and too glamorized.

Here, the abused wife on the lam takes up with a young professor in a small town—I remind you she is still married to the rich bad-guy husband. She begins a new life that is comfy and cluttered, not sterile and stiff like the ultra-cool rich life she shared with the bad guy (played with admirable wimpiness and icy evil by Patrick Bergin). It's the same *FA* infidelity, turned around. And it's the husband, faithful, even if abusive, who's evil, while the adulterers are sweet and endearing—the *FA* for the nineties.

Although *Sleeping with the Enemy* is not as flashy and as jam-packed with loaded guns as *FA*, it served as an exclamation point to my musing on *FA* and the state of the art.

FA opened the door for more film noir à la love/sex/obsession. There's got to be more than blond wild women with knives and crazy husbands with guns. A lot more.

My mind wanders over all of the crazy cinematic couples we've embraced. That couple who did *Last Tango in Paris* '72; Clint and Jessica in *Play Misty for Me* '71; Kit and Holly, as played by the delectable Sissy Spacek and Martin Sheen, in '74's *Badlands*; Warren and Faye's *Bonnie and Clyde* '67; Nicholas Roeg's couple in *Bad Timing*; *A Sensual Obsession* '80; Kasdan's Kathleen Turner/William Hurt steamy *Body Heat* '81; and most recently, those crazy kids in '90's

David Lynch epic, *Wild at Heart*. The list goes on and on. Crazy love, love that kills and steams up the screen with passion, life, and pain.

When cinema breeds more than just an absorbed stare at the dark sides of love and sex and investigates the human frailties exposed by desire, what's not to love? FAs have been around since man and woman first connected. Surviving them is half the fun and remembering them, highly instructive.

And real scary.

Which brings me back, again, to that *FA* ending, the one with the woman in the bathtub with the knife. How she shot up like a rocket after we'd been staring at the whites of her eyes and the little bubbles drifting up from her pale nostrils. How cheap it was, how nasty it was—good old Dan was defending his life and the family's life. But what about that poor unborn baby? Mothers everywhere had to sigh with sorrow. It got me to thinking exactly how I would've ended the movie.

Dearden's choice was to have Forrest kill herself to the strains of *Madama Butterfly* and to ironically frame Gallagher for the murder (his prints on the suicide weapon), but then have Dan's wife, Beth, exonerate him by playing an incriminating tape of Forrest's that shows her suicidal intent.

I would've had the movie end with Gallagher's arrest, the tape somehow discarded, lost, the look on his face as the police cart him away—a glance back at Beth and Ellen, what he has lost. Truly horrific. But would it play in Cincinnati? The realities of the bottom line— $$$$—dictate that many filmmakers yearn to provide what they *think* the audience wants. The era of preview cards has arrived. And the ending that *FA* eventually got was what we wanted.

So we now squirm, in retrospect, to view what *they* say we wanted. It says a lot about us and now it's up to the filmmakers of the nineties to say a lot more.

Chapter

12

Nancy Holder

Nancy looks more than a little like a certain biology teacher I had in high school, only prettier. She always seems to be in a good mood and is the kind of person you automatically trust and who makes you open up and spill your guts, telling her things she certainly doesn't need to know. She never seems to mind. When pressed about herself, she's self-effacing, as if the listener won't be interested. Which is an impossibility.

Nancy dropped out of high school and moved to Germany to become a ballet dancer. Later on, she dropped out of graduate school to write romances and mainstream novels. She has sold fifteen of those. She has also lived in Japan. To be sure, she has a lot to say that is of interest to most people within hearing distance.

Now that she's working in horror and fantasy, she's wasted no time selling more than two dozen short stories to such anthologies as the *Shadows* series (there's that Grant guy again!), *Women of Darkness*, and *Borderlands 2*. Her story "Cannibal Cats Come Out Tonight" is already a classic.

Rough Cut, her latest novel, is about the film industry, and she studied film and filmmaking extensively at the American Film Institute. She knows her stuff.

Nancy lives in San Diego with her "stone fox" husband, Wayne, and their two border collies, Nan and Ron.

Why The Haunting *Is So Damn Scary*

by Nancy Holder

"I haven't seen a damn thing. I just don't like the way it looks."
—Luke Sannerson, in *The Haunting*

Take one: a summer's night on an American military base in Yokosuka, Japan. It is 1963, and my sister and I are running as if for our lives, all the way home. We're too scared to wait ("in the night, in the dark") for the bus; we're amped, sizzling with adrenaline.

Home! Refuge! We fly up the front steps, burst through the doorway, and tumble over the threshold—terrifying my stepmother, who's just inside the door. She drops her purse and starts shrieking at the top of her lungs. We shriek, too, all three of us clinging to each other and screaming in each other's faces.

My sleepy father bolts from the bedroom, shouting "What's wrong? What's wrong?"

"I just got back from the movies!" my stepmother wails.

That was the first time any of us had seen *The Haunting*.

Take two: an autumn evening in 1988, my house in San Diego. It's the night of the monthly "Monster Movie Night," where I throw a party and then show a horror or science-fiction movie, usually so bad everyone calls out jokes and laughs all the way through it. *Chud* was a big hit at Monster Movie Night. *Little Shop of Horrors*, that kind of thing.

But tonight, the room's silent. No one makes jokes. No one gets up to go the bathroom. Midway through the film, I whisper good-byes to a couple at my front door because the husband "can't take any more." And when the movie's over, and the lights go on, people are angry with me. *Pissed*. One says, "That was a *real* horror movie. That one was scary."

And though I laugh and tease them all for being wimps, I've got a minor case of the spookie-ookies myself.

And that was the sixth or seventh time I'd seen *The Haunting*.

Why is this movie so damn scary? Why is it such a chiller that it's listed in video guides as a "cult classic" and that there was a special showing of it at a recent World Fantasy Convention, followed by a panel discussion?

On the surface, it's just another haunted-house story, adapted from the novel *The Haunting of Hill House* by Shirley Jackson. The plot appears to be your standard haunted-house gig: A certain Dr. John Markway (played by Richard Johnson) receives permission from the absentee owner of Hill House to investigate the New England mansion for psychic phenomena. The owner insists that her nephew Luke (played by Russ Tamblyn, Dr. Jacoby on *Twin Peaks*) accompany the doctor. Markway invites dozens of people who've had paranormal experiences to stay with him for two months in the house. However, only two of the many he has contacted accept his invitation—two women who didn't research the history of Hill House before agreeing to come: a stylish, brittle woman named Theodora, "just Theodora" (played by Claire Bloom), and the protagonist of the movie, Eleanor Lance (Julie Harris). They go to the house, and shit, as they say, happens.

Boring, eh? You've heard it, read it, a thousand times. Oh, no, you haven't. A bare-bones synopsis of *The Haunting,* book and film, may rattle like a skeleton of tired clichés—the psychic investigator's attached to the Doubting Thomas, the sinister housekeeper's attached to the Secret, dem bones, dem bones—but *The Haunting* does anything but rattle.

Nor does it roar, and that's one of the most amazing things about it. This is a movie that never jumps out at you. In the immortal words of Stephen King, "She creeps." And creeps, and crawls, and squeezes you too tight, and doesn't let go . . . even after the last foot of film flaps off the reel. It follows you home . . . but it never quite catches you. And that, basically, is why this black-and-white flick, made in 1962, is still so damn scary.

Robert Wise, who directed *The Haunting,* began his career as an editor for Orson Welles and Val Lewton, and he has said that of all the people he worked with, Lewton was his biggest influence. Lewton, of course, is known to horror-film aficionados as a producer of horror pictures for RKO, which he made with "B" budgets but high production values. Wise directed his first three films for Lewton: *Curse of the Cat People, Mademoiselle Fifi,* and *The Body Snatcher.*

From Lewton, Wise learned to create fear, stretch it out, heighten it again, and build upon it until it's almost unbearable. In *The Body Snatcher*, for example, when Wise was still making the transition from editor to director, he achieved this in the film frames themselves—the photographs that whir through a projector, twenty-four (generally) to a second. He did this with his selection of shots and angles, and cutting, while in *The Haunting*, I would posit that he controlled many more cinematic elements to achieve his ends—sound, script, acting, and so on. Let me try to show what I mean first by explaining the Lewton/Wise theory of fright, and then I'll expand on how Wise got more effect for his production dollar out of *The Haunting*, coming later as it did in his career.

In *The Body Snatcher*—one of Wise's personal favorites of his films—two grave robbers, unable to supply their doctor client with enough fresh corpses, have taken to murder. In their black coach, they trail a young street singer, who is singing as she walks through the foggy streets of Victorian London into a tunnel. You hear her sweet voice, the tapping of her shoes, the clop of the carriage horse's hooves just behind her. You see the shadow of the carriage swallowed up as it follows her into the tunnel. You hear her song, her footfalls, the horse hooves; then . . .

Nothing. There's no sound of a scuffle, no thud, no scream. There is no picture, just a black screen. There's nothing to react to, nothing that says "boo!" and allows you to cry out, then laugh a little, and settle in for the next "bit." There is no relief. You sit nervous and tense. When the film cuts to another scene, you are still nervous and tense, but now you get *more* nervous and *more* tense—and when the *next* frightening event occurs, your unease builds on top of that created by the previous scenes—and on and on and on. The lack of resolution this causes in us is like the (alleged) subaudible rumbling on the soundtrack of *Earthquake*—there, always, a constant prod that makes you more and more uneasy.

This was a Lewton trademark, and a technique used by his other directors—Jacques Tourneur, for one. In one of the most memorable moments of the film *The Leopard Man*, we know—but do not see, and barely hear—that a leopard is mauling a young girl. We hear her screams as she pounds on a locked door, and see her mother's rising fear as she tries, and fails, to open the door; and then we hear one gentle thud, and see one slight trickle of blood. Then, the Lewton trademark: *nothing*.

It's like another old movie, one perhaps not quite so classic: *The Tingler*. This movie's premise is that you've got an insectile creature that lives in your spine and feeds on your fear. When you scream, it shrinks. If you can't scream, it keeps growing. And growing. And *growing*.

Lewton taught Wise not to allow you to scream. By the time he undertook *The Haunting*, it was a lesson he had mastered. He wasn't "just" an editor, but a masterful director (he also produced *The Haunting*), and he exploited all the cinematic elements at his disposal to full effect.

One of these elements is the script, the blueprint for the construction of the film and the creation of the characters. As mentioned, it was an adaptation of a novel by Shirley Jackson. It was written by Nelson Gidding, whom Wise had worked with before, and it retained as its "spine" the same question Jackson posed: Who or what is doing the haunting? Like Jackson, Gidding leaves that question open to interpretation (a choice that irritated some reviewers at the time the film came out. Now it's almost always universally praised; in film and video rental guides, for example, words like "underrated" and "cult classic" are used to describe it).

The story centers around Eleanor, a repressed spinster who's spent all her life taking care of her invalid mother. Her mother has recently died, and Eleanor's been living—very unhappily–with her married sister. Dr. Markway's invitation to Hill House is her escape from a dreary life, but she can't escape the psychic burden she's carrying: her mother called for her the night she died, and for the first time, Eleanor didn't answer her summons. She believes she killed her mother, and she is haunted by guilt.

But all was not quite . . . right . . . with Eleanor even before this tragedy: when she was ten, stones rained on her house for three days. Markway's revelation of this to the other "ghost hunters" prompts a definition of the word "poltergeist" and later, of psychokinesis. However, when Dr. Markway brings up the stone anecdote, Eleanor denies it vehemently until he goes on to say that it was the reason he put her on his list of research associates. Rather desperately, she tells him that the neighbors did it; they threw the stones because her mother "wouldn't mix with them." Why wouldn't her mother mix with them? And why is Eleanor so adamant in her denial until faced with the risk of expulsion from her place in the group . . . and from Hill House?

Why did Eleanor's sister refuse to let Eleanor use the car to get to Hill House, even though Eleanor helped pay for it? "There's a perfectly good reason Mother was afraid for you to go anywhere, and I'm sure it still applies," her sister says. The sister's husband chimes in, "We're not going to dig up the family skeleton again, are we?" To which Eleanor responds, "Get out! Before I show you what my nerves can really do!" And they *do* get out.

Wise has said that one of the most interesting parts of the film for him was the relationship between Eleanor and the exotic Theodora, a self-assured, sophisticated woman with a flair for ESP and a penchant for other women. (This lesbian angle is not present, or barely so, in the novel.) It's interesting to note that the first time major supernatural events in the film take place is when Theodora and Eleanor are separated from the men. Why does something bang wildly on the door, demanding to be let in as Theo and Eleanor have climbed into the same bed, clutching each other in terror? And what possesses Eleanor to turn into a tiger and bang on the very same door, refusing to let it in?

Later in the dark, she invites Theo to hold her hand. She believes Theo does—gripping so hard she practically breaks Eleanor's fingers. But then she discovers Theo was nowhere near her and wails, "Whose hand was I holding?" Why does physical contact only happen to her?

During the course of the story, Eleanor falls in love with Markway, an attraction he notes but fails to deal with—he's preoccupied with the investigation. When his wife shows up, all hell breaks loose—and Mrs. Markway is the only person besides Eleanor herself to be controlled by the house—it makes her lose her way, and then it sends her outside—*out,* away from itself. In essence, rejecting her. "The house doesn't want her," Eleanor says. "She's taken my place."

On the other hand, one of the legends that had sprung up around the house is that the old lady who lived there, Miss Abby Craine, died because her paid companion didn't come when she summoned her . . . mirroring the situation between Eleanor and her mother. In fact, when the pounding begins, Eleanor, half-asleep, answers with a rap on the wall and says, "All right, Mother! I'm coming!"

After the arrival of Mrs. Markway, Eleanor goes into a trance of sorts and attempts suicide, but is saved by Dr. Markway. "The house is falling down around me," she thinks; but she also says, "We killed her. You and I, Hugh Craine." (Hugh Craine, the father of Miss Abby, built the house ninety years before.) Chandeliers crash to the floor and the bolts that support the circular stairway Eleanor ascends—ostensibly to jump—yank from the wall.

So, is Eleanor the catalyst or the cause of the supernatural occurrences in the house? Is she having a breakdown, and raining down the stones of her "shattered nerves" on the others? Her jealousy? Both? Or is she merely a focus for ghostly inhabitants who want her to join them?

Wise leaves that up to us. But in praising Lewton's method, Wise says: "He aimed at more than mere exploitable spook shows, and wanted their impact to result from legitimate psychological conflicts. . . . [S]teady pressure was exerted and the people on the screen were thrown off emotional balance, and we hoped, would take the audience with them."[1]

What about the other elements? The photography? What special effects does Wise use to frighten us? What visual form does the haunting take?

None, as one might expect from a Lewton-trained director. One of the most frightening things about the movie is that we never see what's causing all the ruckus. Doors are pushed so hard they bow inward, squealing with the strain. Something hits the walls so hard they shake. Doorknobs turn stealthily, persistently; the sobbing of a child pierces the darkness. The strange, angry murmurings of a something—man, ghost?—waft through the wallpaper.

"Nothing in this house seems to move until you look away, and then you just catch something out of the corner of your eye," Theodora says, and the photography belies that. In an interview on *Entertainment Tonight*, Wise talked about *The Haunting* and the fact that no monster or ghost is ever shown. He believes that what we conjure up in our imagination will be much worse than anything he can show.

"If I knew the monster I could face it," actress Anne Bancroft said in a recent interview in *Lear's*. The fact that no one knows the monster in *The Haunting*—including the audience—makes it unconquerable. How to fight it? How to beat it? How to know when it's gone? These are questions that can never be answered: *there is no resolution*.

Added to this are the literally hundreds of static shots of the house, usually exteriors, with its turrets and its eyelike windows—shots at forty-five-degree angles, shots that loom over you, shots that take you on, of the house that was "born bad . . . leprous, vile, a House of Hades." There are close-ups of statues staring sightlessly at you, shots of the characters startled by their own reflections . . . and entire scenes shown as reflections in mirrors add to the jarring sense of being watched.

Wise was a prominent director at this point—by 1962 his credits included *Blood on the Moon; I Want to Live!; The Day the Earth Stood Still; Run Silent, Run Deep;* and *West Side Story*—yet he shot *The*

1. Samuel Stark, "Robert Wise," *Films in Review* 10 (January 1962).

Haunting in black-and-white. In the script, much is made of the awful colors in the house, but here again, Wise depended upon the audience to exercise its imagination. With his director of photography, Davis Boulton, he went instead for the dark/gray/shaded look of a Lewton movie, in this story about shadows in the mind and the world.

Another cinematic element Wise exploits in this film is his sound-track. In an interview, Wise revealed that this is one of his recipes for success: a "catalog of audible suggestions, of an unusual richness, attaining a sort of delirious paroxysm" (quoting in translation now from the book *Robert Wise*, listed at the end of the essay). The sound effects are elaborate and the music, disjointed and jarring, with tinkles of bells, rolling pieces of metal, and a single melodic line that appears to be Eleanor's theme.

In addition—and this is really an element of the script, although its employment falls into the sound category—Wise used Eleanor's interior thoughts as a series of chilling voice-overs, showing her self-preoccupation, her certainty that the house wants her—her literal self-absorption. "We who walk here, walk alone," Eleanor's disembodied voice tells us at the end of the film.

Which is incredibly disconcerting to us, the audience, since we never really know who or what it is that walks there—and the fact that there's more than one—that there's a "we"—well! That may have never occurred to us. But now the last foot of film is spinning through the projector, and we have to go outside, into "the night, the dark," carrying the film with us, because it's not over yet. *There's been no resolution*.

Take three: right now. It's seven o'clock of a winter's evening. I've been sitting in my office, typing this essay on my Mac and contemplating the fact that I might need to rewatch *The Haunting* to verify some of my assertions. A certain edginess crept over me as I decided yes, I have to do it, have to watch it again. This edginess grew as I pondered whether I should watch it now, tonight, or do it tomorrow morning. Better tomorrow, I decided. It's probably a little late now. On the other hand, I want to get this piece finished, and I usually go to bed around one in the morning, and the film lasts less than two hours. . . .

And the phone just rang, just now, and I swear I jumped a foot. And I startled my dogs, who started barking, and I started laughing (hope that got the Tingler) . . .

. . . and I haven't watched this damn scary movie for at least a year, but just the thought of doing so still completely wigs me out.

That's haunted.
That's *The Haunting*.

Here are some articles and books for further reading:

Film Facts, "The Haunting," September 12, 1963, pp. 181–82 (compilation of reviews).

Grivel, Daniele, and Roland Lacourbe, *Robert Wise* (in French), Paris: Edilig, 1985.

Holland, Larry Lee, "The Haunting," in Frank N. Magill, ed., *Magill's Survey of Cinema*, New Jersey: Salem Press, 1980.

Jackson, Shirley, *The Haunting of Hill House*, New York: Warner Books, 1959.

Knight, Arthur, "Wise in Hollywood," *Saturday Review*, August 8, 1970, pp. 22–25.

Stark, Samuel, "Robert Wise," *Films in Review,* January 1963, pp. 5–22.

Chapter

(Lucky) 13

Joe R. Lansdale

Mention Joe to anyone who's read his stuff and the reaction is immediate and invariable: a smile. People, men and women, get that childlike guess-what-I-got-for-Christmas, honest-to-goodness shit-eating grin. Why/What is it about Joe's work that is so exciting?

Who knows? Who cares?

I do. You do. This son of the Lone Star State and author of the truly weird turns us all on because, though many of his stories stray too far from reality to ever come back, there is something ultimately very real about his writing that taps into our cultural awareness, our social mores, and inevitably, our inner secrets.

And, by the way, he's a funny bastard.

His tales are fairly evenly spread out among the horror, mystery, and western genres, but they share a ferocity and a voice unmistakable as the work of another. His novels include *The Magic Wagon*, *Cold in July*, *The Nightrunners*, *The Drive-in*, and the Batman novel *Captured by the Engines*. His award-winning short stories have appeared in many magazines and anthologies. They include "The Night They Missed the Horror Show" (*Silver Scream*) and "On the Far Side of the Cadillac Desert with Dead Folks" (*Book of the Dead*).

Several of his stories and novels have been optioned for the screen, and he is the author of two screenplays based on his work and of two original off-Broadway plays. He is currently at work on an original miniseries for DC Comics and a new suspense novel.

A Hard-on for Horror: Low-Budget Excitement

by Joe R. Lansdale

(For Russ Ansley)

It's difficult to know precisely where it all began, this love for that third world of films, the low-budget horror movie (and I prefer "movie" to "film" and will use that term from here on out), but I suppose for me it began in my own living room, most likely when I was ten or eleven years old and not reading comic books or playing with my pecker, two favorite boy pastimes just above cussing when your parents aren't around, and poking at something dead you've found with a stick.

I had been exposed to horror before that time, but only in oblique ways, a moment in a fairy tale, ghostly anecdotes told by relatives, an animated corpse in the aforementioned comic book, the odor of a neighbor's outhouse, the Sunday-school terrors of the Bible.

Thinking on it now, I'd have to say the Bible is probably the strongest influence on my attraction to horror. God was always brutally bullying somebody in the Old Testament, showing far less patience and mercy than his minions. Truth to tell, you read the Old Testament, and especially if you're one of those who believe this stuff literally, you're bound to get scared. God comes across in the Old Testament as someone whose caffeine level should be strictly monitored.

In fact, Mr. All-Powerful-Know-It-All, is most of the time just short of rabid. The old boy (and I suppose a case might be made for God as female or as an It, but I think it's pretty clear the celestial force in the Old Testament is presented as male) is always putting folks, who'd rather be left alone to herd their sheep, up to tests, seeing if they'll stab their young'ns if he asks, getting mad when someone like Onan uses the jerk-back method during sexual relations and splatters his seed on the ground. An event that put God in one of his worst humors. God, the old voyeur, wanted that seed in the vagina where it belonged, so he slew Onan for practicing birth control. Maybe sent a thunderbolt up his ass, I don't remember.

Think about it. Guy shits in the woods where you can step on it, it's all right, but if he decides to practice a little birth control, squirts a load of sperm in the dirt, he's out of here. Get out the shovels and put him in the dirt.

The New Testament is only a little less horrifying, what with its reformed approach in the person of a country-boy carpenter named Jesus.

On the surface, Jesus looks like a stand-up kind of guy. But you look at his life head-on, you began to notice he had some defects. He didn't think things through. Maybe it's a parable, I don't know, but one example of his simple-headedness is displayed in the New Testament. Here we have a story about Jesus coming to this burg where there's a fellow full of devils living there. I mean, full of them dudes. He's popping to the eyeballs with them. Slobbering around, short on manners. Being Southern, this last part about manners deeply disturbs me. Nobody likes to have someone around that can't be invited for dinner and be expected to behave, though come to think of it, I don't know a Southerner who hasn't got at least one story about someone dying at the table with a chicken bone or some such lodged in their throat.

Anyway, Jesus got on the job in an instant. He pulled those devils out of that poor infested soul and freed him. 'Course, then he had the devils to get rid of. You can't keep something like that under your hat, so J.C. spotted some innocent pigs wandering nearby, doing pig things, I reckon, and he stuffed those devils into the pigs.

Think on that. You're some piglet cruising along, just eating what you can find, thinking a few minor pig thoughts, and the next thing you know, you need an exorcist. But Jesus had a simpler answer, and any pig hearing of this biblical event for the first time is bound to lose the curl in his or her tail. It's that drastic.

What Jesus did, is he compelled the pigs *he*, his own merciful self, had infested with those devils, to run into a pond. Lickity-split, right there into the water.

This is not part of normal pig activity, brethren. This was achieved by Jesus putting the hex on the pigs, evil eye, something like that. Anyway, the pigs ran into the pond, and the Bible says something like "and they were choked," drowned being a bit less descriptive. It's always important in the Bible that the right words for suffering are chosen, and this precision is something I admire, and this sort of descriptive writing puts God and his biographers clearly and cleanly in the literary arena sometimes described as splatterpunk. It gives the pigs a less welcome title. Deceased.

I used to wake up at night after Sunday school and consider on those pigs. A cruel way to go, that, and pork chops wasted besides. Even the dumbest son of a bitch amongst us, short of a sociopath, would have put those devils in a rock and thrown it in the pond, but not Jesus. As is the general case with the Bible, someone or something innocent needs to suffer, and if you think this doesn't bring us to films, you're wrong.

Scary mythology—Greek, Roman, and those of the aforementioned Testaments—fairy tales, the like, led to horrific pictures in my head, and later they attracted me to the more pleasant horrors of the movies, and the movies in turn sent me to the books, which were the source for many of the films I saw. *Invasion of the Body Snatchers, Day of the Triffids, The Pit and the Pendulum* among them.

My first solid memory of low-budget horror and horror/science-fiction movies were presented to me by a long-haired, good-looking witch named Evilyn who came to me out of Shreveport, Louisiana, every Friday night, courtesy of the boob tube and a program called *Terror!*

Evilyn would come out wearing a slinky black dress with her black hair parted in the middle, say a few words about the movie of the night, then spring it on us.

Those movies ran the gamut, from the classic Universal stuff, *The Wolf Man* (a personal favorite), *Dracula*, *Frankenstein*, etc., to humbler non-Universal efforts such as *I Married a Monster from Outer Space* and *Invaders from Mars*, to William Castle extravaganzas like *Thirteen Ghosts* and *The Tingler*, to Roger Corman's *Attack of the Crab Monsters* and *Little Shop of Horrors*. In other words, a smorgasbord of stuff ranging from the good low-budgets to the indisputable ass wipes of the genre.

And brothers and sisters, I'm here today to witness to you today and say without hesitation, I loved them all.

Let me hear one from the amen corner.

Hallelujah!

Loved every goddamn one of them, from the classy Val Lewton stuff like *The Cat People* and *I Walked with a Zombie,* on down to the slightly off-center ones like *The Beast With Five Fingers* and *The Crawling Eye,* on lower into the sewerish ranks of picture-show produce wherein trees from hell and rocks from outer space threatened innocent civilians who only wanted to marry and raise three kids in a little house next to another house and have a good lawn mower and a barbecue grill in their garage, along with a new Chevy, of course.

And if Evilyn gave me my first dose of cinematic horror, the Cozy

Theater gave me my second dose. Come Saturdays, I practically lived in that sticky-floored, roach-infested theater.

The Cozy showed all kinds of movies, but the kiddie matinee, and the main feature, were quite often men-in-monster-suit movies, apes on the loose, and good stuff like those Corman gems *Diary of a Madman*, based on Guy de Maupassant's "The Horla," and countless other films loosely—quite loosely—based on Edgar Allan Poe stories like "The Pit and the Pendulum" and "The Masque of the Red Death."

Drive-ins gave me my third dose of horror movies, and this one, dear hearts, was as intense as a dose of the clap. Oh man, I loved drive-ins, still do, but now they're as scarce as intellectuals in the political system.

Admittedly, my first drive-in experiences were courtesy of my parents and older brother and his family, and what I saw then was more in the way of Disney films, westerns, that sort of thing, and I loved them, too. But when I was in my teens, I began to go to the drive-in on my own, and that's when the real brain damage took place.

Most of the stuff I saw, and it was not all horror, was just downright bad. But thing was, this way, I was getting to see something I wasn't supposed to see in my living room, something my parents wouldn't want me to see, and finally, there was a certain mystique about the low-budget horror movies, because most likely, one of those dudes passed through town and I missed it, unless it came to a town nearby. I was shit out of luck, 'cause there wasn't any video, and the networks damn sure weren't going to show that crap on television on account of these movies weren't made for art, they were made exclusively as drive-in cannon fodder, produced for one reason only—to separate me, the moviegoer, from his buck.

To some drive-in goers, and I have to speak from a male point of view here, these movies were something to kill time with while pausing between necking with dates, a little breather while putting the clothes back on. Or if you couldn't get a date, you could sit with buddies and watch this crap while you lied about getting a look up Debra Jane's skirt in social studies.

(Let me pause for a historical point of importance. This optical event of boy-eyeball-on-girl-panty was referred to in Gladewater High School as "shooting squirrel."

Write that down, you might need it on a Trivial Pursuit question or something.)

Another thing about the drive-in was it was sort of like a teenage guy itself. It liked dark private places, and it bragged, downright lied actually, about how well it could perform. Compare the lies some guys tell about all the tail they've banged to drive-in advertisements, and you'll begin to see what I mean.

Example: We'd drive on over to the Riverroad in Longview, Texas, and the coming attractions we'd see before the movies, would turn out to be more stimulating than the movie we ended up watching, which, of course, we'd come to see because last week's previews had turned out to be better than the movies we watched then.

In my novel *The Drive-in*, I talked about these kinds of movies and the drive-in experience, and I said this of my mythical drive in, the Orbit:

> Now you're ready. The movies begin. B-string and basement budget pictures. A lot of them made with little more than a Kodak, some spit and a prayer. And if you've watched enough of this stuff, you develop a taste for it, sort of like learning to like sauerkraut.
>
> Drooping mikes, bad acting and the rutting of rubber-suited monsters who want women, not for food, but to mate with, become a genuine pleasure. You can simultaneously hoot and cringe when a monster attacks a screaming female on the beach or in the woods and you see the zipper on the back of the monster suit winking at you like the quick, drunk smile of a Cheshire cat.
>
> Yes sir, there was something special about the Orbit all right. It was romantic. It was outlaw. It was crazy.

For all practical purposes, the drive-in is gone, replaced by cable channels and video. Both are nice, but I still miss being out under that Texas sky, the party or picnic atmosphere drive-ins had, and dammit, I even miss that foul mosquito coil you bought at the concession to ward off the little bloodsuckers. You were supposed to light it and in theory the smoke from it had something in it mosquitoes hated, and they wouldn't come around. This bit of advertisement was in line with the drive-in previews. It lied.

You lit that thing and put it on your dash, and about the only way it stopped a mosquito, was if the ignorant sonofabitch sat on the coil and caught on fire.

But, drive-in, or no drive-in, the low-budget movie is still with us, and though I'm a bit more selective these days, the same attraction remains for me as before.

Other than nostalgia, why is this?

Hell, I don't know, not really, but, let me venture a smidgen of academic analysis—just a little, I don't want to throw up in my trash can here—and toss in a whole bean pot full of opinion.

The low-budget horror film is, on one hand, one of the most maligned forms of entertainment, and on the other hand, is often given a significance far beyond its worth.

As a sometimes writer of stories and novels of questionable taste, meaning fiction that is the equivalent of a dinner guest enthusiastically burping and farting at their host's table between asking why a better beer wasn't stocked for dinner and complaining about the lumps in the gravy, and yet being able to discuss Hemingway and Faulkner and Flannery O'Connor and the Doc Savage book where ol' Doc goes to hell, films of John Huston and John Ford and innovative crap–maker Roger Corman, I am quite aware of these extremes.

Seems many people, knowing my love for low-budget horror movies, think I can't wait to see the next evisceration extravaganza, some exploitation flick that shows in detail how to gut a human being and preserve the body parts, and I must admit I always feel, to put it mildly, distressed. To these folks, any low-budget horror movie with blood and grue is the same as the next, but in my eyes, there is quite a distinction between the *Re-Animator* and *Friday the 13th Part Six Million*, or some of its more brain-damaged cousins that were once the fodder of second-feature drive-in bills, and are now consigned to Made for Video, their packaging commonly appearing to have been designed by malicious children with crayons made of blood and soot and shit and smoke.

Some video packages, however, show a delightful lack of class. Take for instance *The Dead Pit*. This baby has a zombie and a button on the cover. You press the button and the zombie's eyes light up. My wife and I, while eating popcorn and watching this baby, would take turns pressing the button on the box when the theatric excitement slowed up or the backlighting in the movie made you think of a disco-zombie-jamboree. Needless to say, time we turned that little buddy back into the video store, the battery-powered green light behind the zombie's eyes had grown a mite faint.

But this confusion is understandable. The difference between a bad low-budget horror movie and a good one, is at times, difficult to discern. The problem being, a bad one and a good one share the same elements, and at a glance, the distinction between *The Texas Chainsaw Massacre* and *Attack of the Radioactive Testicles from Mars*, may seem slight.

The low-budget horror movie stands on the line of good taste and bad taste, and like a scarecrow in a high wind, flaps its arms and leans first in one direction, then the other. What gives the good film its power is its bravery, its willingness to let the wind blow it across the line of good taste, into that part of the field that is less mannerly and sometimes downright rude.

Possibly that wind will blow off our symbolic scarecrow's hat and sail it into oblivion, tear out some stuffings as well, but the good movie is unwilling to let its support pole topple completely before the wind shifts and redirects it in the direction we call art, and when referring to these movies, or if you must, films, the word "art" more often than not, will be spoken softly and with a cough.

And if we refuse to call bad acting and sloppy effects and stupid plotting art, we can at least say some of these movies, the ones that lost their hat and some of their stuffing, are at their best trying hard to be more than what they appear to be on the surface.

An example being *Street Trash*. You won't get me up on a soapbox expounding on how this little buddy is art. It's kind of a mess really. It rapidly loses its hat to the wind, as well as a large portion of its stuffing, and goes blowing hell-bent for leather over into the field of bad taste and just plain sloppy filmmaking. Still, at its core, I believe it has (cough) artistic intent.

You can feel it. It's clever. *Street Trash* has a sense of irony and satire, a desire to be more than a scarecrow in a high wind. But, like the Oz scarecrow, it needs a brain, but unlike the Oz scarecrow, it never quite gets one.

This aside, it never allows its base pole to come undone, though it does lean precariously far at times, and when the film's over, *Street Trash*'s symbolic scarecrow, minus hat and two-thirds of its stuffing, still has an arm and a leg and a head to nod toward the (cough) artistic side. It's a crippled creature, admittedly, but it's still standing.

It should be obvious by now that my feelings concerning the difference between bad and good, is the ability, or inability, to negotiate the wind. Our movie scarecrows often lose their foundation and go flying off too far in one direction or the other, satisfying neither on an exploitation level or an artistic one.

What the good low-budget horror movie does is attract through exploitation, then, with imagination, cleverness, and greater intent than to appeal to the lowest common denominator, or through a desire to manipulate that low denominator with irony or satire or archetypal imagery, it becomes artistic or shows artistic bents, which is not necessarily the same as becoming art, though at its very best, it can be that, too.

Fact is, any low-budget movie, even the good ones, should make the viewer wonder which camp it wants to be in. That of art or exploitation. That's part of its appeal, and part of the reason these movies are often underestimated, or at times, overestimated.

Big-budget films generally announce which camp they're in early on. They want there to be no mistake. They either see themselves as art, or as a roller-coaster ride—one of those overworked advertising terms used to describe a host of "slick" movies that have less brains than our aforementioned *Street Trash* scarecrow—and they damn well want you to know which one they are before you view the first frame. It's a subliminal way of telling you not to expect much for your dollars.

Enjoying a good low-budget horror movie should be akin to being in love with a good-looking woman with a mysterious past, a past that might possibly include something nefarious. Like murder or voting for Richard Nixon. A little scrambling of intent is what makes the good low-budget movie interesting and thought provoking.

I'm not trying to say that *Night of the Living Dead* and *The Texas Chainsaw Massacre* kept me awake at night pondering the meaning of it all. I've seen far too much attention given to the existentialist nature of these movies, and all I have to say to that is: Bullshit, pilgrim!

But these movies did address some rather primal fears for me far better than most of their filmatic relatives, some sporting fancier credentials.

Saw, like only a handful of other movies, tapped a nerve with me that is more often than not better accomplished with fiction and nonfiction. It touched that part of my brain, the primitive part, that made me realize that at some point the difference between the loving husband and doting father and a fellow with a chainsaw and evil intent, can be uncomfortably close. It accomplished this by simply making its villains a loving and loyal, if quarrelsome, family, and making their victims, if not murderous, less than loving. It takes skill to make a wheelchair-bound victim unsympathetic, but this is managed early on, and quite soon the audience is eager to see a helpless cripple get his, even if his only crime is assholism.

Night of the Living Dead's message is simple as well, but once again, primal. It shows that even the dead get no respect. It makes them a spectacle. Shows that once you're laid to rest in good old Mother Earth, you're going to rot and be full of worms. Not tidy. Once again, good manners have been breached. The director, George Romero, has put his finger on an often unspoken fear that many of us have. Your body is about as much a temple as a sagging, clapboard shithouse. Worse than that, the hero bites the big one in the end, pointing out an even worse horror: It doesn't matter how you live, who you are, there just ain't no such thing as true justice.

There are plenty of other cinematic examples, but I'm pushing my agreed wordage, and it's time for the sum-up.

So, what have we discerned, class?

That Mr. Lansdale is full of doodoo?

Likely. Yet, while I have you trapped mid-paragraph, let me conclude with a summary as to why I, and people like me, have a hard-on, or stiff nipples, for this stuff.

(1) It's primal.

(2) For many of us it's nostalgic.

(3) It's forbidden—less so these days, but that element remains.

(4) It's something to do that's more interesting than polishing the silverware or vacuuming the carpet.

(5) A few of us make our living from writing about this kind of stuff, because like the drive-in movies, we want to separate you from your buck, and I suppose if you're reading this—unless you've borrowed it—mission accomplished.

And you know what? It may not be any of these things.

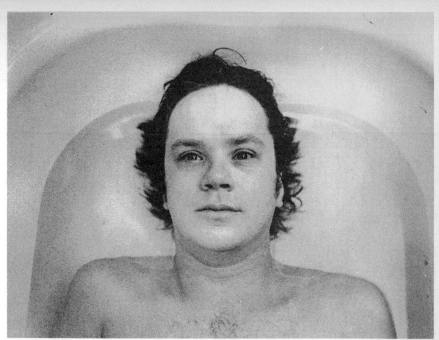

Tim Robbins has a rude awakening in *Jacob's Ladder*.

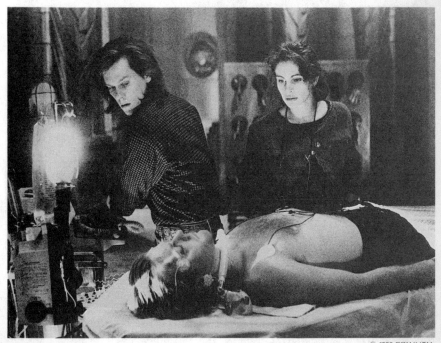

Kevin Bacon and Julia Roberts resurrect Kiefer Sutherland in *Flatliners*.

John Barrymore in 1920's *Dr. Jekyll and Mr. Hyde.*

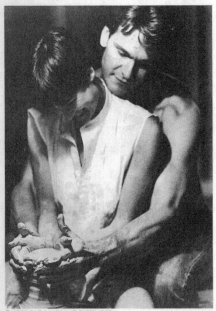

Christopher Stone shows us what he meant by *The Howling.*

The '90s guidelines for safe sex are presented by Demi Moore, Patrick Swayze, and a pottery wheel in *Ghost.*

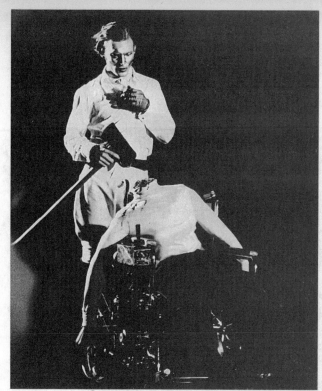

A cutting scene from *Dear Dead Delilah*.

The many facets of Vincent Price, from *The Pit and the Pendulum*.

WHAT MADE THIS THE MOST DIABOLICAL MURDER WEAPON EVER USED?

© 1960 ASTOR PICTURES.

AN ADVENTURE INTO TERROR

peeping tom

CARL BOEHM · MOIRA SHEARER · ANNA MASSEY · MAXINE AUDLEY

EASTMAN COLOR

ASTOR PICTURES presents

Elsa Lanchester and Boris Karloff in a classic scene from the ultimate classic, *Bride of Frankenstein*.

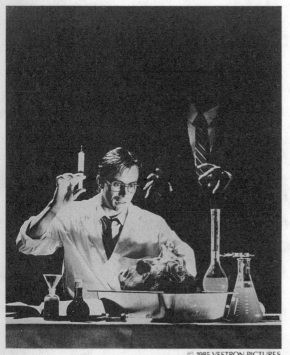

Jeffrey Coombs in H. P. Lovecraft's Re-Animator.

Simone Simon has nothing to fear but herself in the original *Cat People*.

It's only incest if you're human. Or so Malcolm McDowell would have Nastassia Kinski believe in the 1982 remake of *Cat People*.

Michael Berryman, on the hunt in *The Hills Have Eyes*.

Heather Langenkamp gets her first French kiss, courtesy of Freddy Krueger in *A Nightmare on Elm Street*.

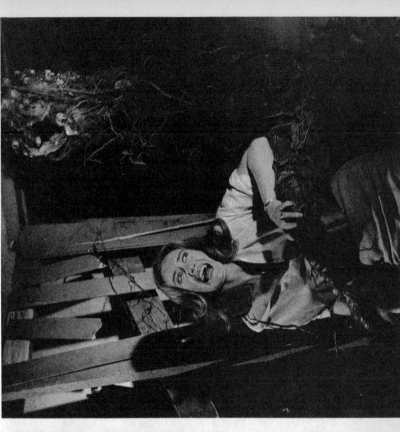

Obviously, Nicole Maurey hasn't neglected her gardening in *Day of the Triffids.*

Julie Harris and Claire Bloom in *The Haunting.*

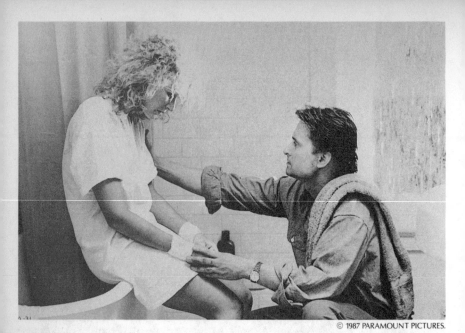

Michael Douglas doesn't know what he's getting into with Glenn Close in *Fatal Attraction*.

Martin Sheen and Sissy Spacek pay for their sins in *Badlands*.

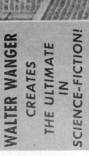

WALTER WANGER CREATES THE ULTIMATE IN SCIENCE-FICTION!

ALLIED ARTISTS presents

INVASION OF THE *BODY SNATCHERS*

KEVIN McCARTHY · DANA WYNTER

with LARRY GATES · KING DONOVAN · CAROLYN JONES · JEAN WILLES · RALPH DUMKE · Directed by DON SIEGEL · Screenplay by DANIEL MAINWARING · Based on the COLLIER'S MAGAZINE Serial by JACK FINNEY

FILMED IN SUPERSCOPE

© 1956 ALLIED ARTISTS.

Christopher Lee and Peter Cushing practicing their javelin throw in Hammer's *The Mummy*.

A wino (Bruce Torbet) suffers a grisly demise in *Street Trash*.

Christopher Lee takes command as Hammer Film's *Dracula*.

Earth vs. The Flying Saucers

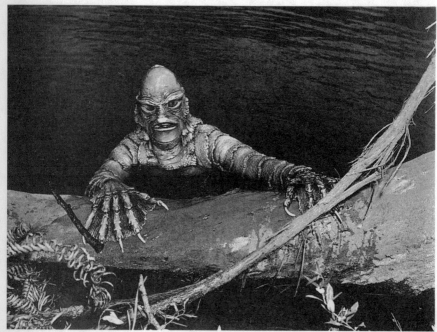

Ben Chapman as *The Creature From the Black Lagoon*

Michael Ironside and Stephen Lack in the mind-blowing finale to *Scanners*.

Jeremy Irons[2] in *Dead Ringers*.

Rory Calhoun is Farmer Vincent in *Motel Hell.*

Bryan Madorsky is served some suspicious meat by his *Parents* Mary Beth Hurt and Randy Quaid.

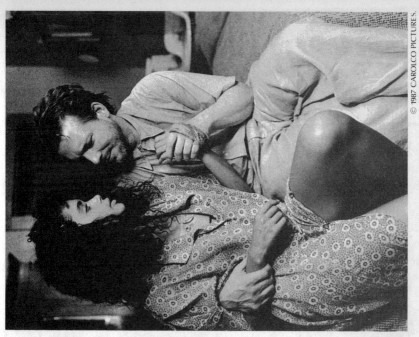

Mickey Rourke and Lisa Bonet in *Angel Heart*.

Speak of the devil. Robert De Niro and Mickey Rourke in *Angel Heart*.

Laurence Olivier and Joan Fontaine in *Rebecca*.

''Who killed...?'' Well, you know. The cast of *Twin Peaks*.

"Maybe in those last few moments, he loved life more than he ever had. Not just his life. Anybody's life. My life." Rutger Hauer and Harrison Ford in *Blade Runner.*

Alien.

Kyle MacLachlan and Isabella Rossellini in a compromising position from *Blue Velvet*.

Michael Rooker and friend in *Henry: Portrait of a Serial Killer*.

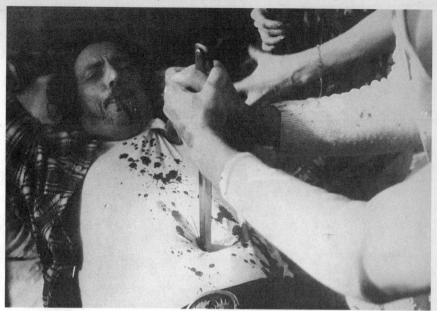

The maniac in *Maniac.*

Suzy Kendall takes care of a peeper in *The Bird with the Crystal Plumage.*

Jessica Harper gets an unwelcome visitor in *Suspiria*.

Deep Red.

"Whoops!" A scene from *I Spit on Your Grave*.

Director Tod Browning and the cast of *Freaks*.

Chapter
14

T. Liam McDonald

The tall, lanky guy with the glasses is Tom, or Liam, depending on when you knew him and where from. Suffice to say that Tom, or Liam, is an extremely busy guy.

Tom (you get the idea) is the editor of *Shadowplays: The Dark Fiction of Charles L. Grant* and the author of the forthcoming mystery novel *Night Without Morning*. His popular interview column "Profiles in Terror" appears in *Cemetery Dance* magazine, and a book-review column, "The House of Fiction," appears in *Gauntlet*. His other nonfiction has appeared in major magazines, including *Early American Life* and such obscure journals as *The Thomas Wolfe Review*.

After receiving degrees in literature and film from New York University, he worked for Universal Television on *The Equalizer* and the revived *Kojak* and for Laurel Entertainment on *Monsters* and *Tales from the Darkside: The Movie*. He is the founder of Incarnate Productions, the independent film company under whose banner he produced his first feature film (the low-budget *Crawdaddys*) at age twenty-one.

Like I said, Liam, or Tom, is a very busy guy.

The Horrors of Hammer:
The House That Blood Built

by T. Liam McDonald

It all began simply enough in the years before World War II, with William Hinds and Enrique Carreras forming a company to distribute select short films. After the war the prospect of making their own movies arose and they began producing feature-length films based on popular BBC radio shows. They struck gold in 1955 with the science-fiction horror of *The Quatermass Xperiment* (USA: *The Creeping Unknown*), and knew they'd stumbled onto a public appetite that needed to be fed. They were Hammer Films, and no matter how many films they produced (hundreds, actually, making them one of the most prolific production houses in the world at the time), be they adventures, historicals, or Ealing-type comedies, their name would always be linked with horror.

There is no true connoisseur of horror movies who is not familiar with Hammer Films. The name is distinctive and calls to mind classic horrors, period sets, and of course, Peter Cushing and Christopher Lee, whose names became inextricably linked with Hammer when they appeared together in *The Curse of Frankenstein* and countless subsequent films. Indeed, many of Hammer's actors appear in one film after another, because Hammer was a "house" studio. Unlike most production companies, which are formed, staffed, crewed, cast, and then dissolved following completion of a film, Hammer was a corporation with a stable of talent that it used for all their projects, which is what contributed to the Hammer look: the consistency of style that marks their films as uniquely their own. Going to work at the Bray Studios, where Hammer shot many of their films during their "golden age" (1957 to 1970) was very much like going to work for any major corporation. You saw the same faces every day and worked the same hours, except that one week you would be making a biofilm about Rasputin, and the next, one of the countless *Frankenstein* or *Dracula* sequels.

In a financial sense, Hammer's approach to horror was to treat it as a commodity, much like AIP was doing in America. This approach led them to choose for their subject matter what could be called the Blue Chip Stock of horror: the sure winners that had already been absorbed into the public consciousness. Frankenstein, Dracula, the Mummy, the Phantom of the Opera, Dr. Jekyll and Mr. Hyde, vampires, werewolves, demons, and zombies: these were all instantly recognizable figures that bore with them certain preconceptions. By popping one of these names into the title (à la *The Vampire Lovers*, *The Scars of Dracula*, *The Curse of the Werewolf*, etc.), they created a set of expectations for the public. People knew the supernatural "rules" that governed these monsters: such as crosses, daylight, and garlic ward off vampires, silver bullets can kill werewolves, and nice Dr. Jekyll turns into nasty Mr. Hyde. Some may consider this approach formulaic and creatively limiting, but a film that comes to the public complete with a history comes complete with a market. Sometimes this allowed the filmmakers to concentrate on character development, style, and the refinement of plots, but more often than not the result was just more-of-the-same. Production qualities, design, acting, and cinematography were always topflight, often compensating for weak plots, but too many of the sequels seem familiar. While any one of the sequels may have stood alone, within a series they became repetitive, diminished reflections of the originals.

Terence Fisher's *The Curse of Frankenstein* was where Hammer's reign of terror began in 1957 and, sadly, the god-awful *To the Devil, a Daughter* is where it would end nineteen years and over five dozen films later. In between there were other movies (mystery, comedy, adventure, war) but none as successful as the horror movies. William Hinds' son Anthony was in charge of production when the proposition to remake *Frankenstein* came to Hammer. Anthony Hinds had a talent for commercially viable, well-crafted, low-budget filmmaking. He picked properties for production with a keen eye for commerce *and* art. Mary Shelley's novel was over a hundred years old and therefore public domain, available for film adaptation. But Universal Pictures had a tight copyright on the film version, and though Hammer was allowed to make a new *Frankenstein* (over twenty years after the Boris Karloff/ James Whale version), it could bear no similarity to Universal's film whatsoever, from sets, to plot, to makeup. So the director, writer, set designer, and makeup artist (Terence Fisher, Jimmy Sangster, Ted Marshall, and Phil Leakey respectively) had to get creative, and as Anthony Hinds would later explain, "what was a pretty average production became great fun."

The elements of the Hammer neo-gothic style are all present in this first *Frankenstein*. The small sets give the impression of being huge and sprawling, and there is a feeling of authenticity in the roomy stone laboratory, with its practical, simple equipment (as opposed to Universal's mildly surreal Teutonic sets) and Victorian decor. As with all gothics, there is the threatened, buxom heroine (Hazel Court) wearing her billowing gowns and doing stupid things, such as entering the monster's lair; and the boring but serviceable "hero" (Robert Urquhart). Dominating the scene is Peter Cushing's Baron Victor Frankenstein, the driven, tortured scientist whom the viewer shouldn't like. After all, the man murders not only friends but innocents, and endeavors to destroy anything or anyone that gets in his way. He has a disturbing clinical ease with the grotesque, and scenes show him probing an eyeball to test its freshness, picking shards of glass from a damaged brain, and sawing open a skull. The baron is extremely unlikable, ruthless and cruel, but in the performance of Peter Cushing, there is an essential, overwhelming sense of humanity and even pity beneath the cruelty. No matter how evil the character is that Cushing plays, the viewer always sympathizes with him. It is something in his manner and nature that is almost imperceptible, but if one were to single out the single most superior element in *The Curse of Frankenstein*, would it not be Peter Cushing's performance?

But that alone would not have catapulted the film and the studio that made it into such extraordinary success. One major element of Hammer's success was simple enough: color. Few horror films (and no British horror films) had been shot in full, bold, bloody Technicolor before. It is what completes the richness of texture, the fullness of the gothic atmosphere. Though horror enthusiast William K. Everson (author of *Classics of the Horror Film*) scorns Hammer films by claiming that color has never been necessary for horror movies and lacks the effectiveness of black-and-white, he has sadly missed the point. Black-and-white, for all its moody effectiveness and evocative atmosphere, has never been able to capture the true grandeur, the pure *gaudiness,* of visceral horror. Even if color is not used to show red blood or putrid flesh, it can be used in evoking the gothic atmosphere in the sets, the costumes, the design, and in the simple *look* of the film. The gothic is a genre of overstatement, of life and emotion pushed to the nth degree. It is sensory overload. The neo-gothic fuses all the classic elements (castles, storms, misty moors) with the new, supercharged medium of film and its ability to depict artfully designed reality. There weren't heaps of violence or buckets of blood in these films. By comparison with today's standards it appears tame, but for the time the sickly color of Christopher Lee's skin and the bright red of the blood was shocking and unprecedented. In the *Frankenstein* films we get Victorian operations and close-ups of brains, eyeballs, and other juicy bits; while the vampire films stick to bloody fangs and the odd staking or decapitation. It was enough to make some viewers rush from the theater and others vomit. Critics scorned the "butchery" of Hammer's films, and trumpeted how this was a disturbing trend and the sign of a sick society. Some wanted it banned, but slapping it with an X Certificate (the equivalent of America's R rating) was enough for the British Film Board. And how did the majority of the audience react?

They loved it, and screamed for more. Hammer was ready and willing to comply, and following the trend of remakes of literary-based Hollywood films, they brought *Dracula* (USA: *The Horror of Dracula*) to the screen in 1958, once again teaming up Christopher Lee and Peter Cushing as, respectively, the title vampire and his nemesis, Dr. Van Helsing. Instead of following in the footsteps of Todd Browning and Bela Lugosi, director Terence Fisher repeated the Hammer formula that was so successful in *The Curse of Frankenstein:* Technicolor all-out gothic horror. There was nothing of the powdered, prissy Bela Lugosi and his ersatz Valentino posing. Christopher Lee is big and savage and *evil*. While never losing sight of the essential tragedy of the character, he never flinches for a second. It is the *ne plus ultra* of Dracula performances. His bloody fangs, his animalistic attacks, his savage silence (in the script his last line is on page thirteen!), his emphasis on the erotic and sensual elements of vampirism all add extraordinary depth to a figure that had become a shadow of Stoker's original character to be laughed at and a subject for pratfalls. Lee had to save Dracula from Lugosi's trivialization and lack of depth.

The grandeur of the film is evident right from the opening credits, with the blaring theme music over the stark image of an eagle (Dracula's symbol), the camera panning over the castle and fading into a shot of Dracula's name emblazoned upon a coffin. Bright red blood drips upon the bronze nameplate, and we cut to the first scene of Jonathan Harker journeying to Dracula's castle. The shot of the blood is symbolically important, not in the context of the film, but in the context of Fisher's (and Hammer's) approach: the shot is not part of the narrative, and figures in no way in the story. It is there merely as part of Hammer's opening statement of purpose, as it were. This is horror, and you will see blood and haunted castles and the living dead and all the elements you asked for. It sets the tone and grabs the viewer right from the beginning. The film falls into a creepy lull as it brings Harker alone into the castle. Dracula is introduced only moments later, after Harker has met a strange, seemingly threatened woman who begs him for help. Christopher Lee appears at the top of the stairs to the sound of his loud, three-note musical motif, then he calmly, elegantly floats down the stairs and crosses the room to greet Harker in the pleasant, mannered voice of an aristocrat. It is striking in its simplicity. Lee's tall, dark, handsome appearance is a notable contrast to Lugosi's short, anemic, repellent character. This is Stoker's Dracula: regal, courtly, with just the slightest hint of the demon in his eyes. He is also brazenly sensual and meant to appeal to women. Indeed: his victims seem to derive an almost sexual enjoyment from his attacks.

With the hugely successful *Frankenstein* and *Dracula* now under their belts, Hammer had proven to Universal Studios its ability to turn out classy, profitable films. The next step was obvious, and in cooperation with Universal, they produced a remake of *The Mummy* (1959). Once again, all the same players were together behind the camera and in front of it. Terence Fisher directed Jimmy Sangster's script, the central production crew was the same, and Lee and Cushing were once again foes. The film begins with a long introduction set in ancient Egypt in which the tongue of the High Priest Kharis (Lee) is ripped out and he is sealed in the tomb of his mummified lover, Princess Ananka, as a punishment for disrupting her burial ceremonies. Flash forward to Victorian times: a party of archaeologists opens the tomb against the warnings of the devout Mehemet, and subsequently bring the full curse of the Mummy down on their heads. Lee, as Kharis/the Mummy, is once again playing a role originated by Karloff, and Cushing is a little more sympathetic this time out (and all the more boring for it) as John Banning, who is determined to stop the creature from carrying out its revenge. The story, as with the original, is a pure revenge fable with no pretenses to being anything else. The Mummy is hell-bent on accomplishing his task. Here neither foe is represented as being wrong or necessarily evil: both the archaeologists that dug up the Mummy and the devoted Kharis have noble goals, one being the quest for knowledge, the other for revenge. It is this clash not only of times but of cultures that provides the driving force of the film, and in the telling of the story it makes more of a statement than any of Hammer's previous period horrors, and shows a sign of an increasing attention to detail and matters of theme.

One of the more unusual stories surrounding the making of a Hammer film involves yet another stable monster film: *The Curse of the Werewolf* (1959), starring a young Oliver Reed. Anthony Hinds had planned to make a film about the Spanish Inquisition. A script was written, the money was raised, and the elaborate Spanish sets were built. Shortly before the cameras began to roll, however, Hinds was informed by the Catholic Church in England that if he made a film about the Inquisition, it would be banned. With such a great deal of money already committed, Hinds had to think fast, and the choice was made to adapt Guy Endore's novel *The Werewolf of Paris* for Spain and shoot it using the Inquisition sets. From such beginnings one would not expect a superior film to evolve, but the Hammer staff was well up to the task and *The Curse of the Werewolf*, their only true venture into the werewolf film, is a genuinely scary and effective horror movie.

Along the theme of the werewolf is the story of *Dr. Jekyll and Mr. Hyde*, which Hammer tried three times to adapt with varying levels of success. The first attempt, a spoof called *The Ugly Duckling* (1959), is best forgotten. *The Two Faces of Dr. Jekyll* followed in 1960, with Paul Massie as the lead who changes from the sympathetic, bearded scientist Dr. Jekyll into the clean-shaven, suave cad Mr. Hyde. With Paul Massie managing to be utterly unengaging throughout and Christopher Lee wasted in a minor role, the film is a total flop in all aspects, being boring, trite, and unscary to boot.

They succeeded a little better the third time out with the offbeat "high concept" *Dr. Jekyll and Sister Hyde* (1971), which at least had the novelty of Ralph Bates turning into Martine *The Happy Hooker* Beswick. Director Roy Ward Baker (who handled the larger films of Hammer's "sexier" period) took the generally silly premise of Dr. Jekyll experimenting with female hormones and turning into the lovely Martine Beswick dreadfully seriously, and missed an opportunity for some well-needed humor. Many of the elements work, such as the struggle between the noble Dr. Jekyll, who has a gentleman's interest in his upstairs neighbor, and the promiscuous, sexually liberated widower Mrs. Hyde, who has a less noble interest in the upstairs neighbor's brother. But these scenes of struggle go on too long and become unintentionally laughable. There are some wonderful, effective scenes in this film, such as the first appearance of Sister Hyde, when Martine Beswick rips open her dressing gown, reveling in her new breasts and the power her sexuality has over men. Tony Calvin and Neil Wilson as Burke and Hare are another highlight, and the scene in which Burke is cast into the lime pit is probably the scariest of the film. But Brian Clemens's script tries to play too many hands at once by incorporating a subplot that sets up Dr. Jekyll as a type of Whitechapel Murderer, thereby strongly reducing sympathy for him and turning him into a kind of warmed-over Baron Frankenstein, luring prostitutes into alleys and removing their glands.

Dr. Jekyll and Sister Hyde came along in the middle of a transitional period for Hammer, when their classy productions were receiving an essential element for the early-seventies film market: sex. Nowhere is this more evident than in a trilogy of vampire films that mark some of the company's highest (and lowest) moments. These are, of course, the notorious Mircalla films: *Lust for a Vampire* (1970), *The Vampire Lovers* (1971), and *Twins of Evil* (1971). Adapted as they were from the classic novella *Carmilla* by the Irish Victorian thriller writer J. Sheridan Le Fanu, they had still more classy Victorian source material. *Carmilla*, with its intimations of both psychological and physical vampirism, and its hints of lesbianism, has been perfect fodder for films, and has been adapted, officially and unofficially, many times.

Unlike previous attempts to film *Carmilla*, however, director Roy Ward Baker (working from a script by "Tudor Gates") succeeded on all fronts, treating the subject with as much explicit restraint and style as it required. For the first time we are given full frontal nudity and overt lesbianism, in sufficient quantities to please and titillate without distracting or becoming cheap. A sense of the truly erotic is mingled effectively with the horrific: not an easy feat. Too often the erotic (or more to the point, the gratuitously sexual) brings a horror film to a grinding halt as we stop the action in order to pop some pretty coed's top. Here, Baker's direction is consummate, and his camera never leers. The sexuality is a natural extension of the story, and when the horror of vampirism is incorporated, often with Mircalla (Ingrid Pitt, in *The Vampire Lovers*) sinking her fangs into some buxom wench's heaving bosoms, the scenes work when they shouldn't. In lesser hands it would be ridiculous and exploitative, but here it is handled with elegant restraint: that Hammer trademark.

All these elements worked spectacularly throughout the first film, with standout acting (from Ingrid Pitt, Peter Cushing, Pippa Steel, and a host of accomplished actors in supporting bits), sets, plotting and effects. One can see the care Hammer took right from the careful choreography and design of the first scene: a gala ball at the General's (Cushing) estate. Into a scene of muted colors and elegant music walks Mircalla, dressed all in blood red. When Emma (Madeleine Smith) coyly suggests to her escort that Mircalla is looking at him, he points out that she (Mircalla) is looking at *her:* the first hint of the lesbianism that will dominate the film. Mircalla feeds on one girl after another, draining the life out of them and plaguing their dreams in the form of a hideous black cat, before she is staked *and* decapitated.

The Vampire Lovers was undoubtedly the finest of the series, with each subsequent one slipping just a little further. Still, *Lust for a Vampire* (directed by Hammer's chief writer, Jimmy Sangster) succeeds on almost all fronts, with Mircalla reborn in the form of Swedish bombshell Yutte Stensgaard and plaguing a girls' school. The film works at times even better than the original, with more locations and more scenes that stand out as downright scary. But a weak performance by Stensgaard, and awful moments such as a lovemaking scene set to the tune of a terrible, out-of-place, early-seventies pop song just kill the mood. Ralph Bates (who appears briefly in this film as a professor who wants to be Mircalla's acolyte) recalled that he and Sangster watched the initial screening in mute horror at this scene, which was added later by the producers for some "contemporary appeal." It didn't work.

For *Twins of Evil* the scene was pushed back to the sixteenth century and witch-hunter times. The novelty casting of *Playboy*'s first twin centerfolds (Madeleine and Mary Collinson) as sisters who come to live with their religious-zealot uncle Peter Cushing was inspired, but couldn't carry the film. In a powerful scene Mircalla is accidentally brought back to life by a drop of blood (of course) and proceeds to convert Count Karnstein (Damien Thomas) into a vampire. The count, in turn, leads the "bad" Collinson girl (Madeleine) into his vampire lair and initiates her into a Sadean world of cruelty and horror. The Collinsons manage to get naked fairly often, but they aren't very convincing actors. Still, the scenes with Count Karnstein and Karnstein Castle are effective, and Cushing brings unusual depth to yet another unlikable character. One more point should be made: None of the "Mircalla" films had any connections in any area of casting or production, with no writer or director associated with all three films. The only actor who appears in all three is the terrific character actor Harvey Hall, who plays supporting bits in all of them. Still, they maintained a fairly consistent similarity of style, which can attest to the singularity of consciousness within Hammer as a whole.

Plague of the Zombies (1966) is another of Hammer's near misses, but an important near miss. It has undoubtedly some of the scariest scenes of any Hammer film, but long periods go on with nothing but drawing-room chatter and there is no sustained mood of dread. This is all the more noticeable when compared with some of the really effective shock scenes that this movie offers. One dream sequence stands out in particular. Among a series of dutch tilts and other odd angles the cemetery roils and heaves, fingers wiggle out of the earth, faces push up through the dirt, and puddles of blood cover the ground as the zombies emerge from their graves. Coming as it did in 1966, *Plague of the Zombies* not only prefigures many of the stylistic touches of *Night of the Living Dead*, but bears a striking resemblance to the atmosphere and scenes of Italian maestro Luchio Fulchi's zombie films (*Zombie, Gates of Hell*, etc.).

Hammer dabbled in other areas of horror, such as witchcraft and demonology, not to mention the dozens of psychological horror and suspense films they produced, such as *Die! Die! My Darling!* (1965), and *The Nanny* (1965). These films would require another whole essay. They were, in many cases, superior to Hammer's straight horror films. Things began to go bad for Hammer in the late sixties and early seventies, following the departure of Anthony Hinds. Their last film was an adaptation of Dennis Wheatley's *To the Devil, a Daughter* (1976), with Richard Widmark in a performance he could have phoned in, and a young, nubile Nastassja Kinski. Widmark spends most of the movie walking around in a comalike daze and mumbling lines from a cue card. It was an inauspicious swan song for a film production company that changed the face of horror. Their classy, elegant, stylish approach mixed with often grisly subject matter and color photography ushered out the trashy garbage of the fifties and lent a new legitimacy to horror that AIP would later emulate in its Corman Poe films. They paved the way for the seriousness and production value of *The Exorcist,* a pivotal film that brought horror to the major studios with a potential for big revenues. This new legitimacy, which would grow in ensuing years into a major Hollywood horror industry, is what ultimately killed them, for their low-budget independence was no match for the muscle of the major American studios. Hammer still exists in some form, having been sold off and absorbed into other companies, but the Hammer of Hinds and Carreras and Lee and Cushing is gone except for the films they leave behind and the path they blazed for horror.

Special thanks to Charles Grant for providing copies of most of the films herein discussed, and to film historian John McCarty for setting the record straight.

Chapter
15

Thomas F. Monteleone

Horror's own "Silver Fox," Tom spent his childhood as an aspiring science-fiction writer and, unsurprisingly, his young adulthood as a science-fiction writer. With the onset of the eighties, he jumped the SF ship and began to write the creepy stuff. Though his work does not fit comfortably into any one category, Tom seems to feel that horror is the lesser of two evils, so to speak.

Tom has been a professional writer since 1972. His short stories now number close to one hundred and have appeared in as many different venues, including his two collections. His entertainment column, "The Mothers and Fathers' Italian Association," currently runs in *Mystery Scene* magazine. His novels include *The Apocalypse Man*, *The Magnificent Gallery*, *Fantasma*, and *Crooked House*.

Tom is also an accomplished editor, having brought us several anthologies including the *Borderlands* series. He has recently begun a small publishing enterprise of his own, Borderlands Press, which will busy itself primarily with horror and dark fantasy limited editions.

He confesses his affection for women who laugh at his jokes, British ales and stouts, comic books, and all kinds of music, and admits to a knowledge that, at fortysomething, he is still "dashingly handsome."

A Double Feature and a Cartoon for 35 Cents: Being a Reminiscence, an Apology, and Maybe an Explanation as to Why They Don't Make Good Horror Films Anymore

by Thomas F. Monteleone

I was ten years old in 1956. One Saturday morning that year, my fourth-grade good-buddy, Tommy Merrow, who lived around the corner, called to see if I wanted to ride bikes into town and catch a DOUBLE FEATURE at the Pikes Theatre. This might not sound like a big deal, but you consider the proposal through the eyes of a ten-year-old kid, we're talking Big Adventure here. Especially since I'd never gone to a movie by myself before—without my parents, that is.

I said, "sure," and didn't even ask him what was playing—it didn't matter—because the idea of hanging out in the movies all afternoon, *without any grown-ups around,* sounded like the best thing I could ever want to do. I was thoroughly in love with movies by then; it was one of the many traits I'd picked up from my father, who'd been taking me to movies since I was maybe four years old. (In fact, one of my earliest memories is the caterpillar in *Alice in Wonderland* blowing smoke-letters from his toadstool perch.)

There was only one problem: like I said earlier, I'd never been to the movies by myself.

My mother didn't like the idea, but Dad puffed on his pipe as he considered it. "Well, maybe we can see if you're responsible enough to do something like this. Maybe it's about time . . ." he said thoughtfully. "But if you screw up, it'll be a long time before you go again."

"Thanks, Dad!" I was already running for the door when he yelled for me to stop. I did, watching him pick up the morning paper.

"What's the matter?" I asked.

"Let's find out what's playing before we go running off, okay?"

I'd been so excited, it hadn't occurred to me he would want to know such bothersome details. He crinkled up the *Baltimore Sun*, folding it over to the movie pages, where all the lurid ads always zinged me with curiosity. "Hmmm," he said slowly. "*Earth vs. the Flying Saucers* and *Creature with the Atom Brain*."

Wow! Just hearing the titles got my heart pounding. They sounded *great*!

"Sounds awful," said my mother.

"Well, they sound pretty good—if you like that kinda stuff—right, son?" My father smiled and winked, because he and I—we *did* like that weird stuff, and I almost wished I was going to the movies with *him* instead of dopey Tommy Merrow.

"Okay, thanks, Dad!"

I was almost out the door when he raised his hand. "Wait a second! There's one more place we'd better check first."

I cringed as he reached for the *Catholic Review*—a newspaper I'm not even sure exists anymore. Back in 1956, all the kids at St. Charles Borromeo grade school had to sell *Catholic Review* subscriptions each September and try to win neat prizes like Schwinn bikes and Gilbert chemistry sets. (I never knew anyone who ever sold enough to win anything better than the Voit scuba mask or the Zebco spinning reel.)

Anyway, back to my father, who was scanning the back pages for a listing of every film (it seemed) ever made, which was produced by an organization called the "Legion of Decency." It was basically what is known as an "index," of films that had either been approved for viewing by Catholics, or had been deemed forbidden fruit, never to be experienced by those loyal to the Vatican. My father—not just a good Catholic, but rather a *super-Catholic* (we had a framed picture of Pope Pius XII in our living room)—held the opinions of the Legion of Decency in the highest, most reverential regard.

I always played dumb when he referred to "the Legion's" list, and he had no idea it was the *only* thing I ever read in the *Catholic Review*. I couldn't tell you how many times I'd read over the catalog of "forbidden" films, then checked the lurid ads in the regular newspapers, wondering what unimaginable wonders and terrors could be found in movies with names like: *Mom and Dad* ("See the actual birth of a baby!"), *Teen-age Crime Wave* ("Teenage terror straight from the sidewalk jungle!"), *Blonde Bait* ("The deadliest bombshell of all!"), *Freaks* ("You won't believe your eyes!"), *Glen or Glenda* ("I changed my sex!"), and the one that *really* intrigued me: *The Third Sex* (now what the hell could *that* be?).

But I digress. Sorry.

Getting back to my father and the Legion of Decency . . . who told me the films I wanted to see were both on the "approved" list. He gave me fifty cents and told me to have a good time. I can't tell you how relieved I was to find out the Legionnaires hadn't found anything too offensive about *Earth vs. the Flying Saucers* or *Creature with the Atom Brain*. I mean, by this time, I was REALLY PSYCHED for going to that double feature.

So finally, I was out the door and on my bike. Tommy Merrow and I rode up to the center of town where the Pikes Theatre is located. We chained our bikes at the big bike rack next to the parking lot and got into line with about two hundred other kids. I can still remember how excited I felt, standing there looking at the movie poster of those saucer ships careening through the skies over Washington, D.C., feeling my heart actually *thump!* in my chest every time I thought about going to the movies without my parents.

Once we got inside and found some seats, the newsreel had already kicked in—something about Ike, but I don't remember. (My total boredom with politics began at a very early age.) My pocket was still heavy with silver, the precious metal was heating up, starting to burn, and I just *had* to spend it on some popcorn and a box of my all-time favorite movie candy: Ju-Ju-Bees.

Anyway, I sat down just as the *Tom and Jerry* cartoon started, and even though I never really was what you would call a fan of movie cartoons (mostly predictable and usually lacking in any real wit), I simply *loved* this one because I was watching in a huge dark place full of screaming, laughing kids just like me. It was great! Not a grown-up in sight and *hours* to do whatever I wanted . . .

. . . which was: to be transfixed by a couple of black and white films that left such deeply graven images upon my memory, it will always seem like I just saw them yesterday. *Creature with the Atom Brain* had a misleading title, though—a trait many films from the fifties and sixties shared. There was no creature, just a bunch of guys in suits (*everybody* in the movies in the fifties wore suits) walking around at night with stitches across their domes where this scientist had replaced their brains with "miniature atomic reactors."

Yeah, right.

Well, it seemed like a good idea at the time, and although the film was a bit on the "talky" side for a bunch of preadolescent hooligans (I always loved that word—long before it was embraced by *Pravda*), there were some great night scenes with the atom-brain-guys walking through the woods and the cops trying to shoot them down. It was an interesting presage of the George Romero classic *Night of the Living Dead*, and while it didn't scare me like some other films did, it left an everlasting impression on me.

But it was the headliner, the second flick, that made the whole afternoon so magical for me. *Earth vs. the Flying Saucers* had everything! A plot that unfolded gracefully, with plenty of suspense, action, and great Harryhausen special effects. There was this great scene where one of the saucers was dogging the convertible carrying Hugh Marlowe and Joan Taylor and it made that weird fluttering/hovering sound (which got accidentally recorded by the tape recorder on the front seat of the car, remember?). And then, several scenes later, when the recorder's batteries gave out while Marlowe was replaying the sound of the saucer, we heard the slowed down sounds becoming intelligible! The saucer was sending them a message, and we heard it begin with that marrow-curdling salutation: "DR. RUSSELL MARVIN . . ." and later we would hear that same scary voice speak to all of us: "PEOPLE OF EARTH . . . ATTENTION."

And the aliens . . . how could we forget those guys when they stiffly teetered out of the ships with their featureless heads (or were they helmets?) and their arms outstretched as they directed their disintegrator beams at all the tanks and artillery pieces? I'll never forget the scene where Donald Curtis tommy-gunned one of the aliens and everybody crowds around as they slowly removed the alien's helmet to reveal its true form. I was peeking through my fingers covering my face at that point and the theater had become this vast space of pure, dark silence. A classic moment. Simply beautiful stuff. I'd always loved SF and horror films, but being there in the dark, washed in the glow of crisp black-and-white images, on my own, I felt finally free to let go and really *participate* in the joy/terror that's part of the outré film experience.

So when the climactic battle scene in Washington with the spinning, careening saucers and Hugh Marlowe's clunky flatbed produce truck finally erupted, I was able to stand up and sail my flattened popcorn box at the screen along with the rest of the crowd. In those pre-Frisbee days, a popcorn box was a pretty fair substitute and the best part was *no parents around* to tell you to stop acting like the kid that you were.

Yeah, it was sweet.

But when the last saucer ship had crashed (each one to the pretestosteroned cheers of the audience) and the credits were rolling and the houselights warmed up, I can remember feeling in some way *changed*. Although only dimly aware of it, I must have had an inkling that I had endured some kind of rite of passage. I wasn't ready for the drive-ins and the freckle-faced girls with the billowy plaid skirts yet, but I had definitely entered a new era of moviegoing. And there would be no turning back.

I didn't realize it then, but I had been lucky enough to be growing up in the golden age of SF/horror/monster movies. For the following decade, an endless parade of black-and-white (and an occasional Technicolor) classics came lurching out of Hollywood and into my neighborhood theater. Their names fall off the tongue with recalled joy like Mediterranean poetry: *Them!*, *The Deadly Mantis*, *Curse of the Demon*, *Beast from 20,000 Fathoms*, *War of the Worlds*, *The Beast That Challenged the World*, *Creature from the Black Lagoon*, *Black Sunday*, *Invaders from Mars*, *The Crawling Eye*, *Cabinet of Doctor Caligari*, *Circus of Horrors*, *The Horrors of the Black Museum*, *Psycho*, *The Thing*, *The Tingler*, *House on Haunted Hill* . . .

Ah, friends, stop me before I go on for a very long time.

What I'm reciting here is a litany some might say should be offered at the altar of misspent youth. But that's bullshit. Credit for my enduring mutant/creative person status lies partially with the sense-of-wonder and fascination-with-being-scared that horror/dark fantasy/SF films deeded to me when I bought all those thirty-five-cent tickets.

My love-affair with SF and horror films has never faltered. If I could have gotten along even half as well with the women in my life, I would be an inordinately happy man (instead of a just regularly happy one). But, you can't have everything, right?

And, you know, when I think back on many of the old films, I realize they worked and left such an impression not just because I was young and therefore impressionable, but also because they were genuinely *scary* in a majority of cases. (Okay, okay . . . I admit that *The Giant Claw* freaked the shit out of me when I saw it in '57 and when I saw it on the USA Channel a year or so back it looked plainly silly with its visible wires and bulging Ping-Pong ball eyes . . . but that was the exception that makes every rule.)

I contend that, in general, the filmmakers of the golden age knew how to scare us and do so with some style. Sure there were certain formulas to follow—the main one being that you never really got a good look at the scary thing for a long while. You had to suffer through lots of tense shadows and strange sounds and blurry glimpses before you saw *anything*, and in the really great stuff like *Cat People* by Val Lewton or George Pal's Martians, you hardly saw them at all—ever.

Which gets me to the first point of this essay, which is clearly this: They *don't* make them like they used to.

I say this at the risk of sounding like an old fart because of one simple fact: There ain't a director out there who can create a horror to compete with stalking terrors locked up in the subbasement of my imagination. Why is that? you might ask. The answer is both obvious and subtle, and it lies, I think, in a semicareful examination of the relationship between horror as film and horror as literature.

The stuff of horror/fantasy/SF is special stuff on the printed page, but it becomes changed when brought into the movie theaters. I don't know about you, but I've rarely caught the film version of a good HDF novel and come away feeling that the film captured the essence of the original material. Sometimes, such as in the case of Kubrick's *The Shining*, you get a totally different emotional feel (and emotional response) to the whole story, so much so, the book and film seem totally unrelated.

In other words, HDF film adaptations usually suck the Big One. But the major question remains *why?*

I'm not sure I have the answer, but I think we can try to shine a little light in some of the darker corners of the problem and see what we find.

Okay, so what's the problem with most HDF films?

Many other writers have examined this problem, often using the works of Steve King as the primary focus. I'm not going to rehash a lot of that discussion other than to note how many of these writers seem to be shocked, actually astonished, that filmmakers can dummy up fine books like *'Salem's Lot, The Shining, Christine, Firestarter,* or *Cujo.* Why not? Filmmakers screw up novels all the time; have been doing it since soon after Edison's dancing bears caught the public eye; and will continue to do it long after we're all gone.

It's unreasonable to expect King's work to be any more immune to the problem than the rest of the books out there.

What we seem to forget is a basic truth about the creation of anything we call art or entertainment or even trash—it is a medium unto itself, and that's it, man. A novel is not conceived or created as a film, but rather as a *book*.

Yeah, I know, seems obvious, doesn't it? But think about it. A book is created most of the time by the imagination and effort of a single mind. A film is the product of hundreds of people's work and is, when actually brought to the screen, in the words of Sam Goldwyn, "a goddamned miracle." As soon as people begin to restructure and reconceive a book as a movie, the work becomes different, changed, and essentially contrasted to the original work.

I think this is especially true in HDF because there is a natural, psychological element—hell, a psychological *requirement*—in horror fiction. The reader must bring to the HDF fiction experience his own nasty little bag of psychological bugbears, his own phobias, hang-ups, and personal problems with the Outer Hull of the World. A good writer of HDF will eventually tap into almost everybody's private fears and sources of trauma. It's called pushing somebody's buttons, and it happens all the time with the good writers, the good books.

The difference in HDF films is simple. All our personal demons and tormented visions are replaced by *someone else's* single ideation of how everything looks, acts, and feels when you are getting scared. It's impossible to count on the filmmaker's vision being very compatible with too many readers' imaginings. It just doesn't happen. That's why they have horse races, friends, and why the tracks make a lot of cake—because we're all different in myriad ways.

So what's the conclusion? Are all HDF films adapted from other sources categorically inferior? Do we just trash them all in our literary smugness?

Nah.

The best thing to do is divorce the literary experience from the cinematic one. Don't expect things from either medium that are unlikely to be delivered. Yeah, right, you're thinking to yourself. How do you do that when you've pulled up to your favorite spot at the summer drive-in with your favorite Sweet Thing and some controlled or uncontrolled substances close at hand, and you're settling in to catch *Groundhog Day IV* and *Night of the Bloodsucking Psychos with Sharp Implements*?

Hey, what're you kidding?

When in that happy situation, you send your cerebrum on a much deserved vacation and you go about venting the urges of your R-complex. Screw film criticism, right?

I guess what I'm really trying to say here (other than copping to a weakness for the horror-movie double features of my flaming youth) is that all the uproar and indignation about how Hollywood and even the Indies are ruining the literature of HDF is a bunch of bullshit. Remember, the printed word perseveres. Even if they make the worst piece of crapola imaginable out of last year's award-winning novel, the film can never diminish the book's greatness because *the movie is not the book.*

Besides, there is a kind of sleazy enjoyment in watching truly bad HDF films. I'm not talking about the endless progression of he's-coming-to-chop-you-up flicks—a particularly odious subgenre that does not really belong in this discussion. These films are nonpsychological in their one-track obsession with killers who kill in supposedly ingenious, but ultimately predictable ways. They are uncommonly dumb, and are fit cinematic fare only for the true Mongoloids among us (people who chain their wallets to their belts and have an affection for Red Man baseball hats spring immediately to mind). The list of bad-but-fun HDF films is practically endless, and I won't bore you with a catalog of all the household standbys because somebody else in this book is probably already doing that.

But, I mean, think about it. . . .

For some reason, we can sit at home on a Saturday night preferring to catch a black-and-white rendition of *The Creeping Terror* or *The Screaming Skull* instead of *Flying Leathernecks* or *Pillow Talk.* We'd rather watch *The Oblong Box* than *The Bridge on the River Kwai*, right? There's a certain charm to the inept theatrics of people like John Agar and Tor Johnson that you just can't get in the average late-night movie on your local independent channels.

And I think stuff like *Fright Night, House, An American Werewolf in London, Alien, Jacob's Ladder, The Fly,* or anything else by Cronenberg show flashes of really good filmmaking. Films that make you react, make you feel, and maybe even think. When a movie works on these levels, you don't find yourself comparing it with the original source material, and that's the way it should be, don't you agree?

Ah good, I thought you would.

I think the biggest problem with contemporary "horror" movies is that they are most often just slasher flicks. When people learn that I sometimes write horror or dark fantasy or suspense, they immediately assume I spend my time writing the twenty-sixth version of *Friday the 13th*, and that's more than a little tragic.

It's insulting. And it's wrong.

The horror film has a long and wonderful tradition in the history of cinema. To have it bogarted by a small backwater subgenre of pinheaded chop-'em-up flicks is to demean the art of scaring—and being scared.

Does this mean I miss my wonderful double features and nickel boxes of Ju-Ju-Bees?

Of course I do. But it also means I never lost the thrill of being so manipulated by a good HDF director that I feel like my emotions have been sent through a goddamned threshing machine. Hey, I admit it: put me in a theater and scare the crap outta me and I'll love you forever.

Chapter

16

Philip Nutman

I have met no one in my life who is as constantly near to exploding with pent-up energy as Phil Nutman. There are many faces this energy takes, that of passion for his craft, anger and impatience with the world around him, and a fierce loyalty to those who stood by him during the remarkable transition he has made from journalist to novelist. These many faces all belong to Philip, and consequently, all look suspiciously like actor John Malkovich. Enough so that, though he'll deny it, past editors have used Malkovich's picture when none of Phil were available.

He was first paid to write at age fifteen when he embarked on a decade-long career as a journalist. From the BBC to his spot as British correspondent for *Fangoria* magazine, Phil has covered the field of horror film and literature as extensively as any other writer. He has seen nearly as many horror films as Steve Bissette, and has even been featured in one or two (*Death Collector*).

The first time I met Phil, he was stubbing out a cigarette (a habit he continues to insist he's quit) between signings of his story in *Book of the Dead*. That story, his first published fiction, has since grown into an excellent novel, *Wet Work*. Phil's short fiction has sprung up throughout the horror community recently and is as in demand as his presence. He is also working on several comic-book projects and his film noir screenplay *Heat Wave* is under option in Hollywood.

The Exploding Family

by Philip Nutman

Of the many writer/directors who tend to specialise in the horror genre, none has been so thematically consistent as Canadian filmmaker

David Cronenberg. Although the critical term "auteur" has been overused (and often unjustifiably so), Cronenberg is one of the very few directors who deserves to be referred to as an "author" due to the unique subject material and personal obsessions present in his work. Even when making a film based on source material not his own (i.e., Stephen King's *The Dead Zone*) he has managed to impose his own vision to such a degree that the end result is undeniably a Cronenberg film.

Thematically, Cronenberg is a critic's dream come true, the richness of the undercurrents present in his films an abundant source of analysis. So much so, there have been dozens of lengthy essays written exploring these themes that have seen print over the past decade as "Canada's King of Venereal Horror" has risen to critical prominence, escaping the confines of the generally-dismissed-horror ghetto. While his explicit sexual metaphors have been much discussed, his interest in the conflict between the mind and body, the tension between conscious discipline and subconscious desires, his transformational metaphor of the "New Flesh," little has been written about family relationships in his films. The obvious exception to this is *The Brood*, his remarkably challenging story of a divorce with a background of psychic trauma in which Nola Carveth (Samantha Eggar) literally gives birth to her rage. But behind the sexual terrors, the psychic battles, the mental and physical decay present in his oeuvre, lies a fairly consistent, if oblique, subtextual commentary on the changing shape of family relationships.

Like any artist who absorbs the undercurrents of the society around him, Cronenberg has reflected the shifting status of the nuclear family in Western culture over the last two decades, from the sexual liberation and social anomie of the seventies to the baby-boomer family decay of the eighties and that decade's flip side, the Moral Majority adherence to "traditional" values (although with his typical perversity, positing the disturbing notion of father, mother, and baby inextricably bound together on the genetic level as Jeff Goldblum urges pregnant girlfriend Geena Davis to "dive into the plasma pool" with him as he mutates into a humanoid fly).

In *They Came from Within* (a.k.a. *The Parasite Murders*, *Shivers*), his first cinema feature, shot in 1975, Cronenberg charts the social decay of a group of nascent yuppies who live in the Starliner Towers, a deluxe condominium complex located on an island outside Toronto, as they come into contact with a species of sexual parasite that liberates their repressed desires, transforming the characters from isolated individuals locked in their own cold materialism to a libidinous gestalt of sexual plague carriers. (Obviously, from a nineties perspective, it's difficult to ignore the chillingly prescient AIDS metaphor.)

Although Dr. Roger St. Luc (Paul Hampton) is ostensibly the film's protagonist, the most interesting characters in the story are Nicholas and Janine Tudor (Allan Migicovsky and Susan Petrie), a bored and boring upwardly mobile couple. Nicholas is so self-absorbed and emotionally cold he could be an automaton, while Janine is the ignored, sexually frustrated housewife privately humiliated by his saturnine sexuality and indifference. Watching these two interact while the venereal plague is literally worming its way throughout the building (the parasites are phallic turds created to replace diseased organs which also act as an extreme aphrodisiac) is realistically painful and acts as a contrast to the visceral carnage erupting across the screen. After being introduced to these characters, one can't help wondering why they are together. They live an empty, ordered life devoid of strong emotional bonds. Nicholas has no time for children and Janine would obviously like them (it is implied she's sterile), but in their environment children are not part of the picture. In fact, we only see one family unit in the film, a mother and young daughter, the father absent, and the other couples depicted in the story all display cool emotional bonds. It is not surprising, considering this chilly, formal environment, that the plague spreads so easily, and that characters—Janine and lesbian neighbour Betts (Barbara Steele) in particular—turn to each other for the most accessible form of human contact: sex.

Just as the sexual revolution of the sixties gave rise to a huge increase in sexually transmitted diseases, so it has been argued by certain sociologists that, in addition to the promiscuous nature of gay sex, the unrestrained carnal life-styles of liberated, "swinging" couples in the 70's helped create the social Petrie dish in which AIDS was able to incubate.

This theme is similarly dealt with in Cronenberg's next feature, *Rabid* (1976), in which hard-core porn star Marilyn Chambers stars as Rose, a young, carefree woman who is turned into a biological vampire through radical plastic surgery designed to save her life after a near-fatal motorbike accident. Irreversibly altered by her operation and confused by her unnatural cravings, Rose becomes isolated from life-affirming human contact and the emotional support of her boyfriend Hart (Frank Moore). Once she escapes from the Keloid Clinic, a private institution in which she has been recuperating, Rose uses her sexual appeal to lure donors into her arms (the archetype of vampire as seductor), though more often than not, Cronenberg shows her as a victim of male sexual attraction—an attempted rape, several sexual pickups. As the plague spreads and her hunger increases Rose becomes further isolated from help. Disturbed by her cravings, and unaware she is the cause of the plague sweeping across the city, she steers clear of Hart and eventually ends up a victim of one of her donors as Hart listens to the attack over the telephone, having made a final attempt to reach her.

Viewed from a reactionary, profamily perspective, the story's underlying metaphor appears to imply women, liberated from social and familial restraints and sexually active (i.e., predatory) are a threat to the social order. Since Cronenberg has displayed himself a liberal thinker, there is no implication this textual reading is a statement of personal belief. Indeed no, for anyone with more than a passing acquaintance with his films is no doubt aware of the strand of irony at work beneath the blood and viscera which led the director to be given the dubious epithet "King of Venereal Horror." Indeed, what he does within the context of the story is investigate our feelings toward sex and play them off against the conventions of the genre. Rose is both sex object and predator, victim and victimiser: the classic misunderstood science-created monster à la Frankenstein on one hand, the succubus vampire on the other, wrapped up in the wholesome Ivory Soap girl-next-door look of Chambers and her public persona as slut goddess. As star of the ground-breaking and phenomenally successful *Behind the Green Door*, Chambers usurped Linda Lovelace's throne as hard-core queen of the early seventies sexual marathons and fast established an almost-legendary reputation as a tireless performer.

It is surely with considerable irony that Cronenberg cast Chambers in the role, and by using the most logical contemporary settings for her character to solicit victims—a porno theater, a shopping mall, etc.—our expectations are fulfilled: Chambers-The-Body is the temptation that leads to death. In light of AIDS *Rabid* has become a disturbing, prescient metaphor for the social—and sexual—decay of the nineties. As critic William Beard stressed in an essay on the filmmaker, "One might suggest *Rabid* allergically depicts the social catastrophe inherent in a culture that encourages sexual impulses without considering what innate forces are being unleashed." Advocates of the family and social unity would applaud loudly.

Until they encounter *The Brood*.

Cronenberg's third feature, made in 1979, takes a substantial leap forward in terms of dramatic material. Having explored the swinging anomie and isolationism of the seventies—the decade in which free love died, kicking its final death throes in orgy clubs like New York's infamous *Plato's Retreat*—the director homed in on the more intimate psychodramas of the family unit itself—or what was left of the conventional perception of it as dysfunctionalism and codependency became the psychotherapeutic buzzwords of a confused and fucked-up generation. Twelve years on, *The Brood* remains Cronenberg's most socially critical and poignant work, in many respects his most personal film because its emotional resonance grew out of the breakup of his first marriage.

Like his previous films, *The Brood* deals with the interdependence of mind and body, the conflict between irrational desire and reason, but focuses on the restrictive, self-serving science of psychotherapy and its potential negative side effects.

Nola Carveth (Samantha Eggar) is a patient of the Somafree Institute of Psychomplasmics, a revolutionary clinic which encourages its patients to psychosomatically actualize their pain, run by ersatz guru Dr. Hal Raglan (Oliver Reed). Effects range from a patient with psychically induced cancer of the lymphatic glands to Nola, who has given "birth" to exterior fetuses that grow and act as the agents of her fury toward her possibly abusive parents (this aspect is never clarified—is it delusion or repressed trauma?), her husband Frank (Art Hindle), and daughter Candy (Cindy Hinds). The direct focus on the family unit, its generational conflicts, and the invocation of Freudian principles creates a complex, multilayered narrative filled with tension. Due to its intimacy it is Cronenberg's most confrontational work.

The character relationships in the film at first appear straightforward. Juliana and Barton, Nola's parents, either deny or reject their daughter's state. Frank is confounded and emotionally wounded by the breakup of the marriage. And little Candy responds through confused passivity. But this simplicity is deceptive. Each character's perception of another, every moral judgment rendered by one family member about another is contradicted or made ambiguous by other details in the film. Nola insists her mother beat her as a child; Juliana denies this, insisting Nola would wake up covered with big ugly bumps. Nola accuses her father of ignoring the situation by pretending it didn't happen. Since denial is a pervasive symptom in abusive families, the audience's emotional identification initially lies with Nola, but once we learn of her ability to psychically actualize her trauma, the question of emotional wounds created by interpersonal tensions and made manifest in physical terms raises its ugly head, rendering moral judgments invalid. Then, the more we learn of Frank's character, the more confused we become and the lines between his sanity and Nola's madness blur. His inability to deal with unpleasant emotions and denial of the situation's seriousness makes us question his grip on reality. Who is the crazy one here—Frank or Nola? Who is at fault—the parents or Nola herself? Whether or not Juliana beat Nola become a moot point, and the question transforms into one of what is psychologically healthy—repression or expression? In many respects the film chillingly illustrates psychotherapist R. D. Laing's theories that mental illness is the reaction of a sane mind to a sick society and that family relationships are the greatest cause of psychic imbalance. The film ends with a disturbing shot of Candy staring straight ahead, shocked into silence by her experiences, her body actualizing her emotional pain in the same manner as her mother. The image is an acute metaphor for the psychological legacy parents can bestow upon their children.

The mother/daughter relationship in *The Brood* is central to the story's dramatic core, while in *Scanners*, Cronenberg's subsequent film, a father/son relationship (of sorts) is tangential to the narrative.

Although perhaps his least thematically successful film, *Scanners* acts as an interesting counterpoint to *The Brood*. If the latter was a horror movie in the Bergman mold—insular, deeply personal, depressing in its claustrophobia and lack of catharsis—the former is a genre story that works rather unevenly through the conventions of action/adventure movies by setting up clearly defined good guys and bad guys, with a Cain and Abel good brother/evil brother twist in the tail. The Scanners of the title are telepathic mutants, the result of the side effects caused by Ephemerol, a tranquiliser developed as an aid for pregnant women, and the plot follows Cameron Vale (Stephen Lack) as he discovers the truth of his origins, encounters a government conspiracy, and finally defeats his malevolent sibling.

Because of its action-oriented nature, however, the film is Cronenberg's least interesting in terms of its social commentary. Once Vale comes to terms with his psychic talent, he discovers a pseudo-extended family of Scanners who have dealt with their freakish nature by banding together, sharing their thoughts and emotions on an intimate level that soothes instead of repulses, as is the case when Scanners usually come into contact with other people's feelings. But as soon as Vale is welcomed into this alternative family unit, the group is destroyed by other Scanners who work for a nefarious government agency. One could suggest this is a metaphor for society eradicating a social unit that threatens the stability of the status quo, but in light of the film's lack of depth when compared with *The Brood*, it would be pretentious to suggest this is the case. The same is true of the father/son relationship (Dr. Ruth, creator of Ephemerol, gave the drug to his wife, using his own offspring as experiments). The film's obvious Oedipal echoes and biblical resonance are there, but only on the most basic dramatic level, incorporating touches of the Macduff subplot from Shakespeare's *Macbeth* and its theme of sibling power play, but in the course of the story's messy construction true dramatic irony is lost.

If his first venture into the commercial action genre was not an artistic success, then *Videodrome* (1982) corrected the balance by plunging its audience back into the dark heart of the director's obsessions, taking the themes of mind/body conflict to their most extreme degree. As much a philosophical thriller as a mystery investigating the pernicious influence of the media on the minds of North America, *Videodrome* rates as one of Cronenberg's most personal films, and as such was a tough nut for mainstream audiences to crack. In terms of this essay, however, the film is somewhat outside the direct scope of what we are considering except for two factors. One, the character of Max Renn (James Woods) acts as a slightly out-of-focus mirror image of Marilyn Chambers's Rose in *Rabid*; and two, the film presents us with a social landscape in which the family unit is almost nonexistent.

Renn is the president of Civic TV, a station catering to the sensationalist tastes of its audience, serving up constant portions of sex and violence. While searching for new programming to boost the station's ratings, Renn taps into experimental transmissions of a show called *Videodrome*, a snuff show featuring sadomasochism and, it appears, actual onscreen torture and murder. Obsessed with tracing the show's source, Renn meets pop psychologist Nicki Brand (Deborah Harry), who entices him into her private world of pain before disappearing at the hands of those behind the *Videodrome* conspiracy. Ultimately, Renn discovers the truth behind *Videodrome* and commits suicide, his mind irreversibly altered by hallucinations created by the subliminal messages transmitted through the show.

A bleak, cold film, *Videodrome* takes the social anomie of *Rabid* and inverts that film's social commentary, reflecting the shift from the anything-goes hedonism of the seventies to the Me Generation self-obsession of eighties yuppiedom. Renn, on one level, is like Rose in that he cannot come to terms with his desires, but while Rose is as much a victim of male sexual attraction and socially ingrained attitudes (woman as prey), Max is a victim of his own perverse longings and self-imposed isolation. Rose at least had a loving relationship with Hart; Renn, on the other hand, only has a brief sexual relationship with Nicki Brand, one that can hardly be described as warm or life affirming. Unlike typical American cinematic narrative structures where there is redemption and resolution through action, usually in connection with a relationship, *Videodrome* is more in tune with European art films (e.g., the works of Ingmar Bergman) and their oblique social commentary. If one adopts a conservative position when "reading" the social text of the film, the conclusion one may draw is that a life devoid of significant relationships leads to the destruction of the individual.

What is important to note at this point is the fact that *Videodrome* was the first of the director's films to end in the suicide of the protagonist, a conclusion that features in his three subsequent features.

The Dead Zone, Cronenberg's next feature based on the Stephen King novel, took the commercialism of *Scanners* one step further. The director maintained a certain thematic unity in relation to his previous films by addressing the conflict between mind and body, and having a protagonist who is a loner, but overall the work is clearly the vision of another creator and lacks the social concerns of the other pictures we have looked at. Again, this is a film that falls outside the parameters of this essay and is only worth noting in relation to the suicidal martyrdom of the protagonist, Johnny Smith (Christopher Walken) and the suicide of corrupt politician Greg Stillson (Martin Sheen). But this theme will be addressed in the essay's conclusion.

Following the considerable commercial success of *The Dead Zone*, Cronenberg's second feature for a major studio (Universal), *The Fly*, was also derived from existing source material; in this case the fifties science-fiction novella by George Langlaan, which had been made into a popular B-movie starring Vincent Price in 1958. Like *The Dead Zone*, which was Cronenberg's first film scripted by another writer, *The Fly*'s original screenplay was by Charles Edward Pogue, but in this case the director took an active hand in the rewrite process, stamping his imprint on the story, taking a hokey concept—scientist transforms into a humanoid fly—and literally transforming it into a story that fits neatly into the Cronenberg universe.

Physicist Seth Brundle (Jeff Goldblum) is a typical Cronenberg protagonist: an outsider who has isolated himself in his own highly disciplined environment, a man whose contact with the real world is tenuous at best. Brundle is married to his life's work, the creation of a matter transporter, but, with the work on the brink of completion, he decides to seek out someone to share his ground-breaking discovery with. The person he decides to reveal this to is science journalist Veronica (Geena Davis), who is understandably skeptical at first, but who soon realizes she has stumbled onto the biggest story of her career, and equally important, a man she finds genuinely warm and considerate. Having ended her long-term relationship with Stathis Borans (John Getz), her editor, an arrogant sexist pig, Veronica finds Brundle's naïveté and honesty ("I don't get out much . . . I don't have a life. . . ." he tells her almost immediately) highly attractive, and within days they become lovers. Having found someone with whom he can share his obsessive passion, Brundle—who is an emotional adolescent—allows Veronica to remold him. Overnight, Brundle changes from a conservative dresser to a passionate, stylish figure, continually animated and suddenly enthusiastic about all life has to offer. But tragedy is just around the corner and ironically follows the scientist's moment of triumph. After successfully transporting a baboon from one side of his lab to another, Brundle is disrupted in his celebration with Veronica by the jealous actions of Borans. When his newfound girlfriend suddenly departs, Brundle puts two and two together and makes six, believing Veronica is still involved with her editor: Perceiving her rapid departure at his happiest moment as a rejection, the scientist throws himself back into his work, decides to experiment on himself, and teleports. The experiment is a success, except for one small detail—a fly enters the telepod seconds before transmission, resulting in man and insect becoming one. Unaware of this, Brundle, who understandably feels like a new man, discovers an appetite for life previously undreamed of. Convinced the transportation process itself is responsible for his increased strength, Brundle encourages Veronica to go through the process herself. Concerned by his suddenly irrational behaviour, she resists. Being rejected a second time, Brundle throws her out, then goes off in pursuit of a suitable mate. But within days the scientist begins to decay, transforming into a full-blown fly just as Veronica discovers she's pregnant. The film ends with Borans saving Veronica from Brundle (who has now transformed into a human-sized insect) as the creature attempts to teleport her so father, mother, and baby can become one. When the teleportation goes wrong and "Brundlefly" absorbs part of the telepod, the mutated human insect urges Borans to kill it.

Much has been written about *The Fly* as a metaphor for people dealing with the death of a loved one suffering from AIDS, and it is hard to deny the parallels between Brundle's physical decay and that of those unfortunate to have contracted such a fatal, debilitating disease, but Cronenberg has rightly denied the story is a conscious attempt at dealing with the subject. In general terms, *The Fly* is about our fears of disease, isolation, bodily decay, and death; from a sociological perspective it reflects the opposite side of *Videodrome*'s self-obsessed yuppie angst and the pursuit of onanistic gratification that denies true intimacy. It is ironic that the Reagan era, which created the environment for such self-interest to flourish, also placed strident emphasis on traditional family values and insisted that the nuclear family is the cornerstone of American society. In *The Fly*, Cronenberg posits the notion of family as a single biological unit. Having learned that a life lived solely around work is empty and meaningless unless you have someone to share it with, Brundle, when faced with isolation through his metamorphosis, cannot go on without Veronica literally being a part of him. Here horror makes flesh of metaphor by painting a picture of total codependency on a genetic level. While it is a ludicrous notion outside the parameters of the story, it is undeniably a disturbing metaphor for the emotional problems many couples have.

Dead Ringers, Cronenberg's most recently released film, takes these themes one stage further in a story that is all the more chilling because it is realistic and loosely based on a true story.

In the late seventies, a pair of successful twin gynecologists were found dead under mysterious circumstances in their New York apartment. Taking this strange occurrence as his departure point, Cronenberg draws a stark picture of codependency and emotional dysfunctioning as he explores the notion of family as a genetic unit without the fantastical mad-scientist trappings of *The Fly*.

We are introduced to Elliot and Beverly Mantle as preteens. They are discussing sex. Elliot, the more extroverted of the two, informs his brother he has discovered what sex is and why humans can't spawn like fish. It's all to do with water. Since humans don't live in water we have to spawn inside the body. Beverly suggests that if humans spent enough time in water, then surely we could spawn like fish. Their interest in the reproductive process and the human body is purely clinical and devoid of emotion. So much so, they think nothing of asking a girl to come sit in the bath with them to see if they can have sex. The girl, who is seated next to a baby carriage, holding a doll, calls them perverts and tells them, "You don't even know what fucking is!" Their response is to raise a collective eyebrow and regard the girl as an alien being.

This concise, somewhat humorous opening sets up the entire balance of what is to come. Elliot and Beverly are a male family unit in and of themselves. They have a cool, analytical joint mind. Women are a rich foreign country ready to be explored, even though it is apparent they consider the inner workings of the female body somewhat disgusting. And it is also clear that ultimately, women will be their downfall.

The film then jumps ahead to Elliot and Beverly's graduation from medical school, two young men (both played superbly by Jeremy Irons) with a brilliant career ahead of them. As the guiding lights of the Mantle Clinic, the twins become leaders of their field, courted by the rich and famous. This delights Elliot, the dominant extrovert lothario who basks in the fame and glory their research bestows upon them. Beverly, on the other hand, is the shy, obsessively studious introvert who does the work that brings them success. Just as Elliot is dependent on Bev for their prominence in the gynecological field, so, too, is Bev dependent on Elliot for human contact: Elliot seduces the women for both of them to enjoy. However, the equilibrium of this psychic and sexual symbiosis is irrevocably disrupted by the presence of actress Clare Niveau (Genevieve Bujold), who comes to them seeking a cure for her sterility. Elliot is the first to bed her, taking delight in Clare's masochism, and encourages Bev to take his place (although the actress is under the impression it is Elliot she's fucking), and Bev and Clare fall in love. Desperate to establish his own identity away from his dominant sibling, Bev is lured into drug abuse by Clare, but this is not the cause of the twins' problems: neither can be whole without the other, and once their roles are reversed—submissive sibling becomes dominant and decisive, dominant brother turns submissive, resentful, and feels rejected—their mental balance is shattered.

The conclusion of the film is one of Cronenberg's most disturbing. The family unit implodes into psychic suicide as their personalities shift back and forth between each other, making it almost impossible to distinguish who is who as they waste away under a severe personality crisis fueled by drug-induced paranoia. It is Bev, though, who finally emerges the stronger of the two, perpetrating the act that kills them both: in an hallucinatory state he surgically opens his brother up in an attempt to free them, killing Elliot. Once he is dead, Bev dies, too, as a result of the separation. Once again the family unit destroys itself.

The recurring use of the suicide motif in the Cronenberg universe is, to say the least, disturbing and depressing. The director's view of familial and interpersonal relationships is bleak. They are, he seems to be saying, hopeless; society is doomed to failure. Man the Social Animal is primarily Man the Outsider, and try as he might to reach out for intimacy, he will inevitably fail.

In the kingdom of the blind no one can see.

Chapter

17

Kathryn Ptacek

Raised in Albuquerque, New Mexico, she has written an historical fantasy series including *The Phoenix Bells*, numerous historical romances under various and sundry names, and five horror novels: *Kachina, Shadoweyes, In Silence Sealed, Ghost Dance*, and the best-selling *Blood Autumn*. Her dark fantasies have won the Silver Medal and Gold Medal awards given by the *West Coast Review of Books*.

Kathy is perhaps the most prominent spokesperson for women in horror fiction, and has shown that in her role as editor of the critically acclaimed, ground-breaking anthologies *Women of Darkness* and *Women of Darkness II*. She is also the editor of *Women of the West*. Her short fiction has appeared in *Greystone Bay, Doom City,* and *A Confederacy of Horrors,* just to name a few. She publishes a monthly newsletter of markets for writers called *The Gila Queen's Guide to Markets* and is currently working on a mystery and another horror novel.

Kathy's work has the enviable tendency to cross any barriers that the word "genre" can place in front of it. She resides in New Jersey with her husband, author Charles L. Grant.

You Are What You Eat/Watch: Cannibalism in Movies

by Kathryn Ptacek

I confess to this secret liking: I enjoy cannibal films.
Really.
And the incredibly silly thing is I'm an almost vegetarian; I don't like

beef-tartar, much less sushi, and boy, my steak or hamburger (on those rare occasions when I order 'em) had better be *well done*.

So, why do I enjoy cannibal films? It's not for the gore (I have a fairly strong stomach, so most things on the screen don't bother me; however, I do have my limits); it's not because I like rare meat. It's because . . . because . . . well, I don't know why I like them so much.

It's just one of those unexplainable things, I guess.

It might be that the cannibal films are tantalizing because cannibalism has long (in Western society, for the most part) been a taboo. Maybe. On the other hand, incest is a taboo, too, but I don't go out of my way to watch films on that. Maybe it's because in a cannibal film you can really play with your food.

Or not.

However, I'm fairly picky about my cannibal films. I don't want to watch those chop/chomp fests from the Philippines. Too much for me; that is not my cup of tea (cup of blood?).

What I like are the ones that are humorous. Yeah, humorous cannibal films. It happens.

My favorites of those are *Motel Hell* and *Consuming Passions*. There have been other cannibal films. I rented *Parents* and watched that; this movie was touted as a dark comedy. Well, maybe it was so black, I just didn't see the humor. It was downright grim; the humor escaped me. Also the cannibalism almost escaped me, too; that wasn't the most obvious part of the film.

There is also the movie *Eating Raoul*, which I saw some years ago and which I enjoyed. When I went to the video store to rent it for this piece, I found they didn't have it. So much for those long-vaunted joys of living in small towns; sometimes it's a pain. There was also some other film I recall seeing not too long ago, some horror-type film (minus humor, though) with John Saxon (who else) as one of a group of Vietnam vets who had returned and years later tendencies toward cannibalism crop up when he decides to take a bite out of the girl next door. This is not a movie to laugh at, unless you count production values, script! the acting, stuff like that. And there was also a movie musical about Sweeney Todd, the demon barber of Fleet Street. He killed his customers; the lady he was in cahoots with made them into meat pies. Yum. I hate the music, so immediately that film was out. And I'm sure there are plenty of other cannibal films, but since I don't know about them, they can't count. Right? Right.

So since I have *Motel Hell* and *Consuming Passions* at home already (yes, I own 'em), I decided to concentrate on those two.

Now, the next step is to give you capsule run-downs on both films.

Motel Hell. This is a 1980 film, starring Rory Calhoun and no one else you've ever heard of. Rory Calhoun used to be on some TV program back when I was a child (I don't recall which one, because I didn't much watch TV, the folks at the mission school being strict about it and all). He was a good-looking young fellow then; he's a good-looking old fellow now. It was done on a low budget (it has that look, but not so low, though, that it's repulsive) and is set somewhere unspecified, but probably in the south because it has that look and feel to it. It certainly didn't take place in the American southwest. The Motel Hell in the film is actually Motel Hello, but the "O" on the neon light keeps flickering on and off. It all boils down to this: Farmer Vincent (Calhoun), who runs the out-of-the-way motel, is famous for his smoked meats. He puts nails down on the highway or shoots out the tires of passing cars, then takes the survivors (yes; gotta have that meat fresh) to his secret garden. There he plants the people, so that only their heads show above the ground; their vocal cords are sliced so they can only make rasping noises. Into this sort of paradise comes Terry, a young woman (blonde, of course). Farmer Vincent starts to fall for the young woman and she for him. But there's another loose cannon here—Vincent's brother, Bruce, the local cop, who has nary an idea about what makes up his brother's famed meats. There's a pesky government man—what other kind is there—and an assortment of folks who are planted. Vincent is fond of saying, "Meat's meat, and a man's gotta eat," and "It takes a whole lot of critters to make Farmer Vincent's fritters." A whole lot of stuff happens after Terry arrives at Motel Hell (and I'm not going to tell you because I don't want to take the surprise away), and at the end there's a scene right out of Romero's *Night of the Living Dead* and a scene more than faintly reminiscent of the duel between Darth Vader and Luke Skywalker in *Star Wars*.

Consuming Passions. This 1988 film is based upon a play by Michael Palin and Terry Jones, who are (as if there were anyone who didn't know) two of those wacky guys who brought us Monty Python's Flying Circus. This film, which is quite well done, takes place in England and stars Freddie Jones, Jonathan Pryce, Sammi Davis, Prunella Scales, and Vanessa Redgrave. This has names; the other film really doesn't. Ian Littleton is starting his new job at Chumley's Chocolate Factory which has just been taken over by a corporation (the representative of which is played to the hilt by Jonathan Pryce). Ian is a bit of a screw-up and doesn't have much confidence in himself; this is not reinforced when just after he enters the factory he accidently pushes three workers into the chocolate vat. The problem with the candy when the corporation took it over was that all things such as milk were taken out and no one much likes the post-takeover product. Once the workers contribute to the chocolate, the candy's popularity rises. Pryce decides to keep Ian on (so he won't blab; but he's too innocent to do such a thing, anyway), but he's put in charge of procurement. Ian starts out getting pound after pound of lamb and veal and pork to pour into the vat. Only no one much likes that. So the next step is to get people for it—he buys corpses from the morgue. All during this time he has found a girlfriend (Sammi Davis; a blonde, of course) and has to help a widow (Vanessa Redgrave) with her bereavement. Of course, things begin to snowball after a while. Again, I don't want to go further; no spoiled endings here.

So, what of these two films. There are a few parallels to be made. As you know cannibalism is a big taboo; which is precisely why these films are fun (the thrill of the forbidden, the attraction of doing something naughty?).

Foremost, in both films the cannibalism aspect is a secret from those who are eating the product, whether it's smoked meat or chocolate. And the funny bit is how much the consumers love the product. There are no cannibals who waylay travelers to gnaw on their bones and toss them out onto the pile in the backyard. You never *see* an act of cannibalism—we aren't treated to the vision of roast haunch of human, or boiled buttocks.

And because the killing/preparation of humans was offstage, as it were, that was a relief. We didn't have to endure minute after minute of full-color, increased-sound scratching, clawing, gnawing, rending, tearing, etc.—you know, the kind of stuff we always see in the zombie films. And by the way, I don't consider zombies cannibals. Yes, they are humans (or were) and are eating human flesh, but let's face it, they're dead; so that becomes something else. Cannibalism, as I define it, is when a living person eats another living (to that moment) person. Digging up stiffs for your afternoon tea doesn't count, either. That's ghoulism. My . . . all these subcategories of one taboo.

Also, in *Motel Hell* there is a thread of morality that weaves through what Vincent and his sister do; you see, they only smoke the very worst people—an older biker with his chick; the Ivan and the Terrible rock group; a "beat" type with his blonde who are both into swinging, S&M,

and a whole lot more. In *Consuming Passions* Ian is a good person, innocent and upstanding at the beginning; but as the movie goes on, his good personality traits begin to deteriorate.

Both films are played for laughs; *Motel Hell* is campy, deliberately so; *Consuming Passions* is funny in the British way, which doesn't necessarily mean there are a lot of belly laughs, but there are silly things going on—in the foreground and in the back as well; and there's a lot of irony, too.

If you haven't ever had the privilege of watching a cannibal film, I recommend these two. Characters and cannibals—what more could you ask for?

Chapter

18

Katherine Ramsland, Ph.D.

The author of *Prism of the Night: A Biography of Anne Rice,* Kathy is often asked how the book came about. She usually replies, "I called her up and asked her." Though slightly more complicated than that, it is quite true that she did call Anne up and ask her.

Her Ph.D. is in philosophy, her M.A. in clinical psychology. Kathy teaches existential philosophy at Rutgers University and has published two books in the field, the latest entitled *The Art of Inner Learning.* Her nonfiction has appeared in *Psychology Today, The Writer,* and *The New York Times.*

Kathy's horror fiction has appeared in *Masques II* and *III, Gorezone, Phantoms* edited by Martin H. Greenberg, and several other magazines and anthologies. (I wonder if her students know that their philosophy professor is so cool?)

She chose well when she decided to write about *Angel Heart.* It's a very complex film, which put her talent and education to the test. She described the experience as "like giving birth." But she chose *Angel Heart* in the first place, so really, they deserve each other.

Angel Heart:
The Journey to Self as the Ultimate Horror

by Katherine Ramsland

The Alan Parker film *Angel Heart* is about a detective who searches for a man who turns out to be himself—to his ultimate damnation. Starring Mickey Rourke and Robert De Niro, this film depicts a paradoxical encounter of the self with itself in an act of terrifying cancellation; it is a metaphor of primal horror. The explicit dynamic of this horror can be interpreted with the help of the *I Ching*, Carl Jung, and self-referential theory.

The film is based on the novel *Falling Angel* by William Hjortsberg, although Parker changes the locale and some of the images. I will be working primarily with the plot developed in the film, but will quote from the novel when it enriches an idea.

The Plot

Harry Angel—a symbol of innocence through ignorance—is hired by the enigmatic Louis Cyphre (Lucifer) through the law firm Winesap and McIntosh (names of apples, symbols of temptation). His task it to locate a forties crooner named Jonathan Liebling, a.k.a. Johnny Favorite. Angel finds himself on a convoluted trail, "looking for a man with amnesia." He encounters several people who knew Johnny: Dr. Fowler, a drug addict; Margaret Krusemark, an heiress into voodoo; Ethan Krusemark, her Satan-worshiping father; Toots Sweet, a jazz musician; and Epiphany, a voodoo mambo who is Johnny's daughter. Each significant character mirrors Angel in some respect—e.g., secrecy, duplicity, or darkness—as he plunges forth on his inward journey, and each is violently and grotesquely murdered after talking with him.

Several times, Harry wants to pull out of the case. "The closest I ever came to death," he claims, "is standing on Second Avenue watching the stiffs go by in a hearse." He grows more confused about the situation as he becomes more clear-eyed. Eventually he realizes that each victim died a symbolic death: Fowler was shot through the eye ("If thine eye offend thee," says Cyphre in the novel, "pluck it out"); Margaret's heart was cut out ("If hearts are steeped against you . . ."); and Toots Sweet was dismembered, then asphyxiated with his genitalia ("If a member offends you . . ."). Harry is horrified, but seduced by the money. He does not realize that he is being carefully unwrapped the way, in one scene, Lucifer peeled an egg.

It doesn't take long to put the pieces together to discover where Favorite is. It seems that Johnny had made a deal with the devil, selling his soul for musical success. Then he had tricked Lucifer out of his due: he'd discovered a ceremony through which he could switch psychic identities with another man and, in essence, become that person. "He needed a victim, someone his own age." So he'd grabbed a soldier in Times Square on New Year's Eve, 1942. With the help of Margaret and her father, "he sliced the boy clean open," tearing out and wolfing down his heart. The body was fed to dogs upstate (in the novel) and Johnny became another person. Then he got drafted, was shipped overseas, suffered an injury, had plastic surgery, and returned with amnesia, claiming he was someone else. Margaret and her father had picked him up at a hospital while he was still in bandages and dropped him off at Times Square the following New Year's Eve.

Harry Angel, too, had celebrated New Year's Eve at Times Square that year, having just been released from the hospital from his stint overseas. He recalls that someone had stolen his wallet and dog tags, and that he'd lost a year of his life to amnesia. As the story unfolds he realizes that *he* was the soldier whose soul Johnny had usurped, and thus that *he* is Johnny, albeit with the memories of Harry Angel. This is confirmed when he finds his dog tags in a vase in the care of Margaret Krusemark. By then, he has been manipulated into committing five murders for which he will die so that Lucifer can "collect his collateral"—Johnny's soul.

The success of the plot involves complicated mechanics of circularity and paradox, foreshadowed through symbolism.

Symbolism

Images from Dante's *Inferno* seem to influence the mood of the story. According to the fourteenth-century classic, the third circle of hell is reserved for gluttons and the ninth for traitors. Johnny was guilty of both, having an enormous appetite for life for which he betrayed the terms of his deal with the devil.

In the third circle, snow, rain, and slush make up the atmosphere. "Angel Heart" begins in snow and winds up in rain. The third circle is also awash with garbage, and one of the inhabitants cries out, "I lie here rotting like a swollen log," echoing the image in the first scene of the film of a dead body in a slushy alleyway garbage dump.

In the ninth circle, three-headed Satan is fixed in ice, eating the souls of the worst of all traitors. Louis Cyphre carries a three-headed cane (in the novel), is described as having "icy stares," and devours one of a trio of eggs of which he says, "Some religions think the egg is the symbol of the soul." The parallel, if not intended, is uncanny.

Aside from apparent references to Dante, the story is filled with subliminal imagery of doubles. Mirrors and portraits are used to emphasize doubles, as are paired objects like two elevators, two nuns, and two dreams. This symbolism serves several purposes that eventually converge into one ultimate image of duplicity: the reversal of innocence into betrayal.

The use of doubles underlines the bifurcated self: the Janus-faced individual ignorant of his own double nature. We get a glimpse of the many business cards Harry uses to change identities, and in one scene, he shatters a mirror into which he is looking; both images symbolize a fragmented self. In the novel, Harry chases a man who turns out to be his twin, and when he asks Margaret to draw up his astrology chart, she tells him: "You switch identities with the instinctive facility of a chameleon changing color . . . and [this] presents a problem when you confront the dual nature of your personality." Epiphany echoes this message: "You are more than one man." No one in this story is what they initially seem, mirroring Harry, who is the epitome of deceptive appearances.

Names, too, possess or suggest double meanings. In the novel there is a man named Vernon Hyde (of Jekyll and . . .) and a secretary named Janice (Janus). Liebling and Favorite mean the same thing, foreshadowing Johnny as a double person, and even Cyphre's name is more than just a clever disguise for Lucifer. A cipher is a method of transforming a text in order to conceal its meaning, which Cyphre does with himself, so it becomes a double entendre. So, too, does Epiphany's name. Epiphany is the season dedicated to the expulsion of evil and is the name of the feast commemorating the arrival of the Magi in Bethlehem (celebrated in France as the Feast of Fools—is it any coincidence that Louis Cyphre carries a French passport?). Epiphany also means the manifestation of a divine being or sudden enlightenment. Since Harry is an "angel" doomed to fall when he gets enlightened, such irony points to the paradox that opens the novel and ends the film: "How terrible is wisdom when it brings no profit to the man that's wise."

The double self is further developed with pairs of opposites, like white/black, cold/hot, and life/death. It depicts a person whose duality displays opposing impulses. Such imagery is constant: milk and morphine in Fowler's refrigerator, a Bible and a revolver, the devil in church. The film dramatizes this contrast: *Falling Angel* is set in New York, but *Angel Heart* takes Harry to New Orleans as well, where heat can more effectively contrast with the northern climate. The film also utilizes fans to represent heat, which show up whenever Lucifer is overtly or covertly present. Such contrasts prefigure ambiguity, a single source issuing into double meaning.

In *Angel Heart,* ambiguity has a dangerous edge, as with the same voodoo rituals that serve both to appease and encourage evil. There are other "dark" mirrors as well. Margaret Krusemark claims in the novel to be her own nonexistent twin—she is a black witch and a white witch—and Epiphany is a half-breed, born of a black woman and a white man. Religious revivals share space with a voodoo altar, and blood from a "suicide victim" looks suspiciously like that of a human sacrifice. Since the opposites presented are so intricately entwined, they set up the possibility of paradox, the foundation of Harry's demise.

A paradox is something with seemingly contradictory qualities that has the appearance of self-cancellation. For example, the paradox "this sentence is false" implies a true claim; yet if true, then it is false. And if false, it is true. Paradox does not actually *cancel* itself, but keeps values fluid and makes possible their reversal. Emerging from the same ambiguous source, they can filter through that source and become their opposite. What seemed true can become false; what seemed good can become evil; an angel can be a devil; the innocent can become guilty; the wise man's wisdom can turn him into the king of fools; and the mamba can be a "virgin Mary" who coupled with the gods to produce a child with the eyes of Lucifer.

It is ultimately through paradox that Harry discovers he *has* no self: "I'm searching for a man who was never there to begin with." This paradox is activated through the circularity of self-reference.

Self-reference

To get clear on the function of self-reference in this film, we can look first to more familiar forms. A movie about making movies is self-referential; so is a book about writing, a discussion about language, or a sentence like "This is a self-referential sentence." Self-reference is a designation within a system and about the system that uses the symbols involved in making the designation; that is, self-reference results from a system circling back on itself.

Angel Heart contains many images of circularity that mirror the structure of self-reference, like the voodoo symbol of a serpent eating its own tail. Harry has dreams about chasing himself. He fathers Epiphany as Johnny, then returns and has sex with her. Johnny picks Harry up on New Year's Eve and returns to the same place on another

New Year's Eve as Harry. The name of Harry's agency is Crossroads, an image of meeting himself, and in the novel, as Cyphre closes in, he says to Harry, "I'm getting to the point, however circuitously."

Self-reference can serve various functions: (1) description ("this sentence is part of the English language"); (2) self-replication ("Copy me"); and (3) self-undermining, as with paradox ("This sentence contains two erors"). The notion of self-reference ties in with Gödel's Incompleteness theorem in mathematics, in which Gödel pointed out that within any system, it is possible to use the symbols to express a paradox: "This formula, expressed with the system S is unprovable within the system S." Thus, the system S is vulnerable to contradiction, which threatens meaning. Since a system is a group of functionally related elements that form a collective entity, we can view the self as a system vulnerable to the threat. Contradiction within the self can become a source for creativity or destruction, but *Angel Heart* emphasizes the darker possibilities through images of doom.

In the novel, Johnny's agent's name is Wagner—a play on the composer who wrote *The Twilight of the Gods,* which seemingly refers to the fall of an angel—Harry Angel. The cop who investigates Angel for murder is named Sterne, which means star, or fate. The film goes back over and over again to a solitary figure in mourning clothes who has cleaned up the blood of a suicide—or a "sacrifice," and Harry witnesses a voodoo ritual in which the practitioners slice the throat of a fowl—an image of what has actually happened to him and what he is doing to others. "I have a thing about chickens," he admits.

Yet why would ambiguity, which can slice both ways, seem inevitably to turn toward doom? Because Johnny has made a deal with the devil. His soul is not his own. Circling back to himself allows Lucifer to invade through the vulnerability within the self to contradiction and, thus, to the disintegration of its essence.

The Self As a Circle

In order to see how contradiction can damage the self, we must examine how the circularity works. For this dynamic, we can turn to the psychoanalyst Carl Jung. He theorized that the self was an entity made up of diverse parts. The ego is the part that organizes conscious activity for continuity and coherence. It keeps things clear and unambiguous. The unconscious holds contents of our personality about which we are unaware. It contains archetypes—recurring impersonal patterns of timeless human experiences that express themselves through symbols, like snakes or caves. One of these archetypes is the Self, which is the archetype of unity and wholeness. Another is Satan, the archetype of Absolute Evil. Thus, the unconscious tolerates ambiguity and contradiction within itself. In *Angel Heart* these archetypes are pitted against one another. Since contradiction threatens the order of the conscious mind, the ego finds ways to divide itself from the unconscious. It develops personas, or masks, through which it connects with the outside world, and uses frightening images to cut itself away from the inner darkness. However, the unconscious will not be ignored.

Ideally, the ego and the unconscious strive for balance, but absolute balance subtracts the dynamic needed for life energy. So the ego also subverts balance; it seeks to be the center of the self by asserting order. The unconscious, which has no structure of its own, then rises up through dreams and personality disorders to throw the ego into disorientation. There is no security, no point of reference. The ego must accept the void or be subsumed. As it begins to assimilate the unconscious, antagonistic elements diminish. The ego is then free to seek wholeness in the archetypal Self, the true center. So the self seeks itself, as Harry seeks Johnny.

This psychological phenomenon is enacted in *Angel Heart*. Harry thinks of himself as a person complete in himself ("I know who I am!"), but in fact, he is carrying around the submerged soul of Johnny. Harry is but a mask, a superficial persona. Throughout the film, evidence of the insistent unconscious is clear. Harry first meets Cyphre in a building in which a religious ceremony is going on—a contradiction. After the ceremony, he looks around in the basement, a symbol of the unconscious. He also absently whistles or plays a tune of Johnny's while claiming he is unfamiliar with Favorite's songs, and the woman wading in the ocean (the unconscious) at Coney Island sings one for him, but he walks away without listening. When he gets to New Orleans, he rents a leaky room—a symbol of a self with no defenses—and the leaks worsen as he comes closer to the truth. By the film's end, he is caught in a torrent of rain.

Harry is like the ego striving to set itself up in its own realm and ignoring a component of itself that will not be ignored; thus, he becomes vulnerable. As time and events pass he grows disoriented. Images flash at him: a room in which a man is screaming, a staircase, and a solitary figure in black. He feels as if things are getting out of control and it's somehow related to Johnny, whom he believes he does not know. It frightens him, just as the unconscious frightens the ego. Whenever he gets close to answers, he is set upon by thugs or dogs, which is like what the ego projects, turning its fears into external threats to keep itself away from the unconscious. Johnny, however, is emerging, shutting out Harry as he performs grisly deeds, and Harry has no memory of what his own hands have done. He is gradually overwhelmed by the force of the unconscious where Johnny resides, ruled by Lucifer.

In the unconscious, the devil is the archetypal Trickster (thus, images from Dante's Inferno gain a psychological flavor). He represents the human potential for destruction at its most seductive. He leads in a false direction and robs his victims of control. Harry cannot escape him because he cannot escape himself. "However cleverly you sneak up on a mirror," Cyphre tells him, "your reflection always looks you straight in the eye." Harry resists, but he eventually remembers how he has murdered each person. Once he acknowledges Johnny, he is lost.

Thus, within the system of self known as Harry Angel, he is vulnerable to the circularity of self-cancellation, partly because his soul is a paradoxical union of opposites: innocence and guilt, light and dark, someone and no one. "I know who I am," he screams, yet he doesn't really, because he is not who he thinks he is.

Moving beyond Jung, we can see more explicitly what this void contains if we look to the *I Ching*—a book that Margaret Krusemark had on her shelf. It chronicles the journey of self into the unconscious.

The *I Ching* is a Chinese philosophy focusing on yin/yang cycles of life and death. Yin and yang represent cosmic forces that govern all things. Yin is negative, weak, destructive, and dark; yang is strong, active, and light. They are opposed, yet inextricable from one another. The archetypes form from combinations of these forces.

According to the *I Ching*, all things move through cycles of change. At birth, spirit becomes physical mass, then reconverts to spirit at death. During life, we are primarily conscious, during death, unconscious. The dead go on a journey before returning again to life, moving through stages where they experience visions.

One of the stages involves horrifying images that are manifestations of the personal psyches (what Jung would call projections of the unconscious). The souls experience physical pain, then come face-to-face with the God of the Dead, who sits in judgment. He is the souls' own hallucinations and he holds up a mirror to them as a complete manifestation of their thoughts and behaviors. It is the horror of the self standing naked and defenseless before its own self-judgment, which is omniscient and uninhibited in the torment it can inflict. This is hell, the inner mentality of the person, where he or she will experience their greatest fears. "The Lord of Death will place round thy neck a rope and drag thee along; he will cut off thy head, extract thy heart, pull out thy intestines, lick up thy brain, drink thy blood, eat thy flesh, and gnaw thy bones; but thou will be incapable of dying" (*The Tibetan Book of the Dead*). The torment is repeated over and over. No self-deception is possible, no rationalization or convenient forgetting. One's deeds are brought forth and the agony begins.

Thus, the journey of the self to itself is the ultimate horror because there is no escape from what we are. Within us all resides the archetype of evil, and the degree to which we manifest it is the degree of our punishment. This horror is brought home to Harry when he meets himself in the form of Johnny, who was described by Evangeline Proudfoot as being "as close to true evil as she ever wanted to come." In the unconscious, he has to confront what he has ignored. Johnny is not another person; Johnny is *him*, and he has to pay for what he is.

Harry Meets Johnny

Both the film and the novel contain hints of possible redemption. "Salvation is within you," reads a church marquee outside Fowler's house. Harry also passes a revival and a river baptism without giving them any thought. "Churches give me the creeps," he says. Compelled unconsciously by the evil soul of Johnny, he bypasses what could save him because he fails to realize that which is within himself for which he needs redemption. He even knocks over a preacher in a parade and breaks a statue of an angel when he struggles with Toots Sweet, foreshadowing his ultimate doom. The images of ambiguity that can yield one of two meanings move inevitably toward darkness; where salvation is possible, so is damnation.

Since Harry is possessed by Johnny, there is no room for innocence. As he discovers this, circling back to himself in his hunt for the missing person, he becomes vulnerable to contradiction and the 'reversal of values. His innocence becomes guilt, and people are revealed to be other than what they seem—Cyphre is Lucifer, Harry's lover is his daughter, the woman in mourning is a man. Harry is canceled out and swallowed by Johnny rising to the surface. And Johnny, who has replaced the archetypal Self with Absolute Evil, has no place to go but down.

"Only the soul is immortal," Cyphre tells him, "and yours belongs to me."

Chapter

19

Anne Rice

It is not enough to say that Anne is one of the most popular novelists of our time. National newspapers have dubbed her "this century's Mary Shelley" and insisted that her fiction will "live on through the ages." It is Anne Rice who, whether she realizes it or not, has raised horror fiction to a level at which, even the snobbiest English professors must admit, it becomes literature.

Her *Vampire Chronicles—Interview with the Vampire, The Vampire Lestat,* and *The Queen of the Damned*—are headed for the silver screen along with *The Witching Hour.* She has begun another series with *The Mummy, or Ramses the Damned.* But she is a novelist by trade, not a horror novelist. *Cry to Heaven* and *The Feast of All Saints* are historical novels. *Exit to Eden* and *Belinda*, written under the pseudonym Anne Rampling are mainstream erotic novels. The trilogy written as A. N. Roquelaure, which began with *The Claiming of Sleeping Beauty* and continued through *Beauty's Punishment* and *Beauty's Release*, are hard-core S&M-laden erotica.

So what can be said about Anne Rice? She is a multifaceted writer of extraordinary talent and depth whose efforts have helped legitimize horror fiction. She is also startlingly consistent in quality, an unusual trait in any author.

Oh, she also loves horror movies.

Anne Rice—The Art of Horror in Film

(As told to Katherine Ramsland)

What I like in horror movies are the ones that are heavily atmospheric, have some degree of elegance, and concern really tragic protagonists. Atmosphere has to do with the way the film looks and the way it's filmed, as well as the script and the character. For example, the scene in *The Bride of Frankenstein* where Dr. Pretorius is sitting in this crypt and the monster walks up and says, "Smoke," and he gives him a cigar. To me that's a fabulously elegant and atmospheric scene because of this lean, handsome, smiling doctor under these gorgeous stone arches with all these graves around him, simply taking the monster in stride. It's wonderful. *That* is atmosphere: building scenes carefully, lighting them so that you go into the mood of the scene and you share the mood of the people on the screen. I've seen horror movies where there was none of that. They're real failures.

The Wolf Man, Dracula, the first *Frankenstein,* and *The Bride of Frankenstein*—all of those movies are squarely in that tradition of having atmosphere and tragic characters. They present the monster tremendously sympathetically. In *Frankenstein,* when the monster visits the old blind man and becomes his friend, and when he "accidentally" throws the little girl into the water, he's presented as really capable of suffering, and at the end of *The Bride of Frankenstein,* when he says, "She dead, she belong with me. You go, you living," or whatever, it's a tragic moment. I love that stuff.

I don't really like horror that doesn't have that, but atmosphere and character don't necessarily exist in the same movie. I mean, you can have a wonderfully atmospheric movie but no character. To me, they have to include all those elements. It has to have atmosphere, some degree of elegance, and really great characters with a tragic dimension.

I feel that most of the Stephen King movies have been undistinguished—they have not had great atmosphere and they have not had great photography and that's been their tragedy. Now, I thought there was great atmosphere and photography in *The Shining,* but the characters didn't add up to anything. They weren't as good as in his books. So there's an example of where that just didn't work, as far as I'm concerned.

Angel Heart is the modern horror classic. It's got atmosphere and there's dimension to the Mickey Rourke character in that film. I thought the suspense, the tension, the photography, the shots of the churches, the glimpses of things in his memory, and the use of New Orleans—it was very atmospheric. Terrific camera work.

Pumpkinhead was, I thought, a wonderful movie. It's what I call a B-movie, a fun B-movie, but it had great atmosphere—the witch's little hut out in the mountains was just fabulous and the mood created by

Lance Henriksen's voice and tone and expression, the way he looked like a mountain man—all of that was wonderful. He's the greatest up-and-coming horror-movie actor that we have. He conveys horror. When he's on the screen, he's low-key and wonderful. He looks unique and has a unique voice. You've got to have people in horror movies that convey a believable response to what's going on. He delivers, emotionally. In *Pumpkinhead,* he really does seem terrified. He goes through all these scenes consumed with anger and rage when he wants revenge on the kids who killed his boy; then he seems consumed with guilt and moral conviction that the monster must be stopped. Those kinds of actors give it weight.

That's what we had in the old days when you go back to *The Bride of Frankenstein*—the people played it totally seriously. They went into the romantic vision and you've got to have that. *Rebecca* is really made by Joan Fontaine. The more I watch it, the more I realize her performance is what makes the entire movie work. I thought *Pumpkinhead* was a great combination of all of those elements.

I loved Cronenberg's *The Fly*. He's a gross-out director. *The Fly* to me was Jeff Goldblum—that's what made it. And *The Fly II*. I'd rank them with *Pumpkinhead* as B-movies. There was something that prevented them from being really great. There was some absurdity and comedy. I've been trying to define B-movie. It's a lighter touch, it's absurd things happening and being given very simple explanations. Now, you could say *Angel Heart* does that, too, but there's a way that *Angel Heart* is so psychologically deep and tense that it's making a demand on you that A-movies demand. In some way, *Pumpkinhead* doesn't do that, and neither does *The Fly* or *The Fly II*. There are moments when you can break up and laugh. It's comic-book fun, like *Re-Animator*—when he gets his head chopped off and he tells his head what to do, and he puts his head on that girl's breast—that's hilarious. It's hard to define B-movies because it doesn't have much to do with budget anymore. For me, the Bs are the ones that are sort of genre movies. They're great, but they're not really transcending. But a movie like *Angel Heart* transcends the genre—I don't think there's a comic moment in *Angel Heart*. There's never a moment when you laugh at the hokeyness of what you're watching. But there is in *The Fly*—the idea of him turning into a fly is preposterous.

I also love David Lynch. I loved *Blue Velvet* and *Eraserhead*. I felt I knew exactly what *Eraserhead* was about, awful as it is. There are moments when the world looks exactly like that. I've been through it.

People seem to be behaving like that, and things seem to be absolutely ghastly, and one thing after another is absurdly grotesque and you feel like hitting people around you and saying, "Don't you see it? Don't you see it? Don't you see how horrible this is?" And they don't. I felt *Eraserhead* was that vision, and *Blue Velvet*, too.

I honestly don't know why kids go for those slasher films. I cannot understand Freddy Krueger, Jason, or Michael Myers. They most resemble mummy movies. I did find *The Mummy* terrifying as a kid—that indefatigable force coming on to get you—and that's what those movies seem to be: they're like the stepchildren of *The Mummy*, but they have no moral sense. Good and bad are killed, it doesn't seem to matter. The force can't be stopped. Nothing protects people from it. Not cunning, not morality, not goodness, not deservingness, *nothing*. There's no depth at all to the monster himself and I just don't like it. To me it's just like a video game—who's he going to kill next?

I thought it was very sad that *Harvest Home* wasn't made into a magnificent film. The way it looks on videotape, it just doesn't have the dimension of beauty that so often happens on the big screen. It doesn't have the same cinematography. I think it could have been a magnificent film. I loved the idea of it. It's very scary, but I'm not sure it would scare me on film if I hadn't read the book. Unfortunately miniseries don't have integrity as a form right now. They jam four or six hours onto a two-hour tape. As long as that goes on, I don't think we can take them seriously. We can't really look at something like *Harvest Home* or *'Salem's Lot* and discuss it the way we can discuss a film. Even when a film is cut, it's not that bad.

The movies I could watch over and over would include *Rebecca*, which does not have a supernatural theme, but is certainly a dark gothic classic film. I've also watched every version of *Jane Eyre* that I can get my hands on—the Timothy Dalton one is magnificent. I've watched *Angel Heart* about five times. *Pumpkinhead* I've watched a number of times, but I think *Pumpkinhead* is more fun. Other B-movies I love are *Re-Animator*—I watch it all the time. I think it's a scream, an absolute howl. I watch *The Bride of Frankenstein* a couple of times a year. I think that is one of the greatest horror movies ever made. The guy playing Dr. Frankenstein is wonderful; everybody in it is great—it's the fullest, richest of the Frankenstein bunch. We really learn about the monster and his capacity for goodness and how he's been betrayed by his maker. I think that movie had the most of the book in it, although it has a silly introduction that ought to be thrown away.

I watch a movie like *The Bride of Frankenstein* over and over to be put in the mood of it. It's like listening to music for me. It's like, "Let's go put in Mahler's Ninth and sink down and listen to that." I want to revisit that mood, I want to be reminded of all of those elements if I'm going to write.

Another movie that I love is *The Thing* with Kurt Russell, for the tension, the suspense, and the interaction between the men as they confront the monster—the way in which macho courage keeps winning out. The most aggressive males survive. I love that. Also, there are no women in it, and to me that's very gutsy. Nowadays, they'd stick some muscular little broad in there, like in *Aliens*. It's gloomy and dark and I love that background music. I also love the theme that you don't know who is one of them.

The same thing in *The Invasion of the Body Snatchers*. That's another of my favorite movies—the Donald Sutherland remake by Kaufman. I think Brooke Adams did a wonderful job. The characters are so good and the photography is excellent—the way they use San Francisco, the way they make it seem claustrophobic and gloomy, and the terrific special effects when those things are growing in the pods. That, to me, is great.

But *The Bride of Frankenstein* is an infinitely greater movie even than those because it has a great theme—a magnificent philosophical theme—and the black-and-white photography was so masterly in that film that it surpasses anything made since.

Another film I really admire is *Frankenstein: the True Story,* written by Christopher Isherwood. I saw that right before I wrote *Interview with the Vampire* and it had an enormous impact on me—almost a frightening impact. I wrote *Interview* with those images from that *Frankenstein* swimming in my brain. When I created Armand, I was remembering Dr. Frankenstein and the monster going to the opera before he started to break out in bumps and began to decay. I was fascinated by all that, and I know that a lot of my writing was seminally influenced.

I love to be scared in these, too. *The Thing,* to me, was really scary. *Alien* is the scariest movie I've ever seen. I watched *Alien* twice with Stan at the Castro Theater sitting on the front row and both times nearly died. I was really crouching down, holding his arm, and I *knew* Sigourney Weaver was going to get into the shuttlecraft, but I was so terrified when she turned and looked around that corner and there was the alien standing there and she ran back and tried to disengage the exploding ship. Oh God! To me, that is one of the greatest masterpieces of all horror movies, Ridley Scott's *Alien*.

I don't think any movie is meant to be watched as many times as I watch movies. They almost all fall apart. I think it's deliberately made to have an impact on the first showing. It's not like a novel, where you can stop and go and stop and go. So when we subject these movies to laser disc and tape and we go over them and over them, we do see all kinds of weak links. Every link is perfect in *Alien*.

However, the only movie I would rank with *The Bride of Franken-stein* as a truly immortal horror flick would be *Blade Runner*—the fantastic Ridley Scott film about the replicants. The thing with *Blade Runner* that hits is when Sean Young goes to play the piano and Harrison Ford walks up and she says something like, "I didn't know whether or not I could play. I took lessons." She knows she's a replicant and she doesn't know whether she really took the lessons or the memories were implanted, and whether she has the skill—to me that's a great scene. It's dark. It's beautifully photographed, everything looks burnished, and there's wonderful Harrison Ford who can play anything. *Blade Runner* is pretty damn near perfect for me. In fact, you almost have to see *Blade Runner* about five times to get everything that's happening.

It's because of movies like *Blade Runner* and *Alien* that I think Ridley Scott is the only person who can make the *Vampire Chronicles*. He's far and away the greatest director to do it. I think our greatest directors are Scorsese, Woody Allen, and Ridley Scott, but Woody Allen and Scorsese wouldn't make this material. So that leaves the magnificent, the great, the untouchable, the incomparable, the inimitable Ridley.

He is the modern master. I wish he would do more horror movies. If Ridley Scott were to get some kind of gig where he could make horror movie after horror movie, like remake *Frankenstein,* remake *Dracula,* do the *Vampire Chronicles,* do *The Witching Hour,* he'd leave us a legacy that we'd be watching forever. It's very sad to me that the Stephen King movies have not, in the main, been given that kind of attention. I think *'Salem's Lot* could have been magnificent.

If I were coaching the making of the films from my books, I would say, first of all, they have to have someone who knows the horror-movie genre. People who don't know the genre tend to create clichés. The scripts I've seen from Hollywood over the years leave me very little hope that anything is going to be done with the *Vampire Chronicles* that will be any good. That's not to say that the present group of writers couldn't do something better, but in general, I think a number of things have to come together for those movies to work.

Number one, they have to be flawlessly conceived vampire films. It is absolutely integral to that work that these are cape-wearing creatures of the night and that they present all the accouterments of traditional vampires: they dress beautifully, they seduce their victims, they cannot go out in the sun. If the writers take away that romance and don't make a good vampire film, they are really misunderstanding the material.

Now the philosophical and psychological elements must be there because a vampire film alone isn't what this film is about. They have to create those characters, Lestat and Louis, and they have to get the tragic dimension and the questing nature of those characters because it's part of the imaginative concept of what a vampire is—that these people would learn something in the immortal state and they would have philosophical agonies. If that is taken out—and it's not present in most vampire movies—that's a terrible failure of imagination. So they must keep in those elements that have made the books work for people: the philosophy, the sense of a moral quest, the tragic ability to feel pain, to feel guilt—they must keep those dimensions to the characters.

The third element that I think is crucial, which has been absent in almost every script I've seen, is that they must keep the characters heroic. These are not stupid, bumbling, idiot characters, and it's amazing how scripts do that to them—make them stupid. This has happened to me all the time with Hollywood. I create a character and they depotentiate that character. They think that in order to make him sympathetic, they have to make him slightly stupid or pathetic. They particularly do this with the vampires, because the vampires are killers. So they feel that to make them sympathetic, they have to make them human. Yet these characters are heroic. My whole thesis is that if you're immortal, and you have preternatural strength, vision, and abilities to think, you're going to be a little bit quicker, faster, better, and smarter than human beings; you will have a greater capacity for pain, and you're going to realize the irony of your position very fast. When the writers take that out, it all falls apart.

There was a script of the vampire Lestat that I saw, where he woke up in the twentieth century, climbed out of a hole wearing a cape, didn't know where he was, and was puzzled when people wouldn't take gold coins. That is *Love at First Bite* foolishness. Lestat decided to come up because of what he heard and he knew within twenty minutes where he was—before he even hit the surface. He was perfectly aware of the fact that people wouldn't be using gold coins. But you take away all that and you have another "stupid immortals" movie. To me, *Near Dark* was a "stupid immortals" movie. We're supposed to believe those people are immortal, yet they burn up on the highway because they forget about morning? That's really stupid. And we have a lot of those movies because of our inability to imagine how smart an immortal would have to be.

Those are the elements that would have to come together: get someone who could make a truly gripping vampire film that would include the elegance, the atmosphere, the scariness, and the seductive quality of the kill. They should go back and watch *Dracula's Daughter*—the moment when she seduces the young girl that she brings to her studio; they should watch the subtlety of that. They need that kind of subtlety, they need that kind of atmosphere, they need that kind of gracious touch to the scenes and characters, and then they need the philosophical depth and they need the heroic dimension.

The movie of *The Witching Hour* would have to transcend genre. If they don't do it with quality, it would just be a hokey mess. If I were coaching, I'd say go watch *The Innocents,* the movie based on *The Turn of the Screw*. Watch that for some of the greatest haunting scenes ever made. Get the dilemma of that tortured woman and her fear as she realizes she's in this haunted house, but also her courage—get that quality. Watch *Rebecca*. Try to get the atmosphere as close as the atmosphere of those two films. Try to show the heroic dimensions of the characters—don't make them weak to make them sympathetic. Make Rowan really strong. Don't decide that for her to be feminine and appealing to the audience she has to be a dingbat or a nurse; make her a brain surgeon and get someone like Julia Roberts to play her— someone who has a tremendous amount of inner strength and stature and a unique voice. Get Eric Roberts to play Lasher. Absolutely—that gaunt, haunted look, tremendous poise, that intensity. Get Tom Berenger to play Michael—he's the easiest part; he just has to be a very sweet, very likable, very indefatigable guy, but definitely show his strength and his attractiveness.

The Witching Hour would be so much easier than the vampires because the characters are human. You're showing human against evil and evil wins. That is much easier to do. The vampires—it's difficult because everyone's a vampire. If you don't get that right, you've got something really disgusting. But even a middling director ought to be able to get some atmosphere in a haunted house, with an old woman and her oil lamp. And with what they can do with special effects today, like in *Ghost*, they ought to be able to do magnificent haunting scenes of Lasher. With the jars and the voices, and all that, they ought to be able to really get it first rate, and there are many quality older actors around who can play Carlotta and Aaron Lightner. The important thing would be to combine those classic elements—the philosophy, the struggle over good and evil, and the elegance, and the atmosphere. I wanted it to be the best, most haunting "old dark house" novel I could write. They have a story, they have a history to that haunting, and they ought to be able to get it right.

Part of my struggle at the machine is to get the words to describe what I can see. But you could convey those qualities with light and subtlety of expression. When Lasher appears and the scene is properly lighted, you can show a character that appears to be the utter embodiment of good and evil, beaming at you and yet terrifying you because he doesn't belong there. That is the big thing with all my books: I see them first very clearly and then I have to get that into words.

One of the reasons I don't protract a scene is because I can't do it. For example, in *The Queen of the Damned* when Mekare kills the queen, it's very quick. I think in a movie, that would be a much longer scene; they will probably convey the violence of that scene much better than I did. I don't mind. That's not my thrust. The same way with Michael's fight with Lasher. That fight can be much longer in film. It can be much more detailed and take more time on screen than it took to read as they fight around the pool and slide around and crash into the water. If they can get the quality of *Angel Heart* in those scenes—the glimpse of a smoldering horrible place, an inferno—it's all subtlety.

I think the core of successful horror films is subtlety. And that's why those scenes in *The Bride of Frankenstein* are so good: they take the time to show the monster's expressions; they let him speak and they develop tension. The camera lingers and the scene blossoms like an evil flower. That's what's needed. You have to show Stella in scene after scene where she appears to be good, and then in that hellish vision, she has to appear to be evil; there has to be a subtlety. That's how I think Lasher needs to be conveyed. Whoever plays that part has to show the capacity for cunning and deception, and yet this near-angelic appearance because he's trying to please the person to whom he's appearing. To me those are the most terrifying scenes I ever wrote. I would love to film the scene where he pushes Cortland down the steps, or where he appears to the doctor, right by him, or where he appears on the porch and he's not real—to me that's what that book is partially about.

I don't think people in Hollywood honestly understand why these books are so popular. I don't think they understand the hold they have on the public imagination. This is the tragic flaw. *Presumed Innocent* is a very good case in point. I had reviewed that book for *The New York Times* and I'd read it with unusual care. I think they rendered that movie very well. In general, they used what the public had responded to in the book and it worked. *Gone With the Wind* did this, and *Jane Eyre* and *Rebecca*—these are amazingly faithful renderings, but in my conversations with some people in Hollywood, I have found that they don't know why my books are popular. They don't know really what makes them work for the readers, and they're eager to gobble up the material for their own purposes.

I think we're in a wonderful period right now. There were about twenty or thirty years there where there were no really good horror movies made, not that I can think of. Hammer studios was making sort of schlocky ones in the sixties and seventies, but that situation began to change, maybe with *The Exorcist,* then *Ghost Story*. I thought *Ghost Story* accomplished a great deal. It wasn't as rich as the book, but it was very interesting, and then of course the popularity of Stephen King and Peter Straub caused more attention to the whole genre. That has produced a lot of bad movies, but it also has produced some wonderful ones. I think all kinds of things are happening. The public is obviously responding very strongly and people have gotten interested again in horror films on all levels, from the very schlocky to the very fine. So to me, this is a very rich and wonderful period. As usual, it's disappointing how unimaginative much of it is, and how imitative, but I have high hopes. I think it's a great time for horror-movie fans. When we go in the video store, we're more likely now than in the past to find something to see.

Horror is important to me and I enjoy it so much and feel so at home with it that I can't see it objectively. I just know that when I'm watching something like *Angel Heart* or *Blade Runner,* I feel an intensity that is several notches above that of a film without those elements. I can't explain it. Perhaps detective freaks love detective films in the same way. I just know that's what turns me on and I can't define it. Critics have written so much on that. I think one critic wrote something about there always being something extra in the horror movie. Someone else said that the horror movie is always erotic. I really don't feel that particularly. But certainly I'm a writer who is obsessed with the erotic and with horror, so perhaps they do work together. I'm so close to it that I can't really feel it. I've tried to analyze it and the explanations I think fall short: I feel like an outsider, I think most people do. I think when we're watching a horror movie, we're watching someone who's a monster, an outsider. We're watching him struggle with that dilemma and it's terrifying. But those explanations sound curiously academic and removed, and I just know that I love the stuff. I absolutely love it. The first movie I remember seeing was *Hamlet,* and the only scene I remember was the ghost scene and the scene with Ophelia floating downstream in the flowers. Those scenes would seem to be seminal in my life and in my work. I remember in high school when I had hardly read one novel in my whole life, I read *Great Expectations* and there was that wonderful gothic stuff with Miss Havisham. I don't think that's the answer, to say, "Well, she saw this and she was influenced by that." The truth is, other people saw those things and they were not influenced. So I don't know the real reason. I just know that it strikes some deep, deep chord in me.

I wrote a story once, called "Die, Die My Darling," in which I tried to describe my sense of it. It was about a bunch of hippies watching TV, smoking grass. One of the hippie women complains about how her intensity puts everybody off. So they're watching this hokey movie called *Die! Die! My Darling!* with Tallulah Bankhead, and there's this scene where Tallulah Bankhead pauses on this gothic staircase and is about to try to murder her daughter-in-law. The hippie freaks out and says, "That's me. I am that woman and I am on that staircase forever and I am always trying, and I am the daughter being killed. I am all those people. That's it! That's it!" There have been many times when I have tried to write something that expresses that feeling of, "There I am, that's it!"

At moments like that, I know exactly what it's about and I know why I feel that I'm in it. Like to write the scene where Louis crawls into that crypt in the cemetery in Montmartre—that feels *so* normal to me, much more normal than sucking blood. Like with the Mayfairs in *The Witching Hour* when Rowan walked in the door of the house. I just loved it. I felt, "Okay, here it is at last. This is really it!" It's *that* feeling. And very few movies get it.

Chapter

20

Paul M. Sammon

Like Phil Nutman, Paul has seen *nearly* as many horror movies as Steve Bissette. He might argue this, and would be right to do so. After all, his book *Blood and Rockets* is the definitive consumer guide to science-fiction, fantasy, and horror films on video. He is also the editor of the controversial volume *Splatterpunks,* an anthology of extreme horror, and the anthology *Die, Elvis, Die!* His fiction has appeared in, among other places, *Twilight Zone* magazine and *The Year's Best Horror Stories* by Karl Edward Wagner.

Paul is firmly entrenched in the motion-picture industry. As a journalist, he has written film history and criticism for such publications as *Omni,* the *Los Angeles Times,* and *Cinefantastique.* As a filmmaker, Paul has produced/edited/directed dozens of documentaries on such films as *Platoon, Dune,* and *Robocop* through his company Awesome Productions. He has worked as a publicist and promotional consultant for every major studio on such films as *Blue Velvet, F/X, Robocop 2,* and *Conan the Barbarian.* Paul is the American coproducer of the Tokyo-based TV series *Hello, Movies!* His screenplay *Stereotypes* has the distinction of becoming the first animated Soviet-American coproduction.

Perhaps more than anything else, Paul is known for his no-bullshit attitude. He doesn't mind ruffling a few feathers when asked for his opinion, as evidenced in his essay "Outlaws." That in mind, the following piece comes as no surprise.

The Salacious Gaze: Sex, the Erotic Trilogy and the Decline of David Lynch

by Paul M. Sammon

The Argument

As the latest filmmaker to successfully transplant the bizarre sensibilities of experimental cinema into mainstream moviemaking—the man who brought the underground into the overground, if you will—David Lynch has produced a body of work long appreciated by horror fans. This peculiar love affair began with 1978's *Eraserhead,* which spurted across movie screens like a diseased nocturnal emission. The gut feeling that Lynch was "one of us" only intensified with the release of *The Elephant Man* (1980), *Dune* (1984), *Blue Velvet* (1986), and *Wild at Heart* (1990); portions of these films embodied primal nightmares, naked and unadorned.

Then came *Twin Peaks.* Lynch's quirky 1990–91 television series not only spawned a phenomenal (if transitory) national fad, it also consolidated a frenzied band of Lynchian cult worshipers more usually attracted to the cinema of Dario Argento, George Romero, and Lucio Fulci. And it's easy to see why horror fans adore David Lynch: it's all those severed ears (*Blue Velvet*) and unnerving fantasy worlds (*Eraserhead*), the gross deformities (*The Elephant Man*), pustule-faced madmen (*Dune*), and vomit crawling with flies (*Wild at Heart*).

Yet like the sixties-born postmodernist architectural movement, whose adherents share no common style or theory beyond a collective borrowing and combining of preexisting styles for the sole purpose of repudiating the stark, simple lines of modernism itself, David Lynch defies easy categorization. He is more multimedia synthesizer than genre purist, a contemporary sensibility so inundated (and fractured) by the unceasing contradictory barrage of today's pop culture that it has healed itself by creating a superficially antithetical—yet centrally integrated—aesthetic.

Make no mistake; there is a core at the films of David Lynch, and a fairly simple one at that. Beneath Lynch's penchant for extreme imagery, classical/pop soundtracks, deadpan wit, and dense, other-

worldly sound effects, behind his postmodernist scramble to assemble a
coherent whole from a cross-generic mishmash—horror films, art
school, ironic comedy, musicals, sitcoms, mystery stories, rock and
roll, science fiction, southern gothics, juvenile-delinquent films,
straight expressionism, and road movies—there lurks a central dynamic. Innocence and corruption are the keystones of Lynch's oeuvre.
These bipolar opposites are then united by a painter's technical
discipline, a surrealist's love of grotesque black comedy, and a
paranoid's fierce devotion to secretive mysteries.

Yet despite his heretofore unchallenged reputation as a uniquely
iconoclastic filmmaker, despite the mainstream accolades he received
for using *Twin Peaks'* extreme weirdness as a means to inject some
much-needed creativity into the lethargic body of network television, a
recent backlash has been building up against David Lynch.

This reaction first surfaced in the generally hostile reviews of Lynch's
latest film, the bizarre mystery/road movie/romance thriller *Wild at
Heart*. For instance, *Film Comment*'s Kathleen Murphy stated that
"David Lynch's paean to arrested development is hollow at heart."[1]
Other critics were more aggressive. Jonathan Rosenbaum, previously a
champion of *Eraserhead* and *Blue Velvet*, saw *Wild at Heart* as a grim
indication that "there's more commercial than artistic logic in the way
that Lynch's career has developed"; this none-too-subtle accusation
suggested that *Twin Peaks'* popularity had seduced Lynch into selling
out his *Heart*.[2]

In one sense, this revisionist critical attitude was to be expected.
Popular American artists who rise from cult obscurity to mainstream
acceptance are peculiarly susceptible to that "tearing down" period that
inevitably seems to follow the critical adulation accorded their earlier,
independent works. Therefore, when David Lynch faced the ax on *Wild
at Heart,* one could have assumed that this was simply another
predictable instance of the American media savaging a previously
praised celebrity, simply because that personality was now enjoying an
unprecedented level of success. (I suppose that this essay could be
accused of the same petty-mindedness. Perhaps this is true; my sole
defense is that the reluctant attacks found in "The Salacious Gaze" arise

1. Kathleen Murphy, "Dead Heat on a Merry-Go-Round," *Film Comment*,
November–December 1990, p. 62.
2. J. Hoberman and Jonathan Rosenbaum, "Curse of the Cult People," *Film
Comment*, January–February 1991, p. 18.

from my *respect* for Lynch's films, and are only partially motivated by Lynch's recent franchising of his idiosyncratic talents.)

Unfortunately, some hard truths lurk around the periphery of the currently fashionable Lynch bashing. The problem is, most of these pejoratives are aimed at the wrong target—David Lynch was actually showing signs of consciously commercializing his vision long *before Wild at Heart*. Aficionados of Lynchian cinema are probably assuming that I am here referring to such projects as *The Elephant Man* and *Dune*, and, indeed, *The Elephant Man* clearly marks that critical moment when Lynch embraced the mainstream.

In point of fact, however, I propose that a canny—and more insidious—melding of the avant garde and the marketplace was also applied to (and, indeed, partly responsible for the success of) the supposedly noncommercial *Blue Velvet*. I would then further propose that this commercialization has become increasingly injurious to an otherwise original cinematic talent. And I would conclude with the sad observation that the cinema of David Lynch has begun to exhibit alarming symptoms of repetition, self-plagiarism, and internal artistic decay, negative signposts that are clearly posted on the downwardly spiraling road that began with *Blue Velvet*, continued with *Twin Peaks*, and recently bottomed out with *Wild at Heart*.

Strong words, considering that these films are among Lynch's most appreciated works. Still, there *is* a pronounced entropic tendency gnawing away at Lynch's latest projects. And nowhere is this potentially self-destructive trait more apparent than in that thematically unified trio that I have come to see as Lynch's "Erotic Trilogy."

The rationale behind labeling *Blue Velvet, Wild at Heart,* and the two-hour pilot film for *Twin Peaks* as an Erotic Trilogy should be obvious. Even the most cursory examination of these three films reveals that "forbidden" heterosexual carnality fuels their dramatic engines; witness *Blue Velvet*'s masochistic lust affair between Kyle MacLachlan and Isabella Rossellini, the secret S&M sex life of Laura Palmer in *Twin Peaks*, the nonstop copulations involving an on-the-run Laura Dern and Nicholas Cage in *Wild at Heart*. But this repeated emphasis on the sexual act merely underlines the most blatant ingredient of Lynch's Erotic Trilogy. *Velvet, Peaks,* and *Heart* share many other similarities; in fact, and in a very real sense, these three films are all the same movie.

It's interesting to note how the rather childish notion of a beautiful, mysterious woman—one with a dark secret—reappears throughout the trilogy, and as a key ingredient. *Blue Velvet*'s Dorothy Valens (Isabella

Rossellini) is not only a seductress, but a helpless victim of blackmail and rape. Laura Palmer (Sheryl Lee) seems to have aroused the entire male population of *Twin Peaks,* which isn't generally aware that their homecoming queen also posed for bondage magazines. *Wild at Heart*'s Lula (Laura Dern) may be "hotter than Georgia asphalt," but her enthusiastic sensuality masks a history of child abuse.

The Erotic Trilogy is also united by genre, with each film belonging (more or less) to the crime/mystery field. (What's going on in *Blue Velvet*'s town of Lumberton? Who shot Laura Palmer? What did Sailor Ripley—Nicholas Cage's character—see or not see concerning Lula's father's death?) Further, *Velvet, Peaks,* and *Heart* are structured as rites of passage. Their leading characters eventually uncover and are threatened by subterranean pathologies festering beneath an otherwise "normal" reality (Kyle MacLachlan's discovery of the corruption within Lumberton and Twin Peaks, Dern and Cage's discovery that "the road" eventually terminates in nighttime accidents and shotgunned heads). Each film in the Erotic Trilogy highlights a terrifyingly primal villain, too; *Blue Velvet*'s Frank Booth (Dennis Hopper), *Twin Peaks*' Bob (Frank Silva), *Wild at Heart*'s Bobby Peru (Willem Dafoe).

Enough—you get the idea. Yet what's rather depressing about the Erotic Trilogy isn't how its blatant self-cannibalization suggests that David Lynch may be running out of ideas; it's not even the fact that these three films evidence an increasing preoccupation with one-dimensional fucking. What *is* disheartening is how the trilogy's sheer *sameness* ominously hints at a newly formulated Lynchian outlook, one whose overwhelming sense of coarsening, calculation, and self-consciousness threatens to seriously dilute the personal visions of this still-exciting artist.

Perhaps the best method of illustrating my fears regarding the recent decay of David Lynch would be to summarize what had gone before. Lynch's early life and films are invested with a remarkably consistent set of obsessional themes, and only by carefully regarding these concerns in their previously pristine state can one fully understand the advancing corruption that has befallen them in the Erotic Trilogy.

So fill up your *Twin Peaks* coffee mug and turn down that *Wild at Hearts* soundtrack, as I attempt to demonstrate how sex, postmodernism, and the Erotic Trilogy have paradoxically contributed to both the rise, and decline, of David Lynch.

The Early Works

David K. Lynch was born January 20, 1946, in Missoula, Montana, and unlike many of his directorial peers, his artistic concerns were not formed by childhood encounters with the cinema; Lynch's first love was painting. Artists Lynch has admired include action painters Jackson Pollock, Franz Kline, and Jack Tworkov. Later influences were Francis Bacon and Edward Hopper, whose combined sense of mutated flesh and urban alienation clearly figure in Lynch's filmic worldview.[3] As a young man Lynch first attended the Corcoran School of Art in Washington, D.C. (on a part-time basis). He then attended Boston Museum School for one year before moving to Philadelphia in 1965, where he enrolled at the Philadelphia Academy of the Fine Arts.

Such biographical knowledge is critical to understanding the influences that both shaped and still permeate Lynch's cinematic work. Indeed, painting (which he successfully pursues today as a second career) lead directly to Lynch's filmmaking, for it was while living in an economically depressed and shabbily industrial section of south Philadelphia that he eventually shifted his focus from art to cinema.

"The only reason I did a film the first time was to see a painting move," says Lynch.[4] Lynch's untitled first film was designed as a continuous loop, lasted under a minute in length, cost two hundred dollars, was shot in 16mm, and consisted of three figures who "caught fire, got headaches, their bodies and stomachs grew, and they all got sick."[5] This film was then projected onto three sculptured surfaces based on casts of Lynch's head, done for him by longtime friend Jack Fisk (husband of Sissy Spacek and later director of *Raggedy Man* and *Violets are Blue*).

---

3. Much of the biographical information on Lynch included herein is derived from the *Eraserhead* chapter of James Hoberman's/Jonathan Rosenbaum's well-researched, recommended 1983 book *Midnight Movies*, as well as from K. George Godwin's definitive analysis of *Eraserhead* (to be found in the September 1984 issue of *Cinefantastique* magazine). The remaining material was personally gathered by this author through interviews with David Lynch. These occurred during Mr. Sammon's research for a long article on *Dune*, which he wrote and then saw appear under the title "My Year on Arrakis: A *Dune* Diary" in the September 1984 issue of *Cinefantastique*.

4. Stuart Schiff, "The Weird Dreams of David Lynch," *Vanity Fair*, March 1987, p. 90.

5. "Eraserhead," K. George Godwin. *Cinefantastique*, September 1984, p. 42.

Lynch's initial cinematic effort caught the eye of millionaire painter H. Barton Wasserman, who gave him money to produce a second film. Wasserman's patronage eventually resulted in "The Alphabet," a four-minute 16mm live-action and animated short that "is a little nightmare about the fear connected with learning," said Lynch. "It's very abstract—a pretty dense little film."[6]

Starring Lynch's then-wife Peggy, "The Alphabet" begins with her lying on an iron-frame bed while wearing large sunglasses over dead-white makeup. The soundtrack erupts with children's voices chanting the first three letters of the alphabet; what follows is a free-associational "narrative," one that includes an animated capital *A* giving birth to two small *a*'s, a pair of lascivious lips in huge close-up (predating a similar image that opens *The Rocky Horror Picture Show*), and an animated cubist portrait sprouting human organs.

Despite its abstracted noncommercialism, "The Alphabet" (which was actually sort of a "film painting") brought Lynch a small measure of local fame. Lynch then applied for and eventually received a total of $7,200 in American Film Institute grants to produce "The Grand-mother," his longest film to date. Running thirty-four minutes, "The Grandmother" was a 16mm surrealist epic filmed in black-and-white and color, one that also mixed live action with animated segments.

Made in 1968, "The Grandmother" 's importance lies in its frontrun-ner status as the first key work in Lynch's expanding filmography, as it clearly encapsulates themes and concerns that have remained with Lynch throughout his career. Using only sound effects and a flamboy-ant, ultra-surreal mélange of hallucinatory images, "The Grandmother" concerns a neglected little boy (Richard White) repeatedly attempting to bond with his uncaring parents, who at one point drop on all fours and bark like dogs. Yet even bouts of desperate bed-wetting gain the boy little more than parental abuse. Dejected, the child plants a strange seed in a mound of dirt, one which will magically create an affectionate grandmother. But in Lynch's universe happiness can be circumscribed and short-lived—the Grandmother sickens and dies, leaving the boy with only his own internal isolation.

In many respects "The Grandmother" resembles Lynch's first two films, since at heart it is only a moving painting. But as I have mentioned, "The Grandmother" additionally demonstrates that Lynch was now attempting to unify his penchant for bizarre imagery with

6. "Eraserhead," K. George Godwin, *Cinefantastique*, September 1984, p. 42.

corresponding themes and plots. Up until this film, Lynch's work had left the impression of a gifted but somewhat naive personality thrilling to the ingenuous, near-pristine act of visually recreating its own preliterate subconscious. With "The Grandmother," it became apparent that David Lynch not only had something to show, he had something to say (and this despite Lynch's well-known insistence that his films flow from an internal torrent of uncensored, abstracted, and nonintellectualized mental images).

The symbolism of "The Grandmother" is too obvious to ignore. Alienation and innocence are represented by the lonely child. A seeming dread of the procreation process and a fascination with skewed biology is variously dramatized by animated lips vomiting out a white liquid at film's start as well as by the birth of the Grandmother herself, whose seed matures into a huge, grotesque plant that ejaculates a full-grown woman amid a welter of fluids. And always, over everything, hovers a trancelike fascination with the conjuring up of completely nonrational universes, ones whose freakishly weird landscapes nevertheless relate to real-world events and social attitudes.

Clearly, whether he was aware of them or not, Lynch was trafficking with deeply personalized matters in "The Grandmother."[7] And if I have gone to such lengths to catalog the thematic high points of this early film—the alienation and the innocence, the morbid ambiguity about human reproduction twinned to a fascination with mutated biologies, the compulsion to invent alien worlds whose outrageous environments trigger altered states of consciousness—it is because Lynch himself returned to and, indeed, solidified these themes with his next project, the feature-length *Eraserhead* (1978).

Most analyses of *Eraserhead* do not focus on its thematic underpinnings, opting instead to examine the film's troubled production history or the fact that it is the premiere representation of Lynch's unique visual signature.[8] This second tendency is thoroughly understandable, as

7. "The Grandmother" was also the initial film on which Lynch worked with Alan Splet, an Oscar-winning sound designer (for *The Black Stallion*). Splet has been an influential artistic collaborator on many Lynch projects; his densely layered, seemingly organic sound effects do much to enhance the atmospheric oddity of Lynch's films.
8. *Eraserhead* was primarily shot in the stables of the American Film Institute, which in the early seventies was located at Greystone Mansion in Beverly Hills. The film took nearly five years to complete, beginning with preproduction in 1971; shooting commenced on May 29, 1972, and it was finished in late 1976.

Eraserhead is, quite simply, an overwhelmingly imagistic masterpiece.

Eraserhead's overall "look" can be described as a suffocating and terrifying expressionism, and along with its seething, sooty imagery comes a painterly attention to composition and light, a fascination with strange surfaces (Lynch's famous "textures"), and an intentionally stylized manipulation of sound. Throughout *Eraserhead* Lynch marshals these techniques (ones he still uses today) to create specific moods, most often a sense of dreamlike illogic or free-floating anxiety. And Lynch is typically more interested in setting up these emotional tonalities for their own sakes rather than making them subservient to the development of a linear narrative.

Yet it is not this film's images that reveal Lynch to be an artist with a clear thematic agenda; that revelation comes with *Eraserhead*'s subterranean narrative and attendant subtexts. The film's mordant plot spotlights nerdish Henry Spencer (Jack Nance), who discovers that the only way to escape his claustrophobically disaffected life (one played out against a nightmarish urban landscape) is to grotesquely murder the monstrously mutated baby he has recently fathered. This action then will unite Henry with his one true love—the ovary-cheeked Lady in the Radiator (Laurel Near).[9]

Basically a study of entrapment, *Eraserhead* also demonstrates that

According to Lynch (as quoted in *Sight & Sound* magazine, "The Heart of the Cavern," by Sean French, Spring 1987, p. 101), "We shot straight for a year and then we were down for a whole year. Then we shot and did the editing and sound piecemeal for the remainder."

9. *Eraserhead* provides some marvelous behind-the-scenes anecdotes. For example, Lynch not only wrote and directed this film, he also built and designed sets, relentlessly worked with Alan Splet on a multilayered, incredibly detailed sound-effects track, and devised the look of such later *Eraserhead* icons as the ovary-cheeked Lady in the Radiator.

Lynch also designed, built, and operated The Baby. An unnervingly lifelike prop, The Baby serves as both the film's symbolic locus and most well-remembered character. From one angle, it resembles a bandage-swathed penis-and-scrotum, from another a weird cross between a giant spermatozoa and a skinned, limbless lamb. Lynch was so obsessed with guarding the origins of this prop and maintaining a veil of secrecy around it that, to this day, he has refused to reveal how he achieved this amazing special effect. Indeed, there is even a rumor (apocryphal?) that Lynch would occasionally blindfold the projectionist who ran *Eraserhead*'s dailies, so that this technician would not be able to see those fleeting moments where Lynch was caught on-screen operating The Baby.

the concerns expressed in "The Grandmother" were not a situational aberration. Henry Spencer lives in an incredibly bleak industrial environment, one totally dominated by decay, malfunction, and entropy ("*Eraserhead* is the *real Philadelphia Story,*"[10] Lynch has said). This alien universe has clear antecedents in "The Grandmother"'s weird world, as do Henry's feelings of loneliness and alienation. A sense of innocence is reflected through Henry's passive puzzlement at the bizarre events unfolding around him. But *Eraserhead*'s most obvious ties to "The Grandmother" are found in its treatment of human reproduction.

The queasiness with which "The Grandmother" associated the birth process has been amplified to become *Eraserhead*'s nauseated central metaphor. Henry's head is knocked off at film's end and replaced with a squalling penis monster, intercourse results in malformed infants, and writhing sperm are crushed underfoot during one of the Radiator Lady's dance routines. This revulsion and fear of sex and its possible aftermath permeates *Eraserhead* and is probably *the* key subtext in Lynch's early works; as we shall see, by the time it resurfaces in the Erotic Trilogy, Lynch's ideas on sex will have become much simplified and inverted.

Eraserhead also adds new themes to the previous Lynchian catalog of alienation, birth fears, and otherworldliness. The first is an abundant sense of mystery, one suggesting that just below the alien surfaces of Henry's strange world lie even darker secrets. The second is a deadpan fondness for black humor; *Eraserhead* may well be pessimistic and despairing, but it is also a perfectly realized comic nightmare. Perhaps the best way to describe how cleverly Lynch here integrated horror and humor is to relate that the first time I saw *Eraserhead*, it genuinely frightened me; the second time, I couldn't stop laughing.

Eraserhead is David Lynch's *Citizen Kane,* a low-budget circus of the absurd whose various components were dominated by Lynch's personality and multifaceted production contributions (script and direction, as well as set, prop, and character designs). It has become justifiably famous as an aberrant entertainment. But for our purposes *Eraserhead* not only best serves as the most fully worked out example of its creator's worldview, it is also Lynch's definitive postmodernist statement. If one of the most oft-noted characteristics of postmodernism is that it recycles earlier cultural forms to serve them up afresh—and in the process triggers a more complex response in the viewer then the material would at first glance seem to merit—then *Eraserhead*'s

10. K. George Godwin, *Eraserhead, Cinefantastique*, September 1984, p. 47.

psychedelic stew of art films, chiaroscuro, Fats Waller organ music, horror movies, urban angst, and cutting-edge wit surely qualifies this motion picture as one of the supreme cinematic achievements of the postmodernist form.

Ironically, *Eraserhead* was so perfectly, hermetically realized that it signified an important closure in Lynch's artistic history. This film now can be seen as the absolute culmination of Lynch's "underground cinema" phase, a dark, triumphant curtain falling over the end of the first act of his film career. *Eraserhead* would be a hard act for *anyone* to follow, and short of simply remaking the same picture, David Lynch now had very few ways to go.

Except commercially.

Which is exactly the direction he chose.

The Elephant Man and *Dune*

Lynch's follow-up to *Eraserhead* was 1980's *The Elephant Man*, and along with *Dune* (1984) it is his most conventional project. This is not to say that *The Elephant Man* is a failure; indeed, it is an eminently enjoyable entertainment. Based on the unfortunate case of one John Merrick, a nineteenth-century Englishman afflicted with a disease so horrible that it caused him to be variously studied and exploited throughout his pain-racked life, *The Elephant Man* heralded Lynch's triumphant transition into the Hollywood mainstream. Popular and fairly profitable, it went on to garner Lynch an Academy Award nomination for Best Director.

Commendably, Lynch also incorporated the previously underground concerns of "The Grandmother" and *Eraserhead* into his first commercial project. *Eraserhead*'s fascination with heavy machinery reemerged in *The Elephant Man* in the many pounding, groaning, steam-powered devices that detail Merrick's story. Another *Eraserhead* characteristic—the love of mystery—resurfaced in Lynch's long, teasing buildup to our first (surprisingly nonexploitative) look at Merrick's ravaged face. Lynch's identification with alienation/the outsider then found literal embodiment in Merrick's twisted flesh, while John Hurt's superbly realized makeup (by British makeup artist Christopher Tucker) likewise represented that ongoing Lynchian fascination with the grotesque. Both "The Grandmother" and *Eraserhead*'s obsession with bizarre worlds here took the form of a seedy, well-designed turn-of-the-century London. And Lynch's disturbing sexual fears appeared in *The Elephant*

Man's opening montage, as Merrick's mother is frightened and/or metaphorically raped by a succession of trumpeting elephants. (Body-function squeamishness is also apparent during a later scene in a public lavatory, where Merrick screams, "I am not an animal!"; is it not the lavatory, after all, where the excretory and reproductive organs are liberated from their customary hiding places, and used within the close proximity of total strangers?)

However, more than simply being an admirable continuation of Lynch's artistic concerns, *The Elephant Man* marks the first appearance of a hitherto unknown Lynchian ability—his keen awareness of, and obvious eagerness to break into, the commercial marketplace. At the time of this film's release, John Merrick's story had been adapted into a successful and much-publicized Broadway play. Lynch cannot have been unaware of this; therefore, the choice of *The Elephant Man* as his first mainstream film was not only the perfect opportunity to graft his outré preoccupations onto a popular property, it evidenced a shrewd understanding of the domestic marketplace. *The Elephant Man* was produced by Mr. Mainstream himself, comedian/producer/director Mel Brooks. The quintessential Hollywood insider, Brooks's involvement with *The Elephant Man* at least *implies* that Lynch harbored a desire to graduate beyond the narrow audiences earlier imposed upon him as a fringe filmmaker.

While *The Elephant Man* may be considered Lynch's most entertaining integration of the mainstream and the personal, *Dune* (1984) is generally perceived as a disaster (although that opinion, this writer maintains, ignores the many strange and wonderful things to be found in this film). Based on science-fiction writer Frank Herbert's enduring ecological masterpiece, *Dune* centers on the clash between four planets for control of a water-poor, narcotic-rich world dubbed Arrakis. Lynch's cinematic adaptation was filmed at Mexico City's Churubusco Studios at a production cost of over $50 million, thereby necessitating a substantial box-office return on producer Dino De Laurentiis's initial investment. Audiences, however, found Lynch's epic mounting of Herbert's story to be either uninvolving or incomprehensible, and the project was a costly flop. (The fact that the two-hour-and-seventeen-minute theatrical print of *Dune* was heavily edited—Lynch had actually shot a still-unseen, near *four hour* version—only added to the general confusion.)[11]

11. A two-part, four-hour version of *Dune* was released by MCA-TV in June

In spite of *Dune*'s box-office failure, it remains another worthwhile example of Lynch's budding mainstream ambitions and continuing artistic concerns; the tackling of such a huge "event movie" may have signaled Lynch's complete break with the underground, but the director still found ways to insert his customary themes. For instance, *Dune*'s Paul Atreides (Kyle MacLachlan) is an inexperienced youth accepted into a nomadic desert tribe named the Fremen, finally set above them by the development of almost godlike powers (another example of Lynch's persistent fascination with innocence/alienation). Bizarre images also saturate *Dune*, not the least of which is the hideously corpulent Baron Harkonnen (Kenneth McMillan). There is a further, evident fondness for intricate machinery, an attraction nonetheless linked to societal decay, as witnessed by the ominous industrialism of the oppressively hostile Harkonnen homeworld. Then there are the countless visions, dreams, and drug-fueled hallucinations that pockmark *Dune*'s story line. As for the ongoing sexual morbidity of Lynch's work, this was objectified in the person of the Guild Navigator, a once-human transformed into a huge, stylized spermatozoa equipped with a vulva-like mouth (the Navigator also looks something like a recycled and bigger version of the *Eraserhead* baby).

In retrospect, *Dune* can be seen as a pivotal moment in Lynch's career. Where *The Elephant Man* had shown him that he could enter the mainstream with most of his personal vision intact, *Dune* thrust Lynch into the bonfire of a major box-office bust and showed him the pain that comes with commercial failure.

A hard lesson, but one that Lynch was obviously determined not to repeat.

The Erotic Trilogy: *Blue Velvet, Twin Peaks,* and *Wild at Heart*

With *Dune*, our survey of early Lynch works comes to an end. For those of you still with me, rest assured that this exhaustive analysis of

1988 as a limited run, syndicated television "event." Assembled under the supervision of MCA-TV Vice President of Special Projects Harry Tatelman, this four-hour *Dune* was put together with little input from Lynch, who not only disowned the project, but had his name removed from the credits. Lynch substituted "Judas Booth" for his screenwriter's card (an amalgam of Judas Escariot and John Wilkes Booth), and then chose "Alan Smithee" for his director's credit, the standard pseudonym routinely used by those members of the Directors Guild who wish to have their real names taken off a picture.

David Lynch's early films (and his initial encounters with the mainstream) was undertaken with a clear sense of purpose.

Two purposes, actually. One was to point out the remarkable faithfulness with which Lynch indulged his multiform interests in alienation, reproduction, strange worlds, black humor, grotesque images, and mysteries (up until *Dune*, anyway). My second intent was to show the uncommon ease with which Lynch eased into the mainstream, as well as the stinging indifference with which his second commercial feature was met.

That indifference raises a question: Could Lynch's commercial ambitions and the failure of *Dune* have melded together to prod this filmmaker toward a reconsideration of how to best profit from his personal obsessions? While only a supposition, this notion of retrenchment and repositioning begins to gain weight if one notices the sudden simplification/objectification of certain Lynchian themes in *Blue Velvet*, the first—and best—film in the Erotic Trilogy.

Shot in Wilmington, North Carolina, for producer Dino De Laurentiis, who gave Lynch total creative control in return for a reduced fee and a reduced budget, *Blue Velvet* will first and foremost be remembered as David Lynch's breakthrough project. A cult and critical hit, the film begins with college-age Jeffrey Beaumont (Kyle MacLachlan) forced to return to his bucolic hometown of Lumberton because of a family illness. Although Jeffrey is attracted to wholesome girl-next-door-type Sandy (Laura Dern), he soon discovers that Lumberton's seeming serenity camouflages perverse and perilous ingredients; severed ears lying in fields, drug-dealing psychopathic rapists (Dennis Hopper as the chillingly deranged Frank Booth), wild nighttime automobile rides, and masochistic femme fatales (Isabella Rossellini as the pathetic Dorothy Valens).

Much has been made of *Blue Velvet*'s menacing mixture of mystery story and art-house surrealism, and indeed, as an entertainment it cannot be faulted; with *The Elephant Man*, *Blue Velvet* is Lynch's tightest, best-constructed project. The story line is studded with disturbing undercurrents (Jeffrey/Dorothy's relationship), bizarre atmosphere (the "moaning corridor" outside Dorothy's apartment), and memorable grotesques (Hopper's simply incredible Frank Booth enjoys sniffing bottled gas before his violent rampages, a substance clearly identified as helium—and *not* nitrous oxide—in *Blue Velvet*'s script).[12] And no one can make a simple shot of rippling blue curtains seem quite

12. The source of my information about the substance Hopper sniffs is myself.

as uncanny as can David Lynch.

But those familiar with Lynch's past work and continuing personal agenda could be forgiven if they began to suspect, midway through the film, that Lynch here may have been more concerned with avoiding the commercial disaster of *Dune* than in enlarging upon his prior artistic statements. Past Lynchian themes most certainly do put in a *Velvet* appearance—Jeffrey is the innocent "outsider" drawn into Lumberton's grotesque criminal underworld through a web of dark sexuality—but overall, one leaves *Blue Velvet* with the feeling that Lynch's recurring obsessions have been commercialized, exploited, and generally made more prurient for mainstream audiences.

The most obvious element distinguishing *Blue Velvet* from Lynch's previous works is the film's setting. Prior to *Velvet* he had explored every world but our own; the avant garde with *Eraserhead*, the period melodrama with *The Elephant Man*, the epic film/science-fiction movie with *Dune*. But as writer Sean French noted in *Sight & Sound*, "*Blue Velvet* is Lynch's first film set either in the present day or in a recognizable version of America."[13] For someone who had previously preferred to work in highly unusual environments, Lynch's significant choice of *Blue Velvet*'s familiar landscape—the quintessential American small town—suggests a filmmaker suddenly willing to explore the safely conventional. Perhaps Lynch felt his previous explorations into the human psyche and strange imaginary universes had been too esoteric, and that the best method of ensuring wider audience acceptance was to ground his newest project in "real life." If this was indeed his game plan, it was a commercially astute one: *Blue Velvet* proved that Lynch could tap into a more tolerant audience by the simple maneuver of anchoring it onto easily recognizable terrain.

Along with *Blue Velvet*'s conventional world came a conventionally linear story line, a "boy detective" one at that. Moreover, Lynch equipped this film with a plethora of mainstream hooks. For despite its justifiably famous sexual pathology and all-pervading mood of weirdness, despite its oft-quoted notion that a deeper darkness waits beneath

I worked on this film (see note 18); I've also read all of *Velvet*'s various screenplay drafts. Those wishing to learn more of what was unexplained or cut from *Blue Velvet* are advised to obtain the trivia-packed "Bluer Velvet" by Bret Wood, a long and informative article that appears in the March/April 1991 (#4) issue of *Video Watchdog* magazine.

13. Sean French, "The Heart of the Cavern," *Sight & Sound*, Spring 1987, p. 104.

the most normal of surfaces (not exactly the most complicated of philosophical statements, by the way), the surprisingly prosaic world of *Blue Velvet* heavily depends on a bevy of time-tested—and clichéd—commercial commodities, ones guaranteed to maximize its box-office appeal. These include a drug-smuggling subplot, pop songs on the soundtrack (by Roy Orbison and Bobby Vinton, two musicians whose very mention screams "middle of the road"), blunt and vulgar language, a despicably hissable villain, and jolts of ultra-violence.

To its credit, *Blue Velvet* managed to integrate these suspiciously commercial elements within a recognizable equivalent of Lynch's prior vision; for example, the goofy absurdist humor of *Eraserhead* reappeared in *Blue Velvet* via Laura Dern's speech about robins as symbols of love. But any lingering doubts engendered by Lynch's setting the film in so prosaic and mercantile a world as Lumberton pales beside the film's radically altered attitude toward sex.

More than any other element, it is *Blue Velvet*'s thematic treatment of sex that signals a sea change—and blanding-out—of Lynch's artistic vision. Before *Blue Velvet*, David Lynch's primary feelings about human sexuality could be summed up in a single world: revulsion. "The Grandmother," *Eraserhead*, and *The Elephant Man* all featured ambiguous reactions to reproduction, children, and the family unit. But with *Blue Velvet*, the bulk of these prior concerns mysteriously disappears. The blackmail of Dorothy Vallens's family may be essential to *Velvet*'s plot, but Dorothy's husband is seen only as a corpse; her child never appears until the film's final moments. Reproductive fears have also become a near nonissue. Frank Booth may growl, "Baby wants to fuck!" during his initial assault on Dorothy, he may even threaten to crawl into Dorothy's womb. But these moments are designed purely to shock. They have no resonance beyond their momentary crudeness and cruelty, are undeveloped and unconnected to the rest of the film.[14]

14. Those who have seen Dennis Hopper's *Out of the Blue*, a 1980 film in which he both starred and directed, will notice a certain similarity between Frank Booth's initial sexual assault on Dorothy Valens in *Blue Velvet* and a corresponding rape sequence between Hopper and actress Linda Manz in *Out of the Blue*. David Lynch reportedly encouraged Hopper to improvise during his assault on Isabella Rossellini; Hopper must have been thinking of *Out of the Blue* during this sequence, because a shot of Hopper chewing on a piece of Rossellini's blue robe while he is bringing himself to orgasm clearly echoes a shot of Hopper chewing on Manz's panties during *Out of the Blue*'s own rape scene.

This sudden reliance on such crass sexual shock treatment is directly linked to a startling implication—while writing *Blue Velvet*, David Lynch seems to have shifted his stance on sexual intercourse from one of personal ambiguity to exploitative endorsement. Given our puritanical heritage, filmed mainstream sex scenes can become instant moneymakers if handled with the right combination of prurience and condemnation (just look at *Last Tango in Paris*). *Blue Velvet* seems aware of this fiscal gambit, as virtually every copulation scene between Jeffrey and Dorothy blends the ardent and the awful.

By way of contrast, Lynch's films prior to *Blue Velvet* were almost puritanically chaste, with a distinct absence of nudity and profanity. There *is* a moment when *Eraserhead*'s reproductive revulsion steps aside to specifically link copulation with poetry (Henry Spencer embraces a compliant neighbor before sinking into a beautiful pool of liquid light, one strategically situated in the middle of a bed). But *Blue Velvet* tellingly dispenses with such visual metaphors to load up on the sundry baggage more normally associated with male-oriented, soft-core pornography: naked flesh (male and female), rapes, sadomasochism, genital-oriented profanity.

This is not to say that *Blue Velvet* trivializes sex, it just finds a decadent way to package it. Lynch colors the film's intercourse scenes with voyeurism, fetishism, and infantile roleplaying, while muddying the moral waters through straight-arrow Jeffrey's attraction to Dorothy's pathetic pleas for a little pain with her pleasure. Yet like the famous black beetles teeming beneath Jeffrey's well-trimmed lawn, below *Blue Velvet*'s so-called sexual sophistication squirms an oddly coarse, dubiously sophomoric lasciviousness.

Gone are the symbolic sexual references of *Eraserhead*'s baby and *Dune*'s Guild Navigator. Instead, *Blue Velvet* offers up the very real, very compliant breasts of Isabella Rossellini, and the bluntly realistic manner in which *Velvet*'s sex scenes have been written and staged is directly antithetical to Lynch's prior (and elegant) sexual subtlety. It's not that the frank sex in *Blue Velvet* is shocking in and of itself; what's startling is the dirty-minded way in which this previously symbolistic director presents fornication. Given Lynch's past, far more imaginative track record in dealing with sexual morbidity, one can only wonder if a piece of his mind fell out somewhere between *Dune* and *Blue Velvet* (maybe Lynch then leaned over to pick up this wayward bit of gray matter and suddenly discovered his penis instead).

Still, *Blue Velvet*'s damp-palmed explicitness does not entirely exclude Lynch's past ambiguity toward sex. Although aggressively *au courant* and invested with a certain degree of cutting-edge posturing, *Blue Velvet*'s insistence on balancing Dorothy's perversity with Sandy's goodness hints that, at bottom, David Lynch may be an affronted traditionalist. Granted, he shows a sickly attraction to the most twisted recesses of the human psyche. But Lynch's seemingly sincere concentration on the relaxed sentimentality of Jeffrey and Sandy's relationship, with all the chirping robins and swelling church organs that go along with that, also suggests that Lynch wouldn't mind if the real world would just shape up and become a whole lot nicer.

Unfortunately, there's all this doggone *wickedness* around to distract him. . . .

Wickedness is the key ingredient of *Twin Peaks*, the second installment of the Erotic Trilogy and the project that finally exposed Lynch to Middle America. A mystery/soap-opera/television series spread out over two seasons on ABC, *Twin Peaks* was originally coconceived by Lynch and television writer/producer Mark Frost (who had previously worked on *Hill Street Blues*). Lynch himself wrote and directed the series' initial two-hour pilot film, a premiere presentation that kicked off a nationwide fascination with the small Pacific Northwest town of Twin Peaks, whose citizens are variously baffled, outraged, and ecstatic over the mysterious murder of the town's supposedly wholesome homecoming queen, Laura Palmer.

Many other critics have recently generated a vast body of analysis on *Twin Peaks*, so there is no need to rewalk familiar ground. Suffice it to say that despite a number of thuddingly bad episodes, the *Twin Peaks* series quickly metamorphosed into an addictive experience. Filled with eccentric characters, quirky humor, and sudden, ambiguous shifts between melodrama and mysticism, it rapidly established itself as one of the most unique mystery programs ever to appear on American television.

Unique, that is, if one hadn't already seen *Blue Velvet*, whose parallels were immediately apparent in the film's premiere episode. One watched this program, in fact, with the growing suspicion that *Blue Velvet*'s success had made Lynch self-conscious and calculating.

Divorced from its fannish adulation, *Twin Peaks* intimates that its ingenuous creator's previous trust in his own subconscious had now been subverted toward a knowing manipulation of the images and emotional attitudes produced by that subconscious. How else to explain the parade of plagiarisms that reveal Twin Peaks to be a recycled Lumberton? Consider the similarities:

Like *Blue Velvet*, *Twin Peaks* is a contemporary mystery story. Like *Blue Velvet*, *Peaks* probes beneath the seemingly placid surfaces of a small town to reveal the societal rot beneath. Like *Blue Velvet*, *Peaks* makes a mysterious woman central to the plot. Like *Blue Velvet*, *Twin Peaks* features a subplot about drug running. Like *Blue Velvet*, *Twin Peaks* is leavened with camp humor (*Peaks*' "*Damn* fine cup of coffee!" imitates Frank Booth's "Heineken? Fuck that! Pabst Blue Ribbon!"). Like *Blue Velvet*, *Twin Peaks* prominently features a close-up of a red-breasted robin. And in the ultimate referent, *Blue Velvet* and *Twin Peaks* share the same leading man: Kyle MacLachlan.

Lynch's television show also pilfers from his earlier works (the dreams of *Twin Peaks*' Agent Cooper seem like shorthand versions of the nightmarish imagery found in *Eraserhead*). But beyond these borrowings, it is Lynch's treatment of sex that testifies to a further weakening of his talents.

The incestuous yearnings of Leland Palmer (Ray Wise) set *Twin Peaks*' plot in motion, and sexual attraction between the series' varied characters is heavily emphasized from episode to episode. Fine. But the *visual* manner in which the vast majority of the female characters are portrayed signifies that *Blue Velvet*'s abrupt sexual realignment (from the symbolic to the onanistic) was no fluke.

Virtually *all* of the *Twin Peaks* women are lit and costumed for maximum glamorous seductiveness, while their characters are written/ directed to suggest a near-continual sense of arousal. One could excuse Lynch here by stating that he's having fun with soap-opera conventions . . . but then there's that insistent imagistic emphasis on a fifties/retrograde sense of glamour spiked with a knowingly contemporary decadence. The salacious gaze that infected *Blue Velvet* has now intensified into *Twin Peaks*' peculiarly adolescent excitement at transforming modern women into the visual icons most associated with soft-core pornography, an excitement grown tumescent by the sight of bare female flesh, by delicious hints of "availability," by moist, painted lips (this fixation was underlined by Lynch's own cameo role on *Twin Peaks*, wherein he played a near-deaf FBI agent named Gordon attracted to a pretty—and much younger—local waitress).

So while there are those who would say that the fundamental contribution of *Twin Peaks* to popular culture is the catch phrase "Who Killed Laura Palmer?", I would contend that the quintessential *Twin*

Peaks "moment" is the shot of Audrey Horne (Sherilyn Fenn) twisting a cherry stem into knots with her tongue.

Of course, all this focusing on *Twin Peaks*' aesthetic chauvinism has obscured the series' very real accomplishments, and I would be remiss not to state that, at its best, *Twin Peaks* is very good television indeed. Beyond its charged, isolated moments (such as that signature shot of a "lone traffic light swaying in the night wind, an audiovisual haiku")[15] *Twin Peaks*' continual use of strange visions and mystical occurrences reminds us that Lynch is still pursuing those spiritual interests he manifested as early as *Eraserhead*. Writing about this trait in *Video Watchdog*, Tim Lucas noted that "Lynch seems . . . preoccupied with body and spirit . . . he is that rare filmmaker capable of making spiritual films without occluding that weightlessness with gravid laws of gods and dogma."[16]

Perhaps. But *Wild at Heart*, Lynch's last entry into the Erotic Trilogy, is all body and no soul.

It's more than ironic that *Wild at Heart* was the recipient of the Cannes Film Festival's prestigious Palme d'Or. Not only did this award imbue Lynch with a newfound respectability (but whoever wanted a talent like Lynch's to be *respectable*?), the Palme d'Or was bestowed upon his worst film.

Based on a novel by Barry Gifford, *Wild at Heart* charts the cross-country flight of two lovers on the run. Lula (Laura Dern) and Sailor (Nicholas Cage) are attempting to escape the assorted murderers sent after them by Marietta (Diane Ladd), Lula's jealousy-crazed mother, and as with *Blue Velvet* and *Twin Peaks*, sex is the high-octane fuel galvanizing the film.

Lula and Sailor are carnally obsessed with one another; Marietta despises Sailor for turning down her own sexual advances. It's this two-pronged sensuality that keeps *Heart*'s plot in motion, but, unfortunately, Lynch seems to have felt that *Heart*'s road-movie framework allowed him to jettison any structural or thematic integrity. For *Wild at Heart* quickly fragments through its own evanescence; barring a few setpieces, this is undoubtedly the shallowest, most self-conscious film David Lynch has yet made.

15. Richard T. Jameson, "Evergreen Velvet," *Film Comment*, March/April 1990, p. 75.
16. Tim Lucas, "Blood 'n Doughnuts: Notes on *Twin Peaks*," *Video Watchdog* 2 (1990), p. 35.

Still, if taken as a loose assemblage of grotesque characters and violent episodes offset by the purity of two passionate lovers bound together by simple-minded pop fantasies and a rebel's disregard for social convention, *Wild at Heart* can be rather superficial fun. One notes the excellent performances by Dern and Cage, savors the rich cinematography (by longtime Lynch collaborator Fred Elmes),[17] sways to the eclectic musical soundtrack (by Angelo Badalamenti, composer for all three films in the Erotic Trilogy), taps his or her foot during a terrifically kinetic sequence in a rock club, and chuckles at Cage's dead-on rendition of "Love Me Tender." There are also two haunting/excruciating sequences that contain some of the best work Lynch has ever done. One has Dern and Cage blundering onto a nighttime roadside accident, the other is Dern's appallingly lewd sexual humiliation by a rotten-toothed character named Bobby Peru (Willem Dafoe, in an astonishingly simian performance).

But on the whole, *Wild at Heart* is a terminally manipulative cul-de-sac. Unlike *Blue Velvet*, which at least had a grubby pathology beneath its Norman Rockwell facade, or *Twin Peaks*, which at the *very* least holds out the promise of an occasionally effective episode, *Wild at Heart* is all surfaces. Rather lifeless surfaces, at that. Most of the film is tired or trivial, and feels like the ultimate Lynchian put-on. Instead of characters, we're given a series of wardrobes tricked out with attitudes, poses, and freakish tics. Instead of sexual heat, we're shown a series of glossy, crimson-lit tableaus shot like perfume commercials. And instead of dramatic resolutions, we're given a *deus ex machina* climax straight from *The Wizard of Oz* (was a fondness for *Oz* the reason Lynch previously named Isabella Rossellini's *Blue Velvet* character Dorothy?).

There *is* a statement struggling to emerge from *Wild at Heart*. This is the notion that Dern and Cage's romantic idealism can never survive the stress of everyday existence . . . but Lynch doesn't follow through on this sole thematic thread. Instead of breaking the lovers apart, which seems to be where the film is headed all along, Lynch reunites them in

17. Like Alan Splet, Frederick Elmes has been a longtime and essential colleague of David Lynch. The principal cinematographer on *Eraserhead* (Herb Cardwell and Anatol Pacanowski also shot portions of this film), Elmes was second unit director of photography on *Dune* and director of photography for *Blue Velvet* and *Wild at Heart*. In this writer's opinion, not enough notice has been given to Elmes's contributions; his lighting effects and compositional sense, in particular, constitute much of what has gone on to become known as the "Lynch look."

a crowd-pleasing but totally arbitrary curtain closer; Cage is smacked in the nose, he hallucinates the arrival of Oz's good witch Glinda (Sheryl Lee), and hightails it right back to Lula.

The desperation of *Heart*'s "we gotta come up with an ending!" is only matched by the remote hauteur that hovers over its perfectly lit, perfectly embalmed sexual sequences. Yes, there is an intense, terrible power generated by a confused Dern semisurrendering to Dafoe's blatant fondling and shouted obscenities, one that's almost too painful to watch. This is a sequence that outdecadents anything in *Blue Velvet*, a stunning "viewer assault" that momentarily cattle-prods this film into gleeful life (it's also about as far as Lynch can go without reverting to erections and insertion shots). But this sole sign of erotic vitality is surrounded by Sailor and Lula's endlessly empty fornication scenes. The sick eroticism that saturated *Blue Velvet* and developed into *Twin Peaks'* parade of *Cosmo* girls has now degenerated into a gauzy series of *Penthouse*-like photo spreads; they may go through the motions, but Lula and Sailor's lovemaking scenes are dead, dead, dead.

What's *truly* dispiriting about *Wild at Heart*, however, isn't the chilly precision of Lula and Sailor's couplings or the film's patchwork narrative; it's the underlying sense of cynical manipulation. If there's one thing we've come to count on in a David Lynch film, it's a sort of cheerfully mordant sincerity. But *Wild at Heart* is all style and no content, an uppercase Film By David Lynch bent on recycling only the most previously effective strategies in the Lynchian bag of tricks. Even the inclusion of such pop icons as Elvis songs and witches from *Oz* seems forced and calculated, weak, obtrusive substitutes for the full-bodied elements that the film sorely lacks—character development, sincere emotion, and unfettered originality.

With *Wild at Heart,* we reach the end of the Erotic Trilogy. And a question. Has David Lynch finally co-opted his individuality to concentrate on how best to market what had previously been known as his maverick, truly iconoclastic artistry?

Read on. . . .

The End

It is, of course, somewhat naive to accuse Lynch of an increasing loss of originality and heart—does anyone *really* expect a financially secure artist to approach his work with the same passions he exhibited as a starving unknown? Still, one used to approach a David Lynch film with the anticipation of entering mysterious new psychological and artistic territories. But instead of the innocence, beauty, and terror previously encountered in projects like *Eraserhead* and *The Elephant Man*, one now senses a superior (and cynical) attitude. From *Blue Velvet* onward, this previously unaffected director has become more mannered, self-imitative, and predictable; one gets the feeling that Lynch is now creating fashionably decadent films for a smugly hip audience, one more concerned with the reassurance that they are "with it" and "wised up" than with watching a good film.

Despite its blemishes, however, the Erotic Trilogy remains a fascinating study of sex and postmodernism. To explain that latter trait, one need only note that the increasing manner with which Lynch littered the trilogy with the detritus of pop culture—trendy beers, sleekly groomed women, Elvis songs, bondage magazines, the *Wizard of Oz*—is highly symptomatic of postmodernism itself.

The most oft-noted characteristic of postmodernist art is that it recycles earlier artistic and cultural forms and doesn't try to disguise this "borrowing." Indeed, postmodernism usually calls attention to its pilfered elements by placing them within figurative quotation marks. Unfortunately, the inherent weakness of postmodernism is not that it is limited to a dependence on a happy synthesis of preexisting elements; postmodernism is basically founded on *stealing*, which means no matter what the final result, the best works of the postmodernists usually come from somewhere else. And in our case, the best elements of the Erotic Trilogy come from the previous films of David Lynch.

Paradoxically, there is little question that *Blue Velvet, Twin Peaks*, and *Wild at Heart* are all well-crafted projects, ones bearing the obvious stamp of an iconoclastic director. Streaked throughout with arresting images, cutting-edge wit, and absorbingly twisted story lines, the Erotic Trilogy is a strikingly mounted thinking person's entertainment, eminently watchable and unpredictable. But as we have seen, a deeper examination of the trilogy indicates—in the aesthetic, not the commercial sense—that each subsequent version of this trio has been less successful than the one before it.

Despite the obvious strictures placed upon Lynch by commercial television, *Twin Peaks* is simply an arch rehashing of the primal abnormalities found in *Blue Velvet*, which in itself was a relatively simplistic study of innocence corrupted. *Wild at Heart*, on the other hand, is a rambling, loosely moored anthology of attitudes and shocks that does not even possess the jokey structural "integrity" of *Twin Peaks*.

Then again, why should David Lynch care about any of this? Right now he's more successful than he's ever been, what with his "Industrial Symphony" video, his weekly series of cartoons featuring the "Angriest Dog in the World," his upcoming coffee-table book of photographs, his October 1, 1990, cover story in *Time* magazine, his coproduced album of ballads (*Floating into the Night* sung by Lynchian protégée Jullee Cruise), and his recent series of Obsession commercials. The Lynchian spin-off machine has been brought up to steam, and with all this attendant success, should we simply write off David Lynch because he's been caught skinny-dipping in the mainstream?

No, but someone should tell him that this success is compromising his vision. And that's truly a shame. For from his earliest independent short films straight through the Erotic Trilogy, David Lynch has obsessively returned to a fascinating nest of personal themes. A film artist in the best sense of the word (although of the American Primitive variety, sort of like Grandma Moses on acid), Lynch has formulated a painstakingly stylistic/thematic working method uniquely his own. In fact, despite the generally negative tone of what has preceded (and will follow) this sentence, I remain a strong supporter and advocate of the films of David Lynch. His projects make me squirm and laugh at the same time, prick my imagination, and disturb my slumber. In fact, the greatest compliment I can bestow upon Lynch is that he makes me dream—with my eyes wide open.[18]

---

18. My regard for Lynch's work extends to his person as well. This appreciation stems from the fact that I worked in a minor capacity on both *Dune* and *Blue Velvet* (I produced/directed a seven-minute film for Universal Pictures titled "Destination Dune," and was employed by the De Laurentiis Entertainment Group to take charge of a special national *Blue Velvet* promotional campaign). Though we never became more than acquaintances, I did have the opportunity to watch Lynch at work in Mexico City for over a year on *Dune*, before then working with the man on a few *Blue Velvet* promotional activities. And my experiences lead me to affirm unhesitatingly that Lynch's reputation as a friendly, unaffected person is fully justified.

Unfortunately, now that I have written "The Salacious Gaze," my relationship with Lynch has probably been jeopardized, an effect no doubt exacerbated by Lynch's memories of the vicious political infighting surrounding me on *Dune*. This uncomfortable state of affairs was partially generated by a certain professional naïveté on my part and resulted in a bitter clash of personalities (*not*

Yet I'm worried about him, too. The Erotic Trilogy seems to be marked by a sensibility increasingly attuned to the mercantile possibilities inherent in a careful packaging of market-ready surrealism. While this tendency might make for a higher media profile and fatter bank account (remember all those *Twin Peaks* merchandising spin-offs?), sad experience has taught us that such a course can be extremely dangerous to one's artistic health (remember the crass franchising of Salvador Dali?).

David Lynch has become admired, well-known, and well-off, and because of that he stands at a particularly crucial crossroads. It is now up to him to decide whether he can successfully assimilate his personal concerns with the dictates of mainstream filmmaking (in the manner of, say, a David Cronenberg), or whether he will continue to dilute and parody his strengths. If Lynch succumbs to this second impulse, he may ultimately become the Andy Warhol of the nineties, a highly visible, commercially successful media celebrity who is also artistically bankrupt.

Yet there is a ray of hope within this gloomy prognosis. Lynch has recently announced that his next film will be the long-delayed *Ronnie Rocket*, a pet project that was stalled by the chapter-11 bankruptcy of the De Laurentiis Entertainment Group, which had been developing the film. Set to star three-foot-seven-inch Mike Anderson (the dancing dwarf of *Twin Peaks*), *Ronnie Rocket* is the bizarre story of an injured interdimensional being trapped by our own universe, and suggests that the simplistic concerns of the Erotic Trilogy may have been a passing fancy.

Let's hope so. Because if the fascinating but increasingly self-parodistic Erotic Trilogy is an indication of the manner in which Lynch intends to work through the next phase of his career, maybe he'd be better off forgetting about sex altogether.

Then David Lynch could get back to some earlier, healthier concerns.

Like mutant babies, pustule-faced madmen, and vomit crawling with flies.

David Lynch's, I hasten to add; on *Dune*, I was victimized by a classically insecure publicist).

In any event, I have taken great pains throughout "The Salacious Gaze" to criticize not the man, but the Erotic Trilogy. David Lynch was always a gentleman to me, and I wish him well.

I also hope his fame does not destroy his art.

Chapter

21

John Skipp & Craig Spector

I confess. *The Light at the End*, Skipp & Spector's first novel, sat on my bookshelf for a long time before I got around to reading it. It wasn't a priority. As a matter of fact, it was a used copy. By the time I read it, I had *The Cleanup* up there with it, and *The Scream* was not far off. But I did read it, and though I don't want to give "the boys" *too* much credit, everything changed.

It wasn't the best book I'd ever read, though a kick-ass novel by any standards and one that I have given as a gift more than once. But it was fun. The stuffy seriousness typical of traditional horror was nonexistent in this book. The novel was a roller coaster filled with gleefully mischievous adolescents screaming their lungs out as they plummeted to an uncertain fate accompanied by a rock-and-roll soundtrack and the good wishes of Bullwinkle Moose. I loved it. At a turning point in my life, it made me smile outwardly, and inwardly it confirmed my feelings about fiction. Though I loved (and still love) traditional horror, my heart was not in writing it. *The Light at the End* made me realize there were other options.

These literary terrorists are also responsible for many short stories, the novel *Deadlines*, the award-winning anthology *Book of the Dead* and its sequel, and their excellent screenplay was butchered into *Nightmare on Elm Street 5*. Skipp & Spector are the Rolling Stones of fiction, the "bad boys" of horror.

Death's Rich Pageantry, or Skipp & Spector's Handy-Dandy Splatterpunk Guide to the Horrors of Non-horror Film

by John Skipp & Craig Spector

Part 1: Introduction

We have a theory. Which is ours. Which we'd like, just briefly, to discuss with you. As with most theories, it's audacious, absurd, and utterly self-serving. But once you get the hang of it, it's also lots of fun. And not without an element of truth.

Stated plainly, it is this:

HORROR IS THE ENGINE THAT POWERS
EVERY MOVIE YOU EVER LOVED.

Before we go any further, we'd like to explain what we *don't* mean by that. We are *not*, for example, saying that horror movies are the only good movies in the world. Nor are we saying that all good movies are horror films. And we are *most certainly not saying* that all horror movies are good. Because, frankly, most of them suck.

But we will start out by stating the obvious: that the horror film, in its finest form, can be a work of art and a thing of beauty. From James Whale's *Frankenstein* to Robert Wise's *The Haunting*, from William Friedkin's *The Exorcist* to Jonathan Demme's *The Silence of the Lambs*, mainstream directors have often drawn on great works of horror fiction to produce their most powerful, lasting work.

And in the brilliant, original visions of genuine genre auteurs like David Cronenberg and George A. Romero, there are routinely moments of such aching acuity, storytelling depth, and sheer honest *transcendence* that the viewer is left going, "Jesus! This isn't just a great monster movie . . . this is a really great movie!"

But if this is true, then how about the converse: that a really great movie of *any* sort—from comedy to romance to grand, uplifting human drama—might be found, upon careful inspection, to carry the seeds of horror in its heart?

This has been our hypothesis, weird as it may sound. And now, with "Skipp & Spector's Handy-Dandy Splatterpunk Guide to the Horrors of Nonhorror Film," we have the means to answer the question.

Along the way, we will run over a hundred films—most of which are *by no means* considered horror movies—through the filter of Death's Rich Pageantry. Then we'll offer up another hundred and fifty or so for *you* to play with. We think you may be surprised by the results.

We'll also include, toward the end, some competitive suggestions for the horror movie industry (which could *use* some good competitive suggestions right about now).

But first—before we even attempt to define what horror *is*—let's take an off-the-wall, analytical look at one of the most highly regarded, non-genre-related films of all time.

Part 2: Exhibit A

In this case, "A" stands for *Amadeus*. And not only is it a textbook case; it even comes with its own recent, personal anecdote.

Once upon a time, not too very long ago, it was a slow Sunday night at the old Skipp homestead in historic Yorktowne, Pennsylvania. Some nice folks we'd recently met stopped by; and as per ancient Skipp custom, they were asked what film they wanted to see.

A quick scan by our guests of the ceremonial video library was, as ever, revealing as hell; you can learn a lot about a person by the films they love . . . and even more by the films they hate. (That's why it's so much fun to pepper the shelves with titles like *Café Flesh, Dr. Butcher, M.D.*, and *Faster, Pussycat! Kill! Kill!* It's a source of great joy to watch the eensy flickers of reaction in their eyes as they register the titles, like the bar-code scanner at a checkout line. You can almost hear the little *meep* sound when something connects, the wacky robot *wonk* that tells us *this-does-not-compute*.)

It didn't take long to figure out that our new friends were not really into horror movies. In *fact*—as they quickly pointed out with equal parts apology, embarrassment, and suspicion—they didn't much care for horror movies *at all*. Which meant no *meeps* for *Hellraiser, Suspiria,* or *The Hills Have Eyes*, big *wonks* for *Dawn of the Dead, The Gates of Hell*, and *The Texas Chainsaw Massacre*. Clearly, cop-with-a-camcorder crime-scene vids and autopsy footage were out of the question.

To their credit, *Jaws* rang a bell. So did *Aliens* and *The Exorcist*. But these were not the picks at the top of the list. The big *ooohs* and *ahhhs* went to: *All about Eve, Sex, Lies and Videotape, Citizen Kane, The Color Purple, Do the Right Thing*, and, perversely, *Pee-Wee's Big Adventure*. Which enabled us to draw a pretty good bead on the range of their tastes.

Then *Amadeus* came up, and they hadn't seen it, and we all knew at once that they'd love it to death. So we turned off the lights. Circulated the ritual refreshments. And settled down, in the darkened living-room theater, to let the twenty-five-inch flickering phosphor-dot screen have its way with us once again.

And this is what we saw:

In the first two minutes—before the opening credits—an ancient and decrepit F. Murray Abraham (in astonishing Dick Smith old-age makeup) tries to kill himself. Rather nastily, in fact: he uses a straight razor to slash his own throat. Next thing we know, he's on his way to a seventeenth-century Viennese insane asylum, where we soon learn that he's the long-forgotten court composer Salieri: a cagey, incredibly bitter old man who's been doomed to outlive his music and fame.

We also learn that he was once a contemporary of Wolfgang Amadeus Mozart. In fact, he claims to have *murdered* Mozart. And it is this story that we—like the priest to whom Salieri confesses—have come to hear.

Now, we're not going to recount the entire story. If you haven't seen it, go *rent* the son of a bitch. It's a superb film, full of sly and startling observations: about genius, mediocrity, and simple humanity; about ghosts, guilts, hauntings, and recriminations; art and commerce; freedom and stricture; love and hate; God and the vacuum. Both Abraham's chilling, heartbreaking Salieri and Tom Hulce's giddy, brilliant Mozart—a manic, tragic, incandescent party-animal savant—are unforgettable. As are everyone and everything else.

(And if you've never been, say, a *big fan* of opera, this here's yer chance: three hundred years of music-appreciation classes couldn't hold a candle to this one picture.)

But the heart of this Milos Forman film—even more than the music, the exquisite costumes and staging, or the fine performances—is Peter Shaffer's screenplay, based on his original stage play. And the core of Shaffer's story is a portrait of steadily mounting madness, a deconstruction of human monstrosity worthy of Edgar Allan Poe. It's the story of a man whom God has supplied with great ambition, a vision sublime, and very little genuine creative talent of his own, a man who, poisoned with jealousy and enraged at his fate, tells God to get fucked by setting out to destroy His own greatest musical instrument.

Then it all goes downhill from there.

It is, shall we say, a *pretty dark little number*.

Of course, everybody loved it: and because it was our umpteenth viewing, we were able to divide our attention between the screen and the faces of our new friends. Which was in itself, a revelation.

Because they sat there—these folks who did not like horror—literally spellbound *in the flickering dark: eyes shining, drinking in every thematic concern, every color and texture and tone. They laughed at the elegantly mounted jokes, shuddered at the grim implications drawn, cried at the senseless sufferings and ignominious ends.*

And all we could think, watching them watch the screen, was, "Jesus! This isn't just a great movie . . . *This is a really great monster movie!*"

Part 3: A Few Last Critical Hairsplitting Clarifications

So, wait a minute. Are we saying that *Amadeus* is a horror movie?

Well, *yes* . . . sort of. But we won't call it that. And here's where and why we draw the line.

Despite its dark heart, its sinister edges, and bounteous, cunning subversions, *Amadeus* is squarely a mainstream film. A *prestige* film, as it turns out, for the System: with eight, count 'em *eight*, Academy Awards, including Best Picture and Best Actor (Abraham). You'll find it listed under "Drama," should you seek it out, because drama is the word that Hollywood has appropriated for marketing "serious" properties.

And that, in many ways, is good. It lets you know where you're standing in the video store. But the moment you start classing drama as a *genre*, you've completely lost touch with the meaning of the word.

Because *drama*, if you check your *Webster's*, is the term originally designed to describe *any story propelled by conflict*. Its two primary faces are comedy and tragedy, like the masks that were worn to stage Mozart's undoing.

Now, we don't know about you, but the last time we looked, there was no "Tragedy" section in the video store. (No "Melodrama" section either, for all those goddamn sappy endings.) And whereas comedy has gobbled up a huge turf of its own—with no real differentiation between, say, a great film like *Harold and Maude* and a sorry pud-wanker like

Fraternity Vacation—*un*funny conflict resolution is spread out over several catagories: the aforementioned "Drama"; "Action/Adventure"; "Martial Arts"; "War"; "Western"; "Romance"; "Science Fiction."

And the subject of this essay: our ol' pal, "Horror."

But, once again, this is the point in the hairsplitting game where the follicles start to scream. Because the pundits, from good ol' Sigmund Freud to Douglas E. Winter, concur: horror is, at root, an *emotion*, not a genre. It's the psychic Cuisenart into which we throw *all of our fears:* about damage and loss; about death and disease; about the failure of our bodies, our minds, and our dreams.

And, getting back to that definition of drama for a second: *where the hell do you think all that conflict* comes *from? K Mart?*

No . . . it comes from *fear.*

That the horror is here, or fast approaching.

That if our heroes don't do *something*, something bad is gonna happen.

Fear is the natural province of horror; and horror is the worst-case scenario of fear. When the worst case goes down, you've got a moment of horror, *no matter what* kind of film you're watching.

It's important, at this point, to note that *only those films that wear their worst-case scenarios on their sleeves* wind up in the "Horror" section.

But horror is the secret ingredient in every conflict-driven film.

Or, as we posited earlier:

> HORROR IS THE ENGINE THAT POWERS
> EVERY MOVIE YOU EVER LOVED.

With this theory now firmly in place, let's step off the blackboard and into the trenches.

Part 4: Using the Handy-Dandy Guide

Our first category is called Dystopian Hells. And though it's top-heavy with science-fiction titles—from the grimly pragmatic *Soylent Green* to the devolutionary payback of *Planet of the Apes*, the dangerous new species of the *Terminator* and *Blade Runner*, to the monstrous, all-too-human Big Brothers of *1984* and *Brazil*—its horrors are by no means restricted to some future time that may never come.

If utopia is the place where everything's great, then dystopia is the place where everything's fucked; and it's no surprise that near-future nightmares like *The Handmaid's Tale* and *A Clockwork Orange* are often found in the "Drama" section, sandwiched in with historical hellholes like the insane asylums suffered by Jessica Lange in *Frances*, Oliver Reed in *The Devils*, or Jack Nicholson in *One Flew Over the Cuckoo's Nest*. Because, in concocting hells, the only thing worse than our possible future has got to be our most *certainly* horrible past.

These stories are spiritual kin to the school of Apocalyptic Visions, where the end of the world comes with both whimpers *and* bangs. They may not come from outer space (as in either *Invasion of the Body Snatchers*), or have metaphysical implications that defy explanation (as in Romero's *Dead* trilogy); but the thermonuclear oblivions predicted by *Threads, The Day After*, and *Miracle Mile* are nothing if not horrific.

At the same time, probably the *funniest* end-of-the-world film ever made would have to be Kubrick's *Dr. Strangelove or How I Learned to Stop Worrying and Love the Bomb*. Which conveniently airlifts us into Black Comedy territory.

And what puts the black into Black Comedy?

Why, that nasty ol' *horror* do!

Consider, just for starters, the suicide gags so central to both sublime entertainments like *Harold and Maude* and wacky ones like *Better Off Dead*. Consider the meditations on madness that inform the core of *King of Hearts, The Ruling Class*, and *How to Get Ahead in Advertising*. In *Little Shop of Horrors*, big plants eat people. In *Parents*, so do Mom and Dad. In *Heathers*, Winona Ryder's tean angst bullshit has a body count; while the bitter recriminations and fatal one-upmanships of the husband and wife in *The War of the Roses* are almost too painful to behold.

And then there are always the works of the legendary Monty Python: hilarious, brilliant, taboo-crunching films that consistently dance with the graphically appalling and the gleefully grotesque. From the Black Knight's flesh wounds in *The Holy Grail* to the live organ transplants and the loathsome, explosive, puke-disgorging Mr. Creosote in *The Meaning of Life*, the Pythons were and still remain the ultimate splatter comedians.

(Indeed, in the *orthodox* horror arena, only a handful of filmmakers have successfully gone to such lengths for a laugh. They include Stuart

Gordon (*Re-Animator*); Sam Raimi (*Evil Dead, Evil Dead 2*); Peter Jackson (*Bad Taste, Meet the Feebles*); Jim Muro (*Street Trash*); Dan O'Bannon (*Return of the Living Dead*); and, of course, Tobe Hooper, whose *Texas Chainsaw Massacre 2* could be subtitled *The Three Stooges Go to Hell*).

It's no coincidence, then, that the movies in our Fringoid Fun category draw a black-humor bead on their horrific hearts. In a world where the fishnet-and-gartered cannibalistic cabal of *Rocky Horror* paved the way for Richard Elfman's whacked-out, Max Fleischer-on-acid *Forbidden Zone* and Stephen Sayadian's twisted, horny, Day-Glo *Dr. Caligari*—a world in which the unbelievable sleazefests of Russ Meyer made David Lynch's *Wild at Heart* possible—humor and horror often wind up rutting together in the cinematic slop.

From there, it's a short, squalid plummet to *Nekromantik*, Jorg Buttgereit's ode to squishy necro love, in which two naked people use their actual genitalia to make it with the greasiest corpse in cinema history; and to *Fingered*, R. Kern's transgressive black-and-white short that features Lydia Lunch with a pistol up her twat. Both of these films owe a nod and a wink to John Waters, whose *Desperate Living, Female Trouble*, and especially *Pink Flamingos* blazed more inroads for sheer aesthetic ugliness than any other filmmaker before him.

But lest we digress, let us now slither past the rest of the Sleaze department—past *Bloodsucking Freaks* and *Frankenhooker, Basket Case*, and *Beyond the Valley of the Dolls*; past *The Gore-Gore Girls* and *Snuff* and *Ilsa, She-Wolf of the SS*; past *Make Them Die Slowly* and *Cannibal Holocaust*—to slightly higher ground. It's a long climb up to the Deeply Symbolic category, but by now the terrain has got to be looking mighty familiar.

Indeed, the distance between *Pink Flamingos* and Peter Greenaway's *The Cook, the Thief, His Wife and Her Lover* is simply a matter of breeding and income bracket. Where *Flamingos* is vile and seedy, *Cook/Thief* is vile and *sumptuous*; but on the issue of *vile*, they come together as two of the most hideous films ever made. (And we mean that in a *good* way. Honest.)

Joining the club is Pasolini's *Salo*, which catapults Nazi pedo/coprophilia into jolting high art. It has spiritual companions in Augustine Villaronga's *In a Glass Cage* and, weirdly, Alan Parker's adaptation of Roger Waters's *Pink Floyd: The Wall* (try 'em as a triple bill sometime). Also falling well within the High Grotesque category are Alejandro Jodorowsky's *El Topo* and, especially, *Santa Sangre*,

which use truly extraordinary visuals and *extremely* physical metaphors to help us negotiate Jodorowsky's profoundly torqued inner
terrains.

In these films, there is no image too intense, too blasphemous or
shattering for the artist to happily hammer us with. These are films that
stop at nothing to get their point across. They also segue nicely to the
What Is Reality? bin: that category devoted to altered states of
consciousness and the ultimate ground of being. From *Altered States* to
Dreamscape, *Brainstorm* to *Videodrome*, *Eraserhead* to *Jacob's Ladder*, these incredible psychic assaults suggest that there is plenty to fear
on the far side of the veil.

And like the paintings of Dali, Robert Williams, or Mati Klarwein,
the best of these films access chunks of the unconscious and bring them
back in their rawest, purest form. Indeed, it's a safe bet that before these
guys captured the images, *nothing like them existed to see* in the poor
old exterior universe. Your whole grip on consensual reality inescap-
ably *mutates* upon exposure to art like this. The world as you know it
is never quite the same.

Which brings us to the place we call the Twilight Zone: that
thoroughly unmistakable pocket of moral surrealism for *regular* folks
that Rod Serling's TV series defined so well. But did he invent that
window in the fabric of reality? And was he the first to gently lob
ordinary people through the shattering glass?

Of course not. In fact, quite a few of the world's most popular films
draw their strength from a frighteningly intimate familiarity with the
Zone. Take, for example, Frank Capra's *It's a Wonderful Life:* the story
of a suicidal guy who discovers what life without him would be like for
the people he loves and the town he'd leave behind . . . in short, a
Dystopian Hell of lovelessness, corruption, and despair.

Serling's motto was "Be careful what you wish for. It just might
come true." And this is certainly true of box-office bonanzas like Jerry
Zucker's *Ghost* and Penny Marshall's *Big. All of Me, The Witches of
Eastwick*, and both versions of *Heaven Can Wait* also fit this bill, if not
the bounty. (And as per any micro-genre, quality tends to run the gamut:
from the mood-drenched, TZ-flavored classic *Carnival of Souls* to the
drooling, insufferable Shelley Long vehicle *Hello Again*.)

Probably the ultimate Zone film is the Alastair Sim version of *A
Christmas Carol*, though any version will certainly qualify, up to
and including the very dark-yet-hilarious, *Beetlejuice*-scented Bill
Murray vehicle *Scrooged*. In each, the spirits of the tortured dead

are everywhere; but worse, the spirits of the *living* are everywhere starved, humiliated, crushed, and sullied. None worse than the spirit of that quintessential human monster, Scrooge: a man stripped of his capacity to love, with only greed and cruel self-interest to lend his life meaning.

And, pal, you can't *get* more fucking horrific than *that*.

Part 5: You're on Your Own/Full Speed Ahead

At this point, we suspect that you're probably pretty well info-glutted, and we're way over our word count. So, to expedite matters, we're breaking the remaining list into patented E-Z© Digestible Chunks. Just add the Secret Sauce, and *watch* how easily Death's Rich Pageantry runs straight through the body of cinematic culture like a rancid burrito.

Now that you've got the hang of it, you too can play. Use our categories, or invent your own. Mix 'em and match 'em. Collect 'em and trade 'em. Have arguments with film-loving friends and foes alike. Then see for yourself if searching for the horrific, black seed of Death's Rich Pageantry in the following titles doesn't change the way you look at the world of films.

Not to mention the world at large.

WAR IS . . . WELL, YOU KNOW!

SALVADOR / PLATOON / BORN ON THE FOURTH OF JULY
APOCALYPSE NOW / JOHNNY GOT HIS GUN / THE DEER HUNTER
FULL METAL JACKET / PATHS OF GLORY
PATTON / THE THIN RED LINE / THE DOGS OF WAR
THE GREEN BERETS / THE DIRTY DOZEN / THE LONGEST DAY
CATCH-22 / THE BOYS IN COMPANY C / HAMBURGER HILL

JUST 'CAUSE YOU'RE PARANOID DON'T MEAN THEY AIN'T OUT TO GET YOU

SEVEN DAYS IN MAY / EXECUTIVE ACTION
THE PARALLAX VIEW / THREE DAYS OF THE CONDOR
FAILSAFE / SILKWOOD / DAY OF THE JACKAL
THE ANDROMEDA STRAIN / COMA

HOMICIDAL HIJINKS
A. LONE WACKOS AND MAD VICTIMS

THE SILENCE OF THE LAMBS / MANHUNTER

THE STEPFATHER / PSYCHO / MAGIC

REPULSION / APARTMENT ZERO

MISERY / MOMMY DEAREST / GAMES

NIGHT OF THE HUNTER / NO WAY TO TREAT A LADY

HEART OF MIDNIGHT / DEAD CALM

SUNSET BOULEVARD / TAXI DRIVER / WAIT UNTIL DARK

TARGETS / HENRY: PORTRAIT OF A SERIAL KILLER

WHATEVER HAPPENED TO BABY JANE?

FATAL ATTRACTION / PLAY MISTY FOR ME

B. CRIME AND PUNISHMENT

THE GODFATHER I–III / GOODFELLAS

MILLER'S CROSSING / STATE OF GRACE

THE LONG GOOD FRIDAY / MARATHON MAN

KING OF NEW YORK / TO LIVE AND DIE IN L.A.

52 PICKUP / EIGHT MILLION WAYS TO DIE

SCARFACE / ONCE UPON A TIME IN AMERICA

MIDNIGHT EXPRESS / SHORT EYES

BLOOD SIMPLE / BODY HEAT / BODY DOUBLE

THE GRIFTERS / AFTER DARK, MY SWEET

THE POSTMAN ALWAYS RINGS TWICE

AT CLOSE RANGE / THE INCIDENT / RIVER'S EDGE

THE UGLY, BITTER TRUTH

WHO'S AFRAID OF VIRGINIA WOOLF?

TALK RADIO / SEX, DRUGS, AND ROCK 'N' ROLL

ALL ABOUT EVE / SOPHIE'S CHOICE

CITIZEN KANE / SEX, LIES AND VIDEOTAPE

MEAN STREETS / THE COLOR PURPLE

DAY OF THE LOCUST / OVER THE EDGE

DRUGSTORE COWBOY / MIDNIGHT COWBOY

BARFLY / THE HUSTLER / THE DAYS OF WINE AND ROSES

DANGEROUS LIAISONS / ALL THE PRESIDENT'S MEN

LOLITA / LENNY / . . . AND JUSTICE FOR ALL

IN THE HEAT OF THE NIGHT / MISSISSIPPI BURNING.
STAR 80 / SMOOTH TALK / WISH YOU WERE HERE
LAST EXIT TO BROOKLYN / THE ACCUSED

BITTERSWEET TRAGEDY / LAST GASPS

ALL THAT JAZZ / WHOSE LIFE IS IT, ANYWAY?
SWEET DREAMS / TERMS OF ENDEARMENT
THE WORLD ACCORDING TO GARP
STEEL MAGNOLIAS / BEACHES
OLD YELLER

YOU WILL NEVER BELONG

TORCH SONG TRILOGY / THE NAKED CIVIL SERVANT
THE BOYS IN THE BAND / DESERT HEARTS
MY BEAUTIFUL LAUNDRETTE / DO THE RIGHT THING
THE ELEPHANT MAN / FRANKENSTEIN / EDWARD SCISSORHANDS
SID AND NANCY / EASY RIDER / THE MAN WHO FELL TO EARTH
KING KONG / MIGHTY JOE YOUNG
OUTRAGEOUS / MY LEFT FOOT
GABY / BIRDY

MADCAP MAYHEM

DIE HARD / DIE HARD II
BEVERLY HILLS COP I & II / 48 HRS. I & II
RAIDERS OF THE LOST ARK / INDY II & III
any Norris / Seagal / Schwarzenegger / Eastwood / Van Damme vehicle.
THE BLUES BROTHERS / ANIMAL HOUSE
LETHAL WEAPON I & II / GHOSTBUSTERS I & II /
ROBOCOP I & II
BATMAN

AGAINST THE WALL

STRAW DOGS / THE WILD BUNCH
DELIVERANCE / SOUTHERN COMFORT
I SPIT ON YOUR GRAVE / MS. 45
DEATH WISH

CREEPY DEITIES

THE EXORCIST / EXORCIST III
AGNES OF GOD / ROSEMARY'S BABY
THE SEVENTH SIGN / THE OMEN
THE BELIEVERS / THE WICKER MAN
THE SERPENT AND THE RAINBOW

KIDDIE KALAMITIES

THE LITTLE MERMAID / ALL DOGS GO TO HEAVEN
BAMBI / DUMBO / PINOCCHIO
CINDERELLA / 101 DALMATIONS
SNOW WHITE AND THE SEVEN DWARFS
HONEY, I SHRUNK THE KIDS
THE SECRET OF NIMH / THE LAND BEFORE TIME
THE WIZARD OF OZ / RETURN TO OZ
THE PRINCESS BRIDE / THE NEVER ENDING STORY

HEARTBREAK HOTEL

WUTHERING HEIGHTS
(We rest our case.)

And this isn't even counting porn, biker flicks, coming-of-age stories, sword and sorcery, martial arts, most foreign films, *all* TV movies, and a thousand other examples for each and every category.

Which means, in these cinema-literate times:

You could watch five movies a day, every day, for a year, and receive your daily adult requirements of murder, mayhem, madness, mortality, gloom, doom, despair, revulsion and revelation . . .

WITHOUT WATCHING A SINGLE "HORROR" FILM.

And this is not a bad thing—in fact, it's a *wonderful* thing, to be inundated with such infinite variety. But since this is a book of essays on horror in film, it's only right that we should address the end of this piece to the horror-film community. Particularly for a genre that's struggling so hard with its reputation—*it is viable? is it dead? is it moral? is it safe?*—the following should hopefully provide some food for thought.

Part 6: Full Circle/Why Most Monster Movies Suck

It is at this point that the two of us, as both writers and lovers of horror in film, *diverge* on one little noncritical issue of taste. Though we're both still crossing the same bridge, toward the same destination, one of us likes to take the low road a whole lot more than the other one does.

Which is to say that Spector believes he could live a full and fruitful life without *ever* having to watch *Three on a Meathook, Bride of the Monster, Biohazard, City of the Walking Dead, Barn of the Naked Dead, Cathy's Curse, Demented, Slumber Party Massacre, Night of the Demons,* or *Microwave Massacre.* He claims that he can literally *feel* the brain cells dying, like sparks flying off a burning building, every time another dimwit dipshit slice-'n'-dice-a-thon trundles across the screen.

Skipp, on the other hand, *lives* for movies like *Guns Don't Argue, Robot Monster, Satan's Black Wedding,* and (especially) Ed Wood, Jr.'s, *Orgy of the Dead*: movies so retarded, so utterly clueless that intellectuals are literally *forced* to hallucinate deeper meaning in them. They—the intellectuals, that is—can't believe, much less accept, that anything could actually *be* that fucking stupid. It's the grim confirmation of their deepest fear.

But there is it—*gasp*—*right before their eyes*.

(In fact, Spector claims that when Skipp dies, it won't be *his* life that flashes before his eyes: it will be the amazing Criswell from *Orgy*— resplendent in cheesy Lugosi-style cloak and hilarious ill-fitting bleached-blond hairpiece—coughing up a silent Thorazine hairball of approval as a woman in a sorry-ass Halloween cat suit performs the most pathetic striptease in human history. And the terrible thing is, Spector might be right.)

But, all aesthetic differences aside, the point where we both come together is this: *We both know it's crap*. There are no illusions.

Which is why we feel comfortable pointing out the following ugly truth:

MOST HORROR MOVIES ARE THE SPIRITUAL
SIAMESE TWINS OF THE LOWEST, MOST INCONTINENT,
AND BRAIN-DEAD GRADE-Z CINEMATIC DRIBBLE
IN THE WHOLE WIDE WORLD.

Which is to say that: when smart people say they don't like horror movies, we shouldn't be particularly surprised. Because the best thing you can say about most of them is that *they tend to underachieve*.

This rankles us no end, principally because we *love* horror movies. We just wish there were more good ones. We suspect we're not alone.

To that end, we'd like to offer up a handful of suggestions for today's horror filmmakers. They're all pretty basic. And they just might be crazy enough to work.

1. *Use quality scripts*. Most horror films, the truth to tell, have zip in the imagination department, creative use of power tools, foam latex and air bladders notwithstanding. And though you can often cite lousy direction, acting, FX, camerawork, editing, lighting, or sound—not to mention no budget—it's not always the case. Indeed, from a production standpoint, a lot of these films are *pretty damn good*. And most of the people who labor long and hard to bring them to life are dedicated and enthusiastic professionals who are doing it because *they* genuinely love movies.

On the other hand, there's almost *always* a shitty script at the core of a shitty film. Nine times out of ten. Shitty scripts are easy enough to spot: they're riddled with holes, rife with coincidence, festooned with clots of ersatz suspense that build toward wholly predictable conclusions, and literally *slopping over* with underdeveloped nonpeople who only become interesting when you think about how to kill them.

And then just barely. ('Cuz face it, folks: if the audience doesn't care about your characters when they're whole, they *sure* ain't gonna care about 'em in pieces.)

Shitty scripts are responsible for most of the straight-to-video stillbirths in the horror-movie field. They throttle rich and poor alike. Shitty scripts, for example, succeeded—where *dozens* of psychic, well-armed, or just plain stupid teenagers had failed—in killing off the incredibly successful Freddy (*Nightmare on Elm Street*) Krueger and Jason (*Friday the 13th*) Voorhees. Well-mounted, big-budget losers like *Leviathan* and *The First Power* sank like stones on the derivative absentee merits of their patently shitty scripts. As did innumerable, far humbler crash-'n'-burn cases.

And while a shitty script is no guarantee of failure—nor a fine script, for that matter, any guarantee of success—the movies that people really love are almost *always* dripping with authenticity, if not actual integrity.

So . . .

2. *Really mean it*. Any good drama demands the courage of its

convictions. Horror movies are certainly no exception to this rule; at the very least, a little sincerity in the screenplay wouldn't *hurt*. Which means not cheating us poor ol' popcorn-munching, ticket-buying movie fans: *not* assuming we're so witless and stupid that we're incapable of seeing that *Titanic*-sized hole in the plot that just sucked every drop of credibility from your pathetically floundering piece-o'-shit picture.

This assumption—often referred to by savvy movie types as the "Roller-Coaster Ride" theory—(i.e., "Come on. They'll never notice. It's a *roller-coaster ride!*")—is the most pernicious, self-defeating and utterly bogus supposition currently undermining Hollywood film. It's an assumption that benefits *no one:* not the lazy, lame filmmakers who fob them off, or the audiences for whom this rickety Cheeze Whiz was intended.

No one likes to be talked down to: even the dimmest cretin will rise commensurate to the level of respect accorded him. And most people, dumb as they might be, are smarter than you think. Given the diminishing returns of the last few years, even the most callous corporate greedhead should know that the percentage in underestimating increasingly cinema-literate viewers is minuscule compared with what could actually be gained by taking the high road.

3. *Don't shoot the messengers*. In all fairness, the writer is quite often not to blame for the film that results from his or her labor; a great script can be hamstrung at any point along the way. Quite often, *no one person* is actually to blame—not the writer, or the producer, or the director. Sometimes it's the *process* that sabotages the film.

Movie making is a collaborative process so convoluted and intrinsically compromising that it's a miracle that any films get made *at all*—no less any good ones. And a lot of fatal judgment calls fall pretty squarely into one of two bins: a) *Seemed Like a Good Idea at the Time*; b) *Couldn't See the Forest for the Trees*.

But either way, when the room goes dark and the screen lights up, it's the story that matters. Fine acting and dazzling special effects and masterful cinematography are all wonderful in the service of a great *story*; but without it, they don't mean squat.

All of which means . . .

4. *Look for the Good Stuff*. There's more to horror than movies with numbers behind the title, desperately rehashing last year's prefab moneymaker. We'd like to suggest that today's horror filmmakers stop

inbreeding for just a minute and take a peek at some of the truly great original modern horror *fiction* currently being produced.

Among contemporary novels that would make great movies, we unhesitatingly recommend: Kathe Koja's *The Cipher*; Nancy A. Collins's *Sunglasses After Dark*; Dan Simmons's *Song of Kali*; Joe R. Lansdale's *The Drive-in*; Ray Garton's *Live Girls*; David J. Schow's *The Kill Riff*; Poppy Z. Brite's *Lost Souls*; Robert R. McCammon's *Stinger*; Ramsey Campbell's *The Face That Must Die;* Iain Banks's *The Wasp Factory;* and John Farris's *Son of the Endless Night*.

Add to this list writers like Elizabeth Massie, Mort Castle, Wayne Allan Sallee, Rex Miller, Edward Bryant, Pat Cadigan, K. W. Jeter, Karl Edward Wagner, Steven R. Boyett, Philip Nutman, Douglas E. Winter, Dennis Etchison, and the multifarious John Shirley, and it becomes clear that Stephen King, Clive Barker, and Dean R. Koontz are not the only guys in the horror kingdom. Excellent as they most certainly are, *they are not alone.* To assume so is to miss out on an inexhaustible supply of fresh, frightening, original ideas that are out there, just waiting for filmmakers of passion, ambition, and vision.

And in the realm of working horror screenwriters, we would be remiss in the extreme were we not to mention guys like Richard Christian Matheson and Mick Garris (*Red Sleep*), Eric Red (*Near Dark*), Charles Edward Pogue (*The Fly*), David J. Schow, again (*Leatherface*), William Goldman (*Misery*), and especially Bruce Joel Rubin, whose *Ghost* and *Jacob's Ladder* were, respectively, the most successful and most challenging supernatural films of the decade to date.

5. *Don't miss out on the lessons of Death's Rich Pageantry.* Which means: Don't hesitate to draw from the *nonhorrific strengths* of your story. Just as all great conflict-driven films gotta have a tiger in their tanks, all great horror gains its substance and soul from the elements that define every *other* form of drama: sexuality (of every bent), the family tree (from parents and children to siblings and primordial ancestors), friendship, community, loneliness, isolation, success and failure, church and state, work and school, economics, politics, love, war, and, above all, simple day-to-day human *survival*.

Because all movies—all *art*—ultimately draw from the same subject matter. And that matter is the substance of life. Life *and* Death's Rich Pageantries are most assiduously aligned at the point where they talk about issues that *count*.

And in the end, quality is purely and solely the measure of *how real* you dared to be.

And what you dared to *do* about it.

Well, thanks for your time. We deeply regret any bile generated or brain cells you may have lost along the way; and we hope that this analysis will prove to be, in the long run, both handy and dandy for you.

So if you find yourself watching, say, *Return to Gilligan's Island* and going, "My God! This is a comic, absurdist, horrific dystopian *hell*!"

Just rest assured: *you're not alone*. We're all in this nightmare together. And the best we can do is to try to help each other sort it out.

Hence, the art of communication.

And all of death's rich pageantry.

Chapter

22

Stanley Wiater

I first became acquainted with Stan in his role as the sometimes official, sometimes unofficial toastmaster of the New England Horror Convention (NECON). I knew I'd seen the name, but it took me a while to realize that, like Phil Nutman, I knew him from the pages of *Fangoria,* where he spent quite a number of years as contributing editor and earned his reputation as the horror genre's leading interviewer.

He has since compiled two volumes of interviews, *Dark Dreamers: Conversations with the Masters of Horror* and *Dark Visions: Conversations with the Masters of the Horror Film.* An acknowledged splatter-film expert and creator of the term "cineteratology," he has also been contributing editor to *Fear* (U.K.), *New Blood,* and *Horrorstruck* magazines. His short stories have appeared in such anthologies as *Masques II* and *III* and *Obsessions* as well as in several national magazines. He has edited two anthologies, *Dark Visions 7* and *After the Darkness.* He reports that he is currently at work on "a series of very disturbing horror books for very little children."

The following essay came to fruition one thoroughly enjoyable night at Monsieur Bissette's house. Steve, Phil Nutman, and I laughed ourselves silly over the video exploits of a flatulent televangelist while Stanley compiled his list, using the Bissette library, and Steve and Phil's brains, as reference points. It was an interesting evening.

Disturbo 13:
The Most Disturbing Horror Films Ever Made

by Stanley Wiater

Any cineteratologist can come up with a credible list of the most frightening movies ever made. The list changes somewhat with each new generation of horror historians, but most can readily acknowledge how *Psycho, Jaws, The Exorcist,* and *Halloween,* to name a few classics at random, have been supremely capable of scaring the hell out of us.

But now consider this: *What if scaring the hell out of us just wasn't the primary intent of the filmmaker?*

Remember what Stephen King once said about the various levels of horror, and how, when nothing seems capable of affecting the audience, you then "go for the gross-out"?

Using that exquisitely unpoetic term, here are *the* films that best instill that unsettling sensation in the gut of any caring, feeling, rational human being. Thirteen movies that go beyond frightening—go beyond being *any* form of cinematic entertainment—and are just balls-to-the-wall *disturbing.* So-called cult films that are so unrelentingly perverse they make us regret having watched them. And, ultimately, make us disgusted to be of the same species of animal portrayed in these motion pictures.

No time for any further warning—here is the ultimate in blood, gore, madness, and depravity, our all-night horror show of horror shows: Disturbo 13. Just remember to

KEEP REPEATING: IT'S ONLY A MOVIE. . . .

1. *Salo, The 120 Days of Sodom* (1977). The last film from controversial Italian director Pier Paolo Pasolini, *Salo* is a well-mounted adaptation of the infamous work by the Marquis de Sade. Updated to World War II when the Fascists have overtaken Italy, this movie is almost unwatchable because it makes a heartfelt attempt to be as disgusting cinematically as de Sade (the man who gave sadism its very name) was in print.

The plot line has a group of adolescents being used as human fodder to satisfy the perverted desires of a band of Fascists who have occupied a castle in war-torn Italy. The Fascists are also using the spoken memoirs of several prostitutes to ignite their already sick imaginations—as then they endeavor to carry out the most perverse scenarios the human mind can devise.

What Pasolini supposedly was attempting to do here was concoct a parallel between the depravity of de Sade with the depravity of the Fascist state which was Italy in World War II. However, Pasolini seems to relish staging the obscene tableaus in all their loathsomeness far more than condemning them. Beyond the numerous rapes (both heterosexual and homosexual) and sexual perversions, we are shown extremely realistic scenes of young people being forced to dine on a meal of cooked shit, people urinating or shitting on one another, or choking on broken glass hidden in apparently edible food.

Whatever his moral intentions may have been, Pasolini wallows so deeply in the filth that it's impossible to do anything but have an automatic gag reflex to the entire motion picture.

. . . IT'S ONLY A MOVIE . . .

2. *Man Behind the Sun* (1988). A very obscure Chinese film—the English credits list only the director (T. F. Mous) and the producer (Fu Chi); no other actors or technical credits are given. The title is also questionable, as the subtitles indicate the literal translation from Chinese would be *Manchu 731 Squadron*. Whatever the title, this is an incredibly grim film, one which purports to tell the true story of the 731 Squadron, a group of Japanese scientists experimenting with biological warfare in occupied China at the very end of World War II.

Just as the Nazi scientists used concentration-camp victims for their hideous experimental efforts to see how much punishment a human body could take and still survive, the scientists of 731 Squadron are shown using the imprisoned natives of Manchu province as their guinea pigs. This is the core of the plot—the vivid demonstrations of these various experiments in human endurance. The handsomely produced film is presented very much like a documentary. Watching this movie is very much like being taken on a guided tour of a factory designed to create hell on earth.

In one unbearable scene, a young boy (the only character the filmmakers have allowed us to develop any sympathy for) is injected with a biological plague. While still alive—to see how fast the plague travels through his body—the young boy is next taken to the operating room. There a group of jovial doctors literally cut him into pieces and put his organs into assorted glass jars. The camera never once moves away from the sight of the scalpels shredding the flesh as the strangers' hands dip inside and cold-bloodedly remove the boy's living organs.

How much of the story is historically accurate I honestly don't know, but the idea that any studio (for this is a major production, not a low-budget exploitation flick) would want to remind us of these unspeakable horrors is something almost beyond imagining.

. . . IT'S ONLY A MOVIE . . .

3. *I Spit on Your Grave* (1980). Originally released—and forgotten–as *Day of the Woman*, this very low budget revenge film received instant cult notoriety when critics Gene Siskel and Roger Ebert lambasted it on their nationally syndicated television show. Why? Written and directed by Israeli filmmaker Meir Zarchi, who shot it somewhere in rural New York, *I Spit on Your Grave* contains perhaps the most prolonged and graphic scenes of rape ever filmed. The plot is incredibly simple and direct: a young woman (Camille Keaton) rents a cabin out in the country. Alone, she is set upon and then brutally and repeatedly raped by four men. That's *the entire first half of the movie:* scenes of this woman being raped and beaten and sodomized by four different men—one of them portrayed as a pathetic mental defective.

The second half of the movie is devoted to showing how this resourceful young woman takes the law into her own hands and fatally dispatches each of her attackers in the most lurid and cruel manner possible. When the last one is dead, the movie just ends.

Some critics have defended this unrelentingly cruel film as a feminist revenge fantasy in the sense that the victim gives her attackers just what they deserved, and then some. However, the fact that the protagonist is a very attractive woman who doesn't hesitate to use her physical attributes to "seduce" the men into compromising positions before attacking them certainly muddies the moral waters. It is one ideal to make a brutal film condemning rape, it is another to portray the four rapists as exhibiting "acceptable" behavior toward women so that a female can later use her sexuality to "naturally" destroy the male.

Whatever *I Spit on Your Grave* is trying to say about rape, about the only conclusion that can be reached from viewing it is that both sexes are thoroughly violated and debased. It's the kind of slimy cinematic experience that makes you want to take a long shower after its final blood-drenched climax.

. . . IT'S ONLY A MOVIE . . .

4. *Bloodsucking Freaks* (1977). This was reportedly first released as *The Incredible Torture Show*—a far more apt title to describe this truly sick film's entire reason for existence. Produced, written, and directed by New York auteur Joel Reed, this very low budget production tries to excuse its nauseating excesses by purporting to be the blackest of black comedies. Unfortunately, the amoral filmmakers seem to be enjoying themselves far too much for *Bloodsucking Freaks* to be anything more than a sadist's red wet dream.

Clearly inspired by the early gore films of Herschell Gordon Lewis, the film has a mad magician named "Sardu" running a Grand Guignol theater off-off Broadway. The theater is a cover so Sardu and company can torture and then slay their unfortunate victims. Not too surprisingly, the victims consist almost entirely of young, naked, attractive females.

When not actually killing women, Sardu passes the time by using their bodies as human dart boards, serving tables, and urinals. Every scene is meant, of course, merely as a huge joke. Check the laughs in this scene: A demented dentist friend of Sardu's first pulls out a woman's teeth with a pair of pliers, then drills a hole into the woman's skull. Inserting a straw into her brain, he then begins to suck the woman's brains out. Get the joke? Reportedly produced by people usually involved in hard-core pornography, and it shows. *Bloodsucking Freaks* is that rare film that is *completely* without redeeming value; it's not even "bad" enough to qualify as offensive camp.

. . . IT'S ONLY A MOVIE . . .

5. *Last House on the Left* (1972). Produced by former porno filmmaker Sean Cunningham (who later went on to produce the first *Friday the 13th*) and the directorial debut of Wes Craven (who went on to direct *The Serpent and the Rainbow, A Nightmare on Elm Street,* and several others) this is one of the vilest films to ever attain respectability as a horror "classic." In truth, its classic status primarily lies in the fact that, as indicated, both men have both since had very successful careers in the genre. Otherwise, this cheap and ugly film would probably be

totally—and thankfully—forgotten. (Although for some inexplicable reason, this is one of critic Roger Ebert's favorite horror films. His review was even used in the movie's posters.)

Supposedly inspired by Ingmar Bergman's classic *Virgin Spring* (!), the story line has a gang of toughs (both male and female) brutalizing, raping, and finally murdering two teenage girls. By chance, they end up at the house of one of the slain girls, and when the parents discover what has happened to their daughter, they naturally become far more vicious and depraved than the trapped gang of punks in exacting their revenge. That the movie was shot on a shoestring budget with a cast of totally unknown "actors" only adds to the gruesome sensation of watching a *cinema verité* docudrama rather than a shameless piece of exploitation catering only to our basest senses. (For example, the story includes one of the cinema's first demises by fellatio/castration.)

In any other genre, *Last House on the Left* would be a credit a first-time director or producer would do their best to make disappear, not be revered as a milestone in splatter-cinema history.

. . . IT'S ONLY A MOVIE . . .

6. *Maniac* (1980). Many movies have used this ultimate horror title over the years. However, accept no substitutes. This is the low-budget gore film that is so completely devoid of any moral perspective that even Tom Savini—who delivered the state-of-the-art special makeup effects—later disowned it. The perfunctory story line has a "mama's boy" (played by character actor Joe Spinell, who also produced the movie and cowrote the screenplay) going about the city slaying various women, scalping them, and then nailing their scalps to his collection of mannequins. Which he then proceeds to bang in a different way.

Not too surprisingly, the entertainment value in *Maniac* is nil. The plot, such as it is, is basically a showcase for Savini's incredibly realistic and gory special makeup effects. The torture and disfigurement and dismemberment of women is shown in loving detail, for those who care to watch the walls run red with their blood. Yet another film supposedly backed by those involved in the hard-core pornography industry, the *Maniac*'s filmmakers' cold-blooded mentality is continually evident in the unrelentingly misogynistic attitude that women are good for only two functions: fucking or killing (and not necessarily in that order). The film's only value may be for someone studying the career of special makeup effects master (and now director) Savini. Producer/writer/star Spinell died before getting a *Maniac 2* under way. Read into that what you will.

. . . IT'S ONLY A MOVIE . . .

7. *Cannibal Holocaust* (1979). Considered the most brutal of the already incredibly savage series of cannibal films produced by Italian filmmakers in the 1970s. The reasons why there first *was* a series of cannibal films (with such Americanized titles as *Trap Them and Kill Them, Make Them Die Slowly, Slave of the Cannibal God*) can't be adequately explored here. (Indeed, cineteratologist Stephen R. Bissette has just written an entire book on the subject.) But rest assured that the basic plot of nearly all of them involves white explorers going deep into the jungles of the Amazon, encountering cannibals, and suffering a most hideous fate.

Of course, being eaten alive isn't always the worst of it, as the female explorers are usually gang-raped, while the men's genitals are cut off or the tops of their skulls are sliced open like coconuts so the brains can then be munched on for dessert. Believe it or not, this is standard behavior in nearly every one of these movies: anyone can be somebody else's next meal.

In *Cannibal Holocaust,* much of the unrelenting gruesomeness lies in the explicit scenes of live animal slaughter. Unlike nearly all of the other cannibal films, these acts are *not* committed by the natives, with the viewer assuming these animals were later eaten by savages in a typically savage manner. Here the slaughter is committed by the explorers as part of the plot. Either way, the very idea of animals being literally butchered as part of a fictional story where human beings are supposedly butchered is morally indefensible, to say the least. The artistic intent of the filmmakers is, of course, to make us suspend our disbelief that human beings are being literally slain as well.

The unending scenes of cruelty are almost indescribable; the only moral lesson supposedly to be learned is that the "civilized" Western explorers are as bloodthirsty as the savages. At one point, two of the explorers gang-rape a native girl. Later she is punished by her tribe by being impaled on a massive pole—which is driven up through her vagina right out through her mouth.

In what it says about the human condition, *Cannibal Holocaust* just gets darker and bleaker and bloodier. It should come as no great shock that the only way for the movie to conclude is for no one to get out alive.

. . . IT'S ONLY A MOVIE . . .

8. *Henry: Portrait of a Serial Killer* (1986). One of the most celebrated "sick" movies in recent years, partially because when the filmmakers submitted it to the MPAA board the film was condemned with an X purely for its "unacceptable moral tone." Whether or not the X was deserved in terms of the standard belief that the rating defines pornography, there can still be no doubt that *Henry* is definitely hard core in its merciless examination of the life and crimes of a serial killer.

Directed by John McNaughton and starring Michael Rooker, the film was made in 1986, but had little commercial exposure until its videocassette release in 1990. The film was shot on a very low budget in Chicago. The story line brings us directly into the boring, lower-middle-class life of a young man named Henry. The sort of guy you wouldn't mind having a beer with once in a while or baby-sitting your kids on short notice. Trouble is, the only way he knows how to enjoy himself sexually is by torturing, raping, and snuffing women. The film opens with the ghastly aftereffects of a bloody murder; the film ends with Henry casually disposing of his latest victim in a moist suitcase by the side of the road.

Though it is far from a wall-to-wall bloodbath, what makes *Henry* so goddamn chilling is the technical quality of the production; the direction and script and acting are all first-rate. For once, the filmmakers were deadly serious in their endeavor to make us all react personally as voyeuristic accomplices to the most violent depths of sociopathic behavior. And they succeed completely—everyone at one time or another has met someone who looks or acts on the surface just like Henry. That's the first moment at which we're terrified by what we're seeing: *Henry* is a cracked mirror held too close to our own darkest reflections.

. . . IT'S ONLY A MOVIE . . .

9. *In a Glass Cage* (1986). Another obscure import, this very well made movie was produced in Spain, apparently by a group of serious filmmakers. Nevertheless, *In a Glass Cage* is a truly loathsome love story, dealing with a former Nazi commandant in the early 1950s who, after a fall, is forced to exist in an iron lung (the glass cage of the title). As his wife cannot care for him alone, she advertises for a male nurse, and the young man who gets the job just happens to be one of her husband's former sexually abused and tortured child victims.

The film has several levels of perversity, not the least of which is the way the Nazi commandant continues to revel in his memories of sexual torture. Meanwhile, the young man at one point becomes so enraptured by the commandant's fantasies that he brings in a procession of young boys the imprisoned man can watch *him* torture. There is also the blatantly stated homosexual love/hate relationship between the two men. This aspect is unusually cruel, with one scene depicting the commandant's iron lung being turned on and off so that, while he is temporarily choking to death, the male nurse can masturbate on his face.

The lush production values, compelling acting, and decidedly unusual plot conspire to keep the viewer from turning away from *In a Glass Cage*. However, any movie that opens with a man viciously whipping a naked boy hanging from the ceiling cannot be construed as anything but seriously disturbing.

. . . IT'S ONLY A MOVIE . . .

10. *Nekromantik* (1988). This German film by Jorg Buttgereit may well qualify as one of the most repulsive movies ever made. The basic plot is enough to turn away all but the most jaded: a young ambulance driver named Rob brings home unclaimed accident victims to show off to his wife. At first he simply collects pieces of the bodies in glass jars. Later on, the couple try to bring some joy back into their listless love life by going to bed with a recently discovered corpse. Since the penis has long since rotted away, they trim off a broom handle, slip a condom over it, and stick it into the groin of the corpse. Then it's a sweaty *ménage à mort*.

For some strange reason, the wife decides to leave him, and Rob unsuccessfully attempts to find sexual release with other women. When he can't, he's forced to murder his lovers before he can become sufficiently aroused to conclude the act. Finally, suicide seems like a sensible turn-on when all else fails. An unrelenting ode to necrophilia, *Nekromantik* is such a black hole of nihilism that if it weren't for the second-rate special makeup effects, it would be all but impossible to sit through.

. . . IT'S ONLY A MOVIE . . .

11. *Ilsa, She Wolf of the SS* (1974). Not the first motion picture to exploit the sadism of the Nazis during World War II and certainly not the last, what is so disturbing about *Ilsa* is that it has become a cult classic. What the attraction may be of a beautiful female commandant (played with gleeful relish by Dyanne Thorne) in a camp where only

female prisoners are endlessly tortured in ghastly "scientific experiments" is certainly open to question. Just the idea of using torture as a form of entertainment is reprehensible enough, but when one realizes that all the tortures depicted in the movie may actually have occurred in the concentration camps, the mind if not the stomach certainly reels. (Add to this the report that the film was shot on the standing set of the television sitcom *Hogan's Heroes,* and the stomach reels as well.)

There isn't a single likable character in the movie—and when Ilsa isn't whipping some naked prisoner, she is shown as a nymphomaniac fucking a different man every night. And any man that doesn't satisfy her insatiable sexual desires is summarily tied down on the operating table and castrated the following morning. Fortunately—if that is the right word—the acting and direction are so over the top that *Ilsa* can perhaps be thought of as "camp"—a Nazi version of *The Rocky Horror Picture Show.*

Amazingly enough, *Ilsa, She Wolf of the SS* is only the first in a series, each movie placing the seemingly immortal Ilsa in a different time period and section of the globe. For those who need to know, they are: *Ilsa, Harem Keeper of the Oil Shieks, Ilsa, Tigress of Siberia,* and *Ilsa, Wicked Warden.* (Originally titled *Wanda, the Wicked Warden* and later transmogrified into an official *Ilsa* movie.) Like the first film, each is filled to vomiting with well-staged scenes of sexual perversion and torture to titillate the fantasies of any true sadist.

. . . IT'S ONLY A MOVIE . . .

12. *Combat Shock* (1984). An extremely personal, overwhelmingly depressing, low-budget film written, produced, and directed by New Yorker Buddy Giovinazzo. Originally *American Nightmares,* it was retitled and reportedly toned down by the notorious exploitation film company Troma so as to secure an R rating and a videocassette release. Even "toned down," the movie is still one of the most uncompromisingly bleak examinations of a person's dead-end existence ever made. (In a critique, Chas. Balun states that the movie had been "thrown out of over fifty film festivals.")

Combat Shock is the tragic story of a wasted Vietnam veteran, living in abject poverty in the Bronx with his wife and baby. Every day is a battle to stay alive; every night is a battle to retain what's left of his steadily eroding sanity. If this weren't bad enough, the couple's baby is not quite human, having been genetically damaged by the aftereffects of agent orange brought home by Dad as an added legacy of lifelong despair.

Combat Shock is so painful because the filmmakers make absolutely no pretense to soothe us with even a moment of happiness for anyone in the movie. Every pitiful character is shown to be hopeless, knowing only drugs and violence and suffering. Incredibly, the man's situation gets even worse—finally concluding with an extended murder-suicide bloodbath after putting the baby into an oven and turning it on high. Nearly unbearable in its raw intensity, *Combat Shock* makes the violence and nihilism in *Taxi Driver* seem like something produced by Walt Disney.

. . . IT'S ONLY A MOVIE . . .

13. *Eraserhead* (1978). Although writer-director David Lynch has gained a considerable reputation in recent years due to such projects as *Blue Velvet* and the television series *Twin Peaks,* his first feature film will forever be his most twisted. Shown originally mostly in art houses and at film festivals, *Eraserhead* is so unfailingly creepy that no one can completely forget it. The movie is structured with the logic of a nightmare, its characters are abnormal people who consume meals that may or may not be still alive, and its protagonists are the parents of a grotesque little baby that is definitely not human. At ninety minutes in length, the movie nevertheless seems to go on forever for anyone trying to anticipate what's going to happen next, and *why*.

Shot in stark black-and-white, the movie shows Lynch at his most outrageous, as unsettling image after unsettling image unspools across the screen like the loosening bandages of a critical accident victim. Cineteratologist Richard Meyers has called it "a live action Monty Python animation made in hell." Whatever *Eraserhead* may be, it can be truly considered one of those films that forever changes your perception of "reality." At the very least, you get the incomparable sensation of being awake in the center of a truly disturbing bad, bad dream.*

KEEP REPEATING: IT'S ONLY A MOVIE. . . .
KEEP REPEATING: IT'S ONLY A MOVIE. . . .
KEEP REPEATING: IT'S ONLY A MOVIE. . . .
DISTURBO 13

*The essayist wishes to thank Chas. Balun and Stephen R. Bissette for being bold enough to preview the titles ultimately selected for the final list of thirteen.

Chapter

23

Douglas E. Winter

Doug is the exception. He may well be the guy who's seen just as many horror movies as Bissette. The most amazing thing about this is that he has an honest-to-god, briefcase and office job. Attorney Winter's colleagues are, no doubt, surprised to learn of their partner's penchant for black clothing and the films of Dario Argento. But his moonlighting as one of Washington, D.C.'s, most respected lawyers does not interfere with his love of horror, on both page and screen, and his love affair with western string ties. He may be the only attorney in America with Dario Argento movie posters on his office walls. Yeah . . . explain that to clients.

He first came to the attention of the horror community at large as the author of *Stephen King: The Art of Darkness*, widely regarded as the definitive discussion of King's work. His criticism, reviews, and interviews have appeared in such wide-ranging publications as the *Washington Post*, the *Philadelphia Inquirer*, and *Harper's Bazaar*. He is also the author of *Faces of Fear*, a history of modern horror fiction. His own short fiction has appeared in such anthologies as *Greystone Bay, Midnight, Book of the Dead, Splatterpunks*, and *Silver Scream*, which contained his acclaimed story "Splatter: A Cautionary Tale." Doug was the editor of the celebrated anthology *Prime Evil* and is now writing a biographical critique of the fiction and film of Clive Barker.

Like I said, he's got this thing for Dario Argento films. But those string ties . . .

Opera of Violence: The Films of Dario Argento

by Douglas E. Winter

I'm in love with the color red. I dream in red. My nightmares are bathed in red. . . . Red is the color of passion, of joy. Red is the color of journeys into the hidden depths of the subconscious. But above all: red is the color of rage . . . and violence.

He is the most important and influential of contemporary directors of the horror film, but few of his motion pictures have appeared in American theaters or video stores. What has found its way to this country is often marred by indifferent distribution and dubbing, and edited mercilessly to lesson the violence—or merely the minutes. The obsessiveness of his art, and his disdain for the conventions of narrative, make him troublesome viewing for the mass market, while his commitment to work in a disreputable genre tempers the growing critical recognition.

His name is Dario Argento, and he is the master of the cinema of delirium, the creator of celluloid worlds seen through the eyes of twisted and tortured souls. An artist of impudent virtuosity and Byzantine complexity, he so stunningly exercises his obsessions that he can only be called a mad genius, one who defies convention—and, at times, belief. A furious and obsessive stylist, Argento's penchant for pyrotechnics of sight and sound suggest a cinematic opera, in which the embrace of violence approaches the classical. His gestures are relentless, sweeping, grand; his texts filled, like those of the great composers, with allusions to his own work and that of his mentors.

Although often called "the Italian Hitchcock," Argento's true influences are the masters of urban noir, Fritz Lang and Carol Reed, and fellow Italian visionaries Riccardo Freda, Mario Bava, and Michelangelo Antonioni. He has influenced in turn more directors of horror film than anyone since Hitchcock himself.

Born in 1940 of Italian/Brazilian descent, Dario Argento is the son of Salvatore Argento, a prominent figure in the postwar Italian film community (indeed, his first memory is said to be of sitting on Sophia Loren's knee). While working as film critic for the Rome daily newspaper *Paese Sera*, Argento was asked to join Bernardo Bertolucci in storyboarding Sergio Leone's gothic western epic *C'era una volta il West* (*Once Upon a Time in the West*, 1968). Their success led each on the winding road to cinematic renown. Argento quickly found work writing scripts for numerous films, from other westerns (*Cimitero senza croci—Cemetery Without Crosses*, 1968; *Oggi a me . . . domani a te!—Today It's Me . . . Tomorrow You!*, 1968; and *Un esercito di cinque uomini—The Five-Man Army*, 1969) to war films (*Probabilita zero—Probability Zero*, 1968; Umberto Lenzi's *La legione dei dannati—Legion of the Damned/Battle of the Commandos*, 1969; *Commandos*, 1969), and even erotica (*Metti una sera a cena—One Night at Dinner*, 1968; *La rivoluzione sessuale—The Love Circle*, 1968; and *Le stagione dei sensi*, 1969).

Argento's screenplay for *Metti una sera a cena* brought him to the attention of Goffredo Lombardo, head of Titanus, a leading Italian film company. Lombardo retained Argento as an assistant responsible for script review and revision. Bernardo Bertolucci urged Argento to read Fredric Brown's innovative psychological thriller *The Screaming Mimi* (1949), and while on holiday, Argento wrote a screenplay inspired by the novel's central theme of murderous misdirection and his love for Mario Bava's *La ragazza che sapeva troppo* (*The Evil Eye/The Girl Who Knew Too Much*, 1962), a film centered on a witness to a murder who cannot identify the killer or even verify that the murder happened.

The result was Argento's directorial debut, *L'uccello dalle piume di cristallo* (*The Bird with the Crystal Plumage*, 1969), produced for Titanus by his father, Salvatore. It was nearly Argento's last film: after viewing the first week's rushes, Lombardo decided to remove him in favor of Ferdinando Baldi; but Salvatore had assured an unbreakable contract. The completed film proved Titanus's leading moneymaker, and Argento's career as a director was established.

L'uccello dalle piume di cristallo was an inspired entry into the then-peculiarly Italian film genre known as the *giallo*, named for the traditionally yellow covers of thrillers when published in Italy. The form had been realized by Riccardo Freda, whose beautiful *I Vampiri* (*The Devil's Commandment/The Vampires*, 1956) signaled the modern renaissance of the horror film, and whose better films, including *L'orribile segreto del Dr. Hichcock* (*The Horrible Dr. Hichcock*, 1962) are profound acts of the visual, studied interplays of light and dark. But it was Mario Bava, Freda's sometime collaborator, who defined and first mastered the *giallo* in *La ragazza che sapeva troppo* and *Sei donne per l'assassino* (*Blood and Black Lace*, 1964). While the former inspired Argento's directorial debut, the latter, a virtually scriptless tour de force of voyeurism, taught him the power of the murderous set-piece.

Just as Leone reinvented the western, Argento took a popular but tiring genre and bent it to his own obsessions, elevating its familiar mythologies to the level of art. It was a step heralded by Antonioni's *Blow Up* (1966) and Giulio Questi's delirious but virtually forgotten *La morte ha fatto l'uovo* (*Death Laid an Egg*, 1967), unabashed "art films" with roots in the *giallo*; but neither was as commercial, or as comprehensible, as *L'uccello dalle piume di cristallo*.

Sam Dalmas (Tony Musante) is a burned-out American writer, cast adrift in Rome, reduced to writing a manual on rare birds for money. "Go to Italy," a friend has told him. "It's a peaceful country, nothing ever happens there." But as Dalmas walks home one evening, he glances into an art gallery and witnesses a man in black struggling with the manager, Monica (Eva Renzi). He rushes to intervene, but is trapped between the glass doors of the gallery entrance—a fish in an aquarium—and must watch, helpless, as the blood-drenched Monica calls to him for help.

As the only eyewitness to what seems the latest attack of a serial killer, Dalmas is drawn into the investigation—at first unwillingly, and then with unnatural preoccupation. The investigating officer, Morosini (Enrico Maria Salerno), has seized Dalmas's passport, but the murderer has seized his imagination. In Argento's world, the police are an emotionless machine, moving forward with patient scientific delibera-tion, capable of solving crime, but incapable of understanding it. It is the artists, and only the artists, who are capable of embracing and confronting the purveyors of murder: the light and the dark, locked in an eternal struggle of creation and destruction, rebirth . . . and death again.

Although the plot of *L'uccello dalle piume di cristallo* now seems synonymous with the name Argento, its archetype is Carol Reed's beguiling adaptation of Graham Greene's *The Third Man* (1947): an American in Europe, a creative talent who is something of a lost soul, is witness to a mystery that defies the authorities and that, in the end, only he can solve. The landscape (for Reed, Vienna; for Argento, most often Rome) is key to the mystery, and the cinematography embraces that landscape so passionately that it comes to express the psychology of the characters. It is said that after viewing *The Third Man*, William Wyler presented Reed with a spirit level to place on his camera so as to forcibly prevent any angle shots. (One wonders what Wyler would have presented Argento, whose nervous and provocative camera work makes Reed seem almost a traditionalist.) The similarities do not end there: in one of *The Third Man*'s most memorable scenes, the killer's hands, seen clutching through a drain, were in fact the hands of Carol Reed; in Argento's films, the hands that wield the shiny, murderous blades invariably are his own.

Although filmed by Italy's leading cinematographer, Vittorio Storaro (whose credits include *1900, Apocalypse Now* and *Reds*), *L'uccello dalle piume di cristallo* is visually the most conventional and claustrophobic Argento. The American version is edited only slightly, excising the sexual overtness of a murder. It is this film that caused Argento to be identified with Alfred Hitchcock, not simply because of its stylish exposition of psychological horror, but also because of its conscious play on the inescapable shadow of Hitchcock. Thus the master's trademarks, including offbeat characterizations and canny plot twists, abound. A suspect is chased into a convention where everyone is dressed like him; a painter who holds an important clue feasts on cats; the prime suspect, Monica's husband, bears a passing resemblance to Anthony Perkins of *Psycho* (1960)—yet all of it is misdirection. Argento manipulates the expectations of the audience with clever patience until the genre is turned inside out: Monica is not a victim at all, but the killer, and what Dalmas has witnessed is a struggle in which her husband has tried to stop her, accidentally wounding her in the process. Even the film's coda is an inversion of Hitchcock, a replay of the psychiatrist's explanation at the conclusion of *Psycho*, which Argento deems so unsatisfactory that even his police detective falls asleep.

In the climax of *L'uccello dalle piume di cristallo*, Dalmas is trapped again, caught beneath a massive plinth—the artist literally weighted down with art, reduced to a helpless watcher on the sidelines of the "real" world. The audience is trapped with him, and it is this aesthetic, an unwilling complicity of viewer and killer, that would inform every Argento film that followed.

After the commercial and critical success of this auspicious debut, Argento mounted his second film, *Il gatto a nove code* (*The Cat O'Nine Tails*, 1970), in which he sought "to transfer to the detective thriller the sort of violence Sergio Leone put in his westerns." Adapted from a story by Argento, Luigi Collo and Dardano Sacchetti, *Il gatto a nove code* is the most straightforward of Argento's films, and yet a virtual paean to the violent flamboyance of Leone and Mario Bava.

Karl Malden plays Franco Arno, a blind aficionado of crossword puzzles who overhears a whispered conversation about blackmail while walking home. Later that night, a break-in occurs at a nearby genetics research facility, the Istitute Terzi; the following day, one of its scientists is killed. As the bodies begin to fall like dominoes, Arno teams with reporter Carlo Giordani (James Franciscus) to pursue the killer, whose identity is tied to the secret files of the Istitute.

From the basis of its title ("That's it, then: nine leads to follow. It's a cat with nine tails") to the identity of its villain, *Il gatto a nove code* is an exercise in the arbitrary, verging on narrative indifference. A harbinger of better things to come, it is Argento's first bending of the cinema of detection into the cinema of delirium. Just as logic is subordinate in the mad schemes of Argento's killers, so too is it subordinate in the cinematic abyss into which he bids us stare. From the camera's opening walk across the Istitute's rooftop—a segue from Orson Welles's *Touch of Evil* (1958) to John Carpenter's *Halloween* (1978) and its myriad successors—to the insistent use of subjective point-of-view camera work and repeated closeups of the killer's eye, *Il gatto a nove code* defined for this and future generations the visual style of the American *giallo*, what for better or worse is now known as the "slasher" film: the audience itself becomes the murderer, or at the very least sees through his or her (or its) eyes—an aesthetic reinforced by Argento's somber finale, in which even the peaceful, loving Arno is proved capable of homicide. And it was here too that Argento first unleashed his ultraviolence, making good on his desire to bring Leone's stylized mayhem into the realm of the modern, culminating in the killer's death, a fall down an elevator shaft, in which his hands are flayed of skin as he grabs at the wire cable in an effort to save himself.

Argento followed *Il gatto a nove code*—perhaps too quickly—with *Quattro mosche di velluto grigio* (*Four Flies on Gray Velvet*, 1971). It is the least successful of his horror films, crippled by a transparent plot and the lobotomized performance of Michael Brandon, a last-minute replacement for Michael York. Based on a story by Argento, Mario Foglietti, and long-time friend and collaborator Luigi Cozzi, *Quattro mosche di velluto grigio* struggles for the kind of bleak urban paranoia masterfully achieved in the films of Fritz Lang (to whom the film was intended as an homage). Unfortunately, Argento seems uncertain of his purpose, jumping from satire to slapstick humor to unsettling horror with distracting abandon.

Brandon plays Roberto Tobias, a progressive-rock drummer who, when followed by a mysterious stranger, confronts the man in an abandoned theater. A scuffle ensues, and the stranger, apparently stabbed, falls to his death. Roberto then realizes that the entire scene has been photographed by a masked onlooker. Soon he is terrorized: threatening letters, the photographs, and finally the onlooker invade his own home, without any apparent motive but mayhem. In due course four people die like flies, and finally it is Roberto's turn. His only salvation is a peculiar friend, played by Italian western star "Bud Spencer" (Carlo Pedersoli), who, in another nod to Fredric Brown's *The Screaming Mimi*, is named Godfrey but called "God" for short.

Brandon's Roberto is a dreadful choice of protagonist—dull, ready to cheat on his wife, Nina (Mimsy Farmer), the moment she leaves home, and blissfully unaware of the obvious fact that Nina is the culprit. Her motive is outré and, given Brandon's sleepwalk of a performance, not entirely unsympathetic: she has married Roberto because he reminds her of her father, a brute who raised her as a boy and committed her to an asylum, then died before she could exact her revenge.

Indeed, Argento brings the viewer perilously close to embracing the killer as the hero of this twisted affair. In one magnificent sequence, the camera literally *becomes* the murderer, plucking a blunt object up and dispatching a victim. Yet despite this scene and its compelling other-worldly sequences—Roberto's recurring dream of a Saudi execution, and Nina's nightmarish memories of the asylum—*Quattro mosche di velluto grigio* does not come alive until its closing minutes, when Nina confronts Roberto. Farmer twists her tame and vapid Nina, a stereotypical Hitchcockian blonde ice goddess, into a vicious and vital madwoman. Only through the intervention of "God" is Roberto saved, and his dream made reality as Nina's escape ends with a slow-motion car crash in which she is beheaded.

Along with Mario Bava's seminal *Ecologio del delitto* (*Twitch of the Death Nerve*/*Bay of Blood*/*Bloodbath*), released the same year, *Quattro mosche di velluto grigio* set the stage for the more popular, but lesser "slasher" films that would follow a few years later. Bava and Argento each created cat-and-mouse games between themselves and the audience in which narrative succumbed to aggressive, serial violence. But unlike their American counterparts and imitators, neither Bava nor Argento is relenting: their killers are neither subhuman nor superhuman, of the sort found in *The Texas Chainsaw Massacre* (1974) or *Nightmare on Elm Street* (1984).

Argento's loose "animal trilogy"—bird, cat, flies—is in retrospect a benchmark in the cinema of horror: a summation and reinterpretation of the psychological thriller that would set the course for most every such film to come, from John Carpenter's *Halloween* to Brian De Palma's *Dressed to Kill* (1980) and Jonathan Demme's *The Silence of the Lambs* (1991). At its heart was a repudiation of the film of detection—and, more important, the cinema of conventional explanations and outcomes. In the grand tradition of Edgar Allan Poe, science—and, more often, pseudoscience—is intrinsic of each of the "animal" films: in *L'uccello dalle piume di cristallo*, cursory voiceprints; in *Il gatto a nove code*, the XYY chromosome as an indicator of violent and criminal tendencies; in *Quattro mosche di velluto grigio*, the idea that the last thing one sees is imprinted on the retina of a corpse. And the very inadequacy of these "rational" explanations only reinforces the growing sense that logic has fallen pray to madness, not simply in the minds of the murderers, but in our minds as well.

The trilogy also established an iconography that is now peculiar to and recognizable as Argento: murderers in black who strike from the shadows; gloved hands and shiny blades; twisted art and music and architecture; explanations that are impulsive and not always adequate; a world of danger and deception, where seeing is not believing, and the oneiric is supreme.

The "animal" motif of these early films was deliberate; Argento wanted to explore "the instinct which prevails in human reasoning, which can be more irresponsible than a creature's instinct." The pervasive influence of his trilogy can be seen in the immediate surge in popularity of thrillers infused with sex and horror—and animal imagery. Indeed, the early seventies produced a virtual bestiary of titles, including Lucio Fulci's *Una lucertola con la pelle di donna* (*A Lizard in a Woman's Skin*, 1971) and *Non si sevizia un paperino* (*Don't Torture the Duckling*, 1972); Paola Cavara's *La tarantola dal ventre nero* (*The Black Belly of the Tarantula*, 1971); Riccardo Freda's pseudonymous *L'iguana dalla lingua di fuoco* (*Iguana with the Tongue of Fire*, 1971); Sergio Pastore's *Sette scialli di seta gialla* (*The Crimes of the Black Cat*, 1972); and Antonio Margheriti's *La morte negli occhi del gatto* (*Seven Deaths in the Cat's Eye*, 1973). More than a decade later, Christian Plummer's *Assassino al cimitero Etrusco* (1982) would be retitled *The Scorpion with Two Tails* in order to evoke the Argento mystique. Even

Argento's 1975 masterwork *Profondo rosso* would be retitled by some distributors as *The Saber Tooth Tiger*.

In the meantime, Argento had moved on, creating a series of thrillers for Italian television, *La porta sul buio* (*The Door of Darkness*, 1972), and directing two episodes pseudonymously. He then wrote and directed a film set in the 1848 Italian revolution, *Le cinque giornate* (*The Five Days of Milan*, 1973), which remains unreleased outside of Italy, and seems thankfully to have exorcised the comic impulses that marred *Quattro mosche di velluto grigio*. Argento's brief hiatus from the horror film ended in 1975 with the release of an undisputed masterpiece, *Profondo rosso* (*Deep Red/The Hatchet Murders*).

Where the "animal trilogy" proceeded from the generic imagery of the *giallo*, embracing and then inverting its conventions and expectations, *Profondo rosso* signaled Argento's leap of faith from film as a commercial construct into art. It was here that he fractured the closed circle of traditional narrative and took his imaginings into the open-ended realm of dreams. *Profondo rosso* also marked Argento's transition from suspense to splatter, its set pieces insistently bathing the viewer in blood; more importantly, it was a transition from the insular, cloistered world of murder and detection into the realm of supernatural horror, and beyond—into magic.

The screenplay of *Profondo rosso*, adapted by Bernardino Zapponi (cowriter of Federico Fellini's *Roma* and *Satyricon*) from a story by Argento, twisted the *giallo* into the mad baroque vision that is uniquely Argento. It is a narrative filled with doubling and deception, looping back on itself with nightmarish deliberation. Unfortunately, the American release of *Profondo rosso* is missing its more outlandish violence and some twenty minutes of exposition.

While visiting Rome, pianist Marcus Daly (David Hemmings) witnesses the brutal murder of a psychic, who, only hours before, had warned her audience of the presence of a palpable evil. Drawn into the investigation by the police and a feminist reporter, Gianna Brezzi (Daria Nicolodi), Daly is soon stalked by the mysterious killer. From this by now typical beginning, *Profondo rosso* skews into a maelstrom of madness as blood-drenched as its title suggests.

First there is Rome itself, neither the pastoral landscape of guide-books nor the gritty urban sprawl of the "animal trilogy," but a city seen by a madman: a fantastic maze of monuments tainted an unnatural red that alienates and belittles its human occupants. Then there is Argento's resourceful gift for allusion: from the casting of David Hemmings, invoking that classic antimystery, *Blow Up*, to the discomforting artwork that haunts the fringes of almost every key frame. Finally there is the text: a mélange of precognition and hauntings, in which that most vindictive of ghosts, the past, pursues the present with vicious glee. Although the film's resolution, like that of *L'uccello dalle piume di cristallo*, is based upon what Daly saw but failed to understand, the viewer, like Daly, is finally left stunned, disturbed, gazing at nothing but his own reflection in an ever-deepening pool of red.

In the "animal trilogy," there is logic—though sometimes tenuous and twisted with madness, intercut with flashbacks, dreams and phantasms, still there is logic; scene follows scene in conventional and comprehensible film narrative. With *Profondo rosso*, Argento's film-making itself begins to warp like the broken minds of his killers. The camera is nervously alive; the colors, as the film's title suggests, are deeper, more garish, stained; the landscapes verge on the imagined, in the vein of Robert Wiene's *Das Cabinet des Dr. Caligari* (1919). And at last Argento eschews explanation: the psychic's powers are real; an animated puppet performs a terrifying dance as prelude to a grisly murder.

Profondo rosso also is notable for its soundtrack. Like Sergio Leone, Argento uses music less as backdrop or filler than as an intrinsic, if not overt, element of his art, offering both cues and clues. Not surprisingly, Argento's "animal trilogy" was scored by Leone's renowned collaborator, Ennio Morricone, who delivered schizophrenic soundscapes where childlike melodies were fractured by scathing, discordant jazz.

With *Profondo rosso*, Argento moved to the furious rock scores for which he is most well known, and in so doing virtually abandoned the notion of soundtrack as counterpoint in favor of its use as narrative, often replacing dialogue as his favored means of aural exposition. Early in the film the viewer witnesses an extended series of sweeping close-ups of objects identified with the killer, a scene set solely to music—an interplay of sight and sound that prefigures the music videos of the Eighties.

When his first choice for the *Profondo rosso* score, pioneer metal-heads Deep Purple, proved unavailable, Argento turned to the Italian progressive rock band Goblin, led by keyboardist Claudio Simonetti, who created for him the kind of stylized synthesizer score that is now the staple of horror film: minimalist piano and synthesizer sequences; cannonades of sampled cellos, violins and voices; shrieking guitars. Goblin's accompaniment for *Suspiria*, with its relentless bass line, childlike synth lead, and whispered cries of "Witch," is possibly the loudest soundtrack ever presented.

In later films Argento diversified, working with such rock legends as Keith Emerson (*Inferno*), Brian Eno (*Opera*), and Bill Wyman of the Rolling Stones (*Phenomena, Opera*)—and, more recently, with the great Bernard Herrmann's heir apparent, Pino Donaggio (*Due occhi diabolici*); but he has never lost his penchant for Simonetti's aggressive keyboards or for headbanging guitars as punctuation for his most violent junctures. Argento's later scores, particularly *Phenomena* and *Opera*, are almost unnervingly schizoid tapestries, pitting Simonetti's uncharacteristically romantic piano work against the frenzied guitars of Iron Maiden's "Flash of the Blade," the ambient atmospherics of Eno against the lush arias of Verdi.

Contributing to the sonic wonder of Argento's films—at least for unsuspecting American audiences—is the Italian cinema's standard practice of postdubbing: sound, including dialogue, is not actually recorded until after filming is complete, lending an otherworldly and often hollow quality to the soundtrack. Not until *Opera* (1987) would Argento film with direct sound, and even then he relied heavily on postdubbing.

Argento's embrace of film-as-nightmare would reach its zenith in his next and arguably best films, *Suspiria* (1977) and *Inferno* (1980). Written by Argento and his then-love, Daria Nicolodi, these interrelated epics of the imagination are lurid, violent fairy tales inspired by Thomas De Quincey's visionary essay *Suspiria de Profundis* (and, in particular, its chapter "Levana and Our Ladies of Sorrow"). Virtually devoid of conventional narrative, the films find their momentum, if not reason for existence, in luscious and flamboyant setpieces of violence.

Suspiria, Argento's most well known picture, was shot by Luciano Tovoli on the last of the IB Technicolor stock in Italy, creating a canvas painted bright with primary colors: blue, green—and, inevitably, red. Its intensity begins with its infamous opening act.

A ballerina, Susy Bannion (Jessica Harper), travels to the celebrated Tanz Akademie of Freiburg-im-Breisgau, West Germany, in order to perfect her skills. She arrives in a blue apocalypse of rain, and witnesses a young woman's frenzied departure. Words, disjointed and meaningless, are carried on the wet wind: "secret . . . irises." The student runs from the great house, and the point of view shifts suddenly to her as she seeks asylum with a friend. In an astonishingly violent vignette, an intruder bursts through a window of the upper-story apartment and stabs her repeatedly, climaxing in close-ups of the knife entering her beating heart; then she is hung by the neck, falling through the colored glass of an atrium skylight. The glass rains down, slicing her friend to death.

"Bad luck is not made by broken mirrors, but by broken minds," a psychologist tells Susy, but Argento's insistent imagery disputes his rationalist's diagnosis: the first deaths suggest a world of shattered glass, and neither Susy nor the viewer can escape Argento's insistent hall of mirrors. From Susy's claustrophobic taxi ride to the killer's shiny blades to the shard of mirror whose reflection stuns Susy as she goes to her first dance class, there is no doubt that we are being taken through a looking glass into a wonderland of hallucination and horror.

There is a mystery in *Suspiria,* to be sure; but for once it is not one of murder. The identity and motive of the killer are secondary to a greater mystery of space and time. The Tanz Akademie once housed a witch, and it is haunted by her memory, if not her presence. That there is killing is inescapable, but Argento pushes his setpieces to impulsive, insane heights. A blind pianist is attacked by his own seeing-eye dog; maggots rain down from the *Akademie*'s ceilings; a dancer's exploration of the house ends in an attic filled with barbed wire; rooms are hidden within rooms; and somewhere in the upper reaches of the house waits the "Black Widow," the dark Mother of Sighs.

In the film's final seconds, as Susy staggers in wild-eyed triumph from the ruined Akademie, we are no longer certain whether the film is literal, a dream . . . or the imaginings of a broken mind. The Tanz Akademie is a hyperrealist construct of contour and color, a landscape worthy of Drs. Caligari and Leary. It is presided over by two wicked wardens whose faces are icons in the Argento pantheon: the ballet instructor Madame Tanner (Alida Valli, the dark heroine of *The Third Man* and Hitchcock's *The Paradine Case*, 1947) and Madame Blank (Joan Bennett, a stalwart of Fritz Lang's American period). Jessica Harper plays Susy's dance of delirium with wide-eyed perfection, a feverish little girl lost in a dollhouse of tortured dreams. The best of Argento's heroines, she is a fallen angel whose beauty and terror are as fragile as glass.

It was in *Suspiria* that Argento took the supernatural horror film out of the realm of fantasy and into one of the marvelous and miraculous. It was here, too, that Argento first displayed the cinematic legerdemain for which he is famed, dropping a wire-guided camera from the heights of a government building to portray the swoop of the angel of death.

There would be no turning back, as with each subsequent film Argento sought to up the ante: central to *Tenebrae* is a sustained and unedited louma crane shot in which a camera moves out of a bedroom window, over the wall and roof of a house, down the opposite wall, in through another window, and finally comes to rest on the scene of a murder. For the opening sequence of *Phenomena*, Argento found the largest crane in Europe and mounted a towering vista of the Italian Alps. *Opera* is a nonstop excursion of camera wizardry, in which the lens swoops and swerves with nervous abandon, virtually never stopping, climaxing in a raven's-eye view of the action, in which a camera literally is flown through the upper reaches of an opera house.

With *Suspiria*, the setpiece became the hallmark of Argento's work—all else, story included, succumbs to an insistent visual whirlpool, drawing the viewer hypnotically, irresistibly, into a feeling of inescapable helplessness, if not participation. Just as Argento himself wields the silver blades that paint his bloodred canvases, his viewers become his accomplices—an aesthetic that reaches its zenith in *Opera*, where the ingénue Betty is repeatedly bound and gagged by the mysterious murderer, her eyelids taped open as she is forced again and again to watch others die. "In the end," Argento tells us, "it is you, the spectator, who kills . . . or who is murdered."

Suspiria would prove to be the most successful of Argento's films at the box office, and no doubt remains his most-remembered work. He turned next to George A. Romero's long-awaited sequel to the zombie classic *Night of the Living Dead* (1968). As producer and script consultant for *Dawn of the Dead* (1979), Argento's contributions to the film primarily involved financing, the screenplay, and the Goblin score; he also supervised the European edit (*Zombi*), which is slightly shorter than the American cut and has a juiced-up soundtrack.

By the time of *Inferno* (1980), Argento's prowess for the setpiece had reached the stage where he could dispense with plot entirely, creating a masterwork driven solely by the accumulation of violent imagery: a film that unfolds with the instinctive (il)logic of nightmare. A thematic sequel to *Suspiria, Inferno* is the second of a projected trilogy that, following the breakup of Argento and Nicolodi, may never see completion. The story, such as it is, is subsumed utterly in style, an architectural wonderwork on the scale of its obvious inspiration, the Alain Resnais/Alain Robbe-Grillet collaboration *L'Année dernière à Marienbad* (*Last Year at Marienbad*, 1962).

While living in New York City, poet Rose Elliot (Irene Miracle) discovers an occult book, *The Three Mothers*, and learns that her baroque apartment tower is one of three great houses built by Varelli, a mysterious alchemist-architect based upon the legendary Fulcanelli. In these houses—in Freiburg, New York, and Rome—lurk the three wicked stepmothers of mankind, matrons of the world's sorrows: Mater Suspiriorum (the Mother of Sighs), Mater Tenebrarum (the Mother of Shadows), and Mater Lachrymarum (the Mother of Tears).

Rose writes of her discovery to her brother Mark (Leigh McCloskey), a music student in Rome, but the letter is read by his girlfriend (Eleonora Giorgi), whose search for a copy of the book ends in death. Rose is also killed, and when Mark travels to New York, the murders increase with nightmarish imperative; no one is safe, and no one knows why. As Mark wanders in bewildered despair, at last literally stumbling over the solution, Argento creates a baroque architecture of fear to match that of his great house: a furnished room entirely underwater; a floor between floors; and, ultimately, a house within the house, a Chinese puzzle box constantly unfolding.

For bravado alone, *Inferno* must rank among the greatest of contemporary horror films, a visual feast of hallucinatory proportions. All the borders of sanity have been systematically erased. It is also notable as Mario Bava's final film; he handled certain visual effects, while his son Lamberto, who made his directional debut later that year with *Macabro* (*Macabre/Frozen Terror*), served as assistant director.

After the sheer dementia of *Inferno*, Argento created his most tightly plotted film, *Tenebrae* (*Sotto gli occhi dell'assassino*, 1982), released here as the radically edited *Unsane*. Although a return to the *giallo* and the *Third Man* archetype, *Tenebrae* is another undeniable step forward, Argento taking firm control of conventional narrative while opening an introspective vein in bright sprays of blood.

A writer of suspense fiction, Peter Neal (Anthony Franciosa), is touring Italy to promote his new novel when a series of horrific murders occur, all tied to the book. Neal, his agent (John Saxon), and assistant (Daria Nicolodi) are drawn into the investigation. Midway through the film, the prime suspect, a television talk-show host (John Steiner), is slain; Argento's brilliant twist is that there are *two* murderers: Neal has solved the crimes, killed the killer, and taken his place, using the killer's techniques to pursue his own ends.

Gone is the opulent color of the *Three Mothers* films; in its place is a landscape that is cold, white, sterile, modern. With its unabashedly voyeuristic cinematography by Luciano Tovoli, *Tenebrae* glories in the throes of its female victims: each is the subject of a prolonged courting ritual that leads to a violent consummation—and death. The camera leers, lingers, loves; and the film's closing minutes, a virtual bath of blood, rank among the most gripping in contemporary horror.

Argento is known for his sensationalistic quote: "I like women, especially beautiful ones. If they have a good face and figure, I would much prefer to watch them being murdered than an ugly girl or man." ("The perpetration of death," he has noted, "being the clearest act of love.") *Tenebrae* proves to be his most self-reflective, self-critical work, imputing these very motives to his killers. In its opening act, the pages of Peter Neal's book are literally shoved down the throat of a flirty shoplifter. A feminist reporter soon confronts Neal, charging that the women in his books are nothing but "victims, ciphers"—a charge often leveled at Argento himself. When Neal finally gloats over his murder spree—"It was just like writing a book"—Argento admits in clearest terms to the personal demons powering his art.

Later efforts seem even more critical of Argento's aesthetics, and those of the horror film generally. In *Demoni* (*Demons*, 1985), produced and cowritten by Argento but directed by Lamberto Bava, rabid violence spreads from a motion-picture screen to the audience and finally to the world outside. Its sequel, *Demoni 2 . . . L'incubo ritorna* (*Demons 2*, 1986), used television as the agent of infectious destruction. In *Opera*, a director of horror films, clearly based upon Argento, notes sarcastically: "I always jerk off before I shoot a scene." When murder strikes, his girlfriend observes: "All this turns you on, doesn't it? You're a sadist . . . " And in *Due occhi diabolici*, a photographer tortures and kills a cat for his lens, confirming that murder and art may be inseparable—that, as Argento's glorious setpieces have suggested all along, murder *is* an art.

"I have no secrets," Argento tells us. "Violence is a means of communication, a way of expressing myself." But as his alter ego also notes in *Opera*: "I think it's unwise to use movies as a guide for reality."

Phenomena (1985), whose American version, shortened by nearly one-half hour, was retitled *Creepers*, sought to merge the diverging paths of Argento's enthusiasms by creating a truly supernatural *giallo*. Written with Franco Ferrini and intended as an autobiographical look at the dark side of adolescence, the result is a visually stunning but otherwise disappointing mish-mash whose technical flair is overcome by a ludicrous story.

A film star's daughter, Jennifer Corvino (Jennifer Connelly), is exiled to the Collegio Wagner, a boarding school in Switzerland presided over by the shrewish Mrs. Bruckner (Daria Nicolodi). In one of Argento's more heavy-handed devices, Jennifer has a preternatural affinity with insects, and ultimately, like Stephen King's psychokinetic children, she learns the art of controlling her power. Alone, misunderstood, and haunted by violent dreams, Jennifer befriends a crippled entomologist, Professor McGregor (Donald Pleasance), and becomes both hunter and hunted in a mystery surrounding the deaths of McGregor's assistant and several other schoolgirls.

Beautifully filmed by Romano Albani, *Phenomena* opens with a pastoral view of the Alps gone awry, climaxing with the beheading of a schoolgirl (played by Argento's daughter Fiore). From there it reels back and forth, threads of *giallo* intertwined with threads of teen angst, enlivened only by Pleasance's hammy antics and a succession of heavy-metal murders. Still, there are moments: the film's entomological solution foreshadows *The Silence of the Lambs*, and its visual treats include a watery pit of body parts and maggots, and the compelling revelation (echoing Nicholas Roeg's *Don't Look Now*, 1973, itself clearly influenced by Argento) that again there are two killers: Mrs. Bruckner and her tiny, bestial son.

Although hopelessly confused, the excesses of *Phenomena* are alone often compelling and make the film worthy of repeated viewing. Argento pledges great belief in *Phenomena*, for reasons no doubt extrinsic to its content; in addition to its autobiographical elements, the film also acted as a kind of personal watershed. In its frames, he would kill off characters portrayed by his onetime lover, Daria Nicolodi, and both of his children—an obvious metaphor, Nicolodi has suggested, for the changes then occurring in his personal life.

In the mid-1980s, Argento was approached by the Sferisterio Theater of Macerata to direct a stage version of Verdi's *Rigoletto*. When word of his rather sordid plans created something of a scandal, he was replaced by a more traditional director. (It was not the first time that Argento's ventures into the mainstream were met with controversy: in 1986, at the invitation of fashion designer Trussardi, he directed a promotional video in which runway models were stabbed to death and dragged away in body bags.) But the seed of his next film had been planted: "It was the look backstage at Sferisterio which excited me—all gray movement, dramatic lighting and never knowing what was lurking in the shadows."

The result, cowritten with Franco Ferrini, was *Opera* (1987), what

Argento calls "an aria of violence beyond imagination." Aggressively decorated and filmed, it is a virtual showcase of modern camera technique and technology. Argento used his first non-Italian director of photography, Ronnie Taylor—Richard Attenborough's favorite cameraman and winner of an Oscar for *Gandhi*—and the result is a visual splendor rarely obtained in the cinema of the macabre.

Ian Charleson plays a director of horror films slated to stage that most haunted of operas, Verdi's *Macbeth*. Life imitates art: Vanessa Redgrave stormed off the set of *Opera* in the manner of the fictitious opera's prima donna, leaving Argento to create a brilliant opening scene where the camera replaces her, the story shot entirely from her point of view . . . until she is struck by a car, raising the curtain on her understudy, the ingénue Betty (Cristina Marsillach).

Betty's debut as a pistol-toting Lady Macbeth, standing watch over a wasteland of crashed airplanes, smoke-stained soldiers, and a cascade of ravens, is a resounding success; but there is an operatic phantom lurking somewhere in the shadows. He is a vicious and fetishistic killer who has engineered Betty's debut, but for reasons that would be utterly alien to Gaston Leroux's romantic Phantom: It is not Betty, but her role—as Lady Macbeth and, as the viewer learns in time, a surrogate for her dead mother—that holds this phantom in thrall.

In *Opera*, the act of seeing is fatal. The phantom (not unlike Argento himself) compulsively forces Betty to witness his deeds; Betty's agent (Daria Nicolodi) is killed while staring through an apartment peephole; and the identity of the killer is known only to the ravens, who, like the camera, can speak to us only through their eyes. And Argento adopts the finale of Thomas Harris's novel *Red Dragon* (1981), which had been rejected in Michael Mann's film adaptation, *Manhunter* (1986), as his own, reaffirming his warning that what is seen, like that which is not seen, cannot be believed.

Even the mysterious killer proves nothing but a mad pawn of vision, his murderous spree inspired by his mistress, Betty's mother, a voyeur who commanded him to kill for her. When his eye is plucked out by the swirling ravens, Argento's most biblical retribution, we learn that the killer is the police inspector (Urbano Barberini). "Look at me," he cries. "A monster!"

Argento thus takes the *giallo* full circle: the police are criminals, the sinners saints, and in the film's closing moments the viewer finds Betty's protestations—"I'm not like my mother, not at all"—less than convincing. Notably, the generally available English-language version, sometimes known as *Terror at the Opera*, concludes as a freeze-frame captures Betty after this denial of her capacity for violence; but in the Italian theatrical release, Argento's finale is optimistic. The scene continues into a fantasia as Betty falls to the ground and, on hands and knees, embraces the flowers, the grass, the dirt, finally urging a salamander to "go free."

Argento's most recent work is a collaboration with George A. Romero, *Due occhi diabolici* (*Two Evil Eyes*, 1990), in which each director adapts a story by Edgar Allan Poe. Romero's contribution, *The Facts in the Case of M. Valdemar*, opens the film. It proves surprisingly tepid, little more than a big-budget episode of his television series *Tales from the Darkside*, and may be the reason that the film has not been released in the United States. Argento's *Il gatto nero* (*The Black Cat*), on the other hand, is outrageous, compelling and, along with Federico Fellini's *Toby Dammit* in *Tre passi nel delirio* (*Spirits of the Dead*, 1968), among the very best of the countless Poe-derived films.

Harvey Keitel plays Rod Usher, a photographer based loosely on Wee Gee, the "Naked City" lensman of 1940s New York murder scenes. Usher's obsession with scenes of horror mirrors Argento's own: an editor urges him to photograph something other than death, to "show the skeptics you've got an eye." But Usher is haunted by, indeed addicted to, the imagery of violence. A black cat appears mysteriously on his doorstep and is adopted by his live-in girlfriend, Annabel (Madeleine Potter); the cat seems to stalk him, taunt him, like the conscience he apparently lacks. Usher's attempts to photograph the cat twist into a compulsion, and finally he tortures and kills it for the eye of the camera.

When the photographs feature prominently in Usher's latest book, Annabel decides to move out; but the cat, proverbially, has come back. In a drunken stupor, Usher kills Annabel and walls up her corpse (and, unknowingly, the cat) inside his house. When the police arrive to investigate Annabel's disappearance, the cries of the cat become the tell-tale heart by which Usher's crimes are revealed.

While Argento traditionally aligns his artist/detectives with the forces of good—even *Tenebrae*'s Peter Neal mimes righteousness and, in his own twisted way, pursues it—Rod Usher is bad to the bone, the inevitable conclusion of Argento's inward-spiraling tour of the destructive side of creativity. "It is the depravity that's in all of us," Usher says during the film's opening credits. "Perversity is one of the prime impulses of the heart. Who's never done something wrong just because it was forbidden? To be evil only for the love of being evil . . ."

The black cat of countless lives is more than Usher's conscience—the white spot at its throat echoes the ever-watchful neighborhood priest, who is black, and thus white only at the collar. Argento suggests that more primal forces are at work, that bad luck indeed is caused by something more than broken minds, evil and good coexisting in an eternal struggle for balance. In the painfully bleak finale, Argento ups the ante for this much-adapted tale: the black cat was pregnant, and gave birth inside the walled tomb; its young have survived by feeding upon Annabel's corpse. Once he is found out, Usher's escape proves impossible. Although he kills the investigating policemen, he has been handcuffed to one of them and loses the key. When he tries to leave through an upper window, he falls, suspended in an agonized purgatory between sky and earth, heaven and hell, literally the hanged man of the Tarot.

The image befits Argento as his film career enters the 1990s: like Usher, he is an artist whose singular obsessiveness has left him hanging in the balance. Commercial and critical success have eluded him, at least when measured by the new Hollywood's mania for shopping mall audience acceptance, self-serving awards and quotable reviews. Each new film seems damned to a kind of purgatory for Argento's effort to elevate his violent concerns and, with them, horror film itself, to an artform.

Nevertheless, in his native Italy, Argento is a cultural icon, his identification with things horrific on a level as lofty as that reached by Stephen King in America. His likeness can be found on a regularly published comic magazine, *Profondo rosso,* and his production company owns a chain of shops by the same name, devoted to horror and science-fiction merchandise. He has directed and starred in a television commercial for Fiat, and served as a contributor and creative consultant to two television series, *Giallo* and *Turno di notte.*

Having recently celebrated more than twenty years of filmmaking, Dario Argento is this generation's most pervasive influence on the film of mystery and horror. Certainly he has changed the look and intensity of these genre like no one since Hitchcock. His films read like a veritable sourcebook for the commercial American thriller cinema of the late Seventies and Eighties: *L'uccello dalle piume di cristallo* clearly influenced the elevator murder in Brian De Palma's *Dressed to Kill*, and the killer's hacking through the door in Stanley Kubrick's *The Shining*

(1980), among many other lesser films. John Carpenter's *Halloween* borrows freely from *Il gatto a nove code* and *Quattro mosche di velluto grigio*, and the latter film provided the blueprint for the slow-motion decapitation in Richard Donner's *The Omen* (1976). The coloration of *Suspiria* and *Inferno* influenced George A. Romero's *Creepshow* (1982) and, in turn, Warren Beatty's *Dick Tracy* (1990). The louma crane shot in *Tenebrae* was replicated in De Palma's *The Untouchables* (1987). And the list could go on and on.

The Argento touch may be found in films as disparate as Nicholas Roeg's *Don't Look Now* (1973), Lucio Fulci's *Sette note in nero* (*The Psychic,* 1977) and   . . . *E tu vivrai nel terrore! L'Aldila* (*The Beyond/Seven Doors of Death*, 1981), Carlo Vanzina's *Sotto il vestito niente* (*Nothing Underneath*, 1985), Donald Cammell's *The White of the Eye* (1987), Clive Barker's *Hellraiser* (1987), and the Coen brothers' oeuvre—most recently, *Barton Fink* (1991)—not to mention the emerging Hong Kong cinema of terror, including Tsui Hark's *A Chinese Ghost Story* (1987). Argento's assistant directors and collaborators have moved on to substantial careers of their own, within and without of his shadow—not only Luigi Cozzi and Lamberto Bava, but more recently Michele Soavi, whose debut in *Deliria* (*Aquarius/Bloody Bird/Stage Fright*, 1986) was followed by the magnificent *La Chiesa* (*The Church*, 1990) and *La Setta* (*The Sect*, 1991), the latter films produced and cowritten by Argento.

The unmade Argento films are intriguing to ponder. Early in his career, he sought repeatedly, without success, to option Agatha Christie's *Three Blind Mice*. After completing *Suspiria*, he discussed a remake of *The Phantom of the Opera*. He allegedly turned down Stephen King's *The Stand*, and more recently proposed a version of *Frankenstein* set in Nazi Germany. And, of course, speculation continues about when, if ever, he will undertake the finale of his "Three Mothers" trilogy.

Where Dario Argento's camera will turn next is uncertain at this writing, but one thing is clear: He will show us things that we have never seen.

for Jessica Harper and Tony Williams

interview material courtesy of
Alan Jones and Michele Soavi

Filmography

1966 *Scusi lei e' favorevole o contrario?*, figuration
1968 *C'era una volta il West (Once Upon a Time in the West)*, cowriter
    Cimitero senza croci (Cemetery Without Crosses), cowriter
    Metti una sera a cena (One Night at Dinner), cowriter
    La rivoluzione sessuale (The Love Circle), writer
    Oggi a me . . . domani a te! (Today It's Me . . . Tomorrow You!), cowriter
    Probabilita zero (Probability Zero), cowriter
1969 *Un esercito di cinque uomini (The Five-Man Army)*, writer
    La legione dei dannati (Legion of the Damned/Battle of the Commandos), cowriter
    Commandos, cowriter
    La stagione dei sensi, cowriter
    L'uccello dalle piume di cristallo (The Bird with the Crystal Plumage/The Gallery Murders/Phantom of Terror), writer and director
1970 *Il gatto a nove code (Cat O'Nine Tails)*, cowriter and director
1971 *Quattro mosche di velluto grigio (Four Flies on Gray Velvet)*, cowriter and director
    Er piu, coproducer
1972–73 *La Porta sul buio (The Door of Darkness)* (television miniseries), producer, including: *Il Tram*, writer and director (as *Sirio Bernadotte*); *Il vicino di casa (The Man Upstairs)*; *Testimone ocular (Eyewitness)*, cowriter and director (as *Roberto Pariante*); and *La Bambola (The Puppet)*.
1973 *Le cinque giornate (The Five Days of Milan)*, cowriter and director
    L'albero dalle foglia rosa, coproducer
    Carioca tigre, coproducer
1975 *Profondo rosso (Deep Red; The Hatchet Murders; Suspiria 2)*, cowriter and director
1977 *Suspiria*, cowriter and director
1979 *Zombie (Dawn of the Dead)*, producer and cowriter
1980 *Inferno*, writer and director
1982 *Tenebrae (Sotto gli occhi dell'assassino/Unsane)*, writer and director
1985 *Phenomena (Creepers)*, producer, cowriter and director

Phenomena by Claudio Simonetti (music video), producer and director

Valley by Bill Wyman (music video), producer

Demoni (*Demons*), producer and cowriter

1986 *Demoni 2 . . . L'incubo ritorna* (*Demons 2*), producer and cowriter

1987 *Opera* (*Terror at the Opera*), producer, cowriter and director

Giallo (television series): *Gli incubi di Dario Argento*, contributor and creative consultant

1988 *Turno di notte* (television series), contributor and creative consultant

1989 *La Chiesa* (*The Church*), producer and cowriter

1990 *Due occhi diabolici*: *Il gatto nero* (*Two Evil Eyes: The Black Cat*), coproducer, cowriter and director

1991 *La Setta* (*The Sect*), producer and cowriter

ABOUT DARIO ARGENTO

1986 *Dario Argento's World of Horror*, directed by Michele Soavi

1987 *The Making of 'Opera'*, directed by Giovani Torinesi

Chapter
24

Chelsea Quinn Yarbro

Quinn stands out from the rest of the contributors to this book for one very simple reason—she does not like horror movies. Or so she claims.

Among her many achievements, she is best known as the chronicler of the adventures of the Count de Saint Germain, a vampire with a strong foothold in history. His story extends through five novels, from *Hotel Transylvania* to *Tempting Fate*, in which he took on villains from Nero to Hitler, and a short-story collection. He is a supporting player in Quinn's trilogy about Olivia, also a vampire and Saint Germain's one true love, which included *A Flame in Byzantium*, and his history is recounted in her latest, *Out of the House of Life*.

Quinn's many short stories have appeared in the anthologies of Charles L. Grant as well as *Cutting Edge* and quite a few others; some were collected in *Signs and Portents*. (Her story "Disturb Not My Slumbering Fair" from *Terrors* is a longtime favorite of mine.) She is an accomplished historian, and the majority of her novels apply this knowledge extensively and with an understanding few can match. Her books are just as likely to be found in the "Horror" section as they are to be found in "New Age" (*Messages from Michael*), "Science Fiction" (*False Dawn*), "Fantasy" (*To the High Redoubt*), and "Mystery" (*Bad Medicine*).

She may not like horror films, but she loves *Freaks*.

On Freaks

by Chelsea Quinn Yarbro

There are certain times in life when the mind is especially ready for certain books and films. Seen or read at other times, they will still have impact but not the power they possess at those unique times. This is about one of those times, a window when the alchemy was right, and how it worked later on.

It was November of 1957 when I first saw Tod Browning's *Freaks*. I was fifteen, and had in the previous eighteen months read *Dracula*, *Frankenstein*, and most of the short stories of Wilde and Poe, so in a way I was primed for the film because I was already familiar with monsters and was beginning to think about what made them monsters. I went with three friends and one set of parents to one of the small "art houses" specializing in a wide variety of European films. Occasionally they showed American films as well, if they were old enough and not too political, those being days when the specter of the HUAC still hung over Berkeley.

There was a double bill that night, and I was looking forward to the first film, one I had already seen and loved—and love to this day—Cocteau's *La Belle et la Bête*. The second film was *Freaks*. Certainly *La Belle et la Bête*, with its sympathetic, all-too-human monster, set me up for *Freaks*. But Cocteau's film was a fairy tale, far removed from the real world. *Freaks* was solidly anchored in the here and now of a traveling carnival.

The first thing that impressed me—and repelled the friends I was with—was that the freaks of the film were not masterpieces of makeup and special effects, as Cocteau's Beast had been, but actual human beings, real people with severe physical abnormalities. I supposed they had come from the setting of the film—that is, a carnival—because they were able to perform so well. Clearly they were used to appearing in public; I thought then they were incredibly courageous. I still think so.

It is a tribute to Browning—and to the lead, Harry Earles, who reportedly suggested the project—that within the first fifteen minutes of the film, the freaks become so familiar and recognizably human that the beautiful, venal Cleopatra (Olga Baclanova) and her strongman lover (Wallace Victor) appear the unattractive oddities. When Cleopatra plots to marry the midget Hans (Harry Earles) in order to get the fortune he will inherit, it is she who seems the most inhuman, and Hans the victim of the monster! The wedding scene, with the freaks merrily chanting "we accept her" shows their camaraderie, their close-knit and affectionate fellowship. Cleopatra's revulsion is therefore all the more offensive. And revealing. When she and her lover start to poison Hans slowly, no one in the audience ought to be surprised.

There is a contrast to the casual cruelty of most of the other carnival folk and the outright malice of Cleopatra and Victor, and that is provided by Frozo the clown (Wallace Ford) and his lady Venus (Leila Hymans); these two are accepted by the freaks, dealing with them as they would with anyone else, seeing the humanity in them instead of their physical distortions. At the time I first saw the film it struck me that a clown, who is already an abstraction of humanity, would be the one figure who could fit comfortably into both the normal world and the world of the freaks. By being a clown, Frozo is a perfect interface.

It is through Frozo and Venus that the audience gains the most insight into the action of the characters and comes to sympathize—perhaps even empathize—with the freaks. Frozo and Venus treat the freaks like family. And the audience is persuaded to go along with them, to identify not with the beautiful trapeze artist and her muscular lover but with the midgets and dwarfs and bearded lady and living torso and pinheads.

The freaks, for all their chanting of acceptance, do not entirely trust Cleopatra, and they take to watching her. She can go nowhere in the carnival without someone watching her. The omnipresent eyes watching Cleopatra are an odd counterpoint to the carnival audiences, who come to stare at the freaks.

As they discover what Cleopatra is doing to Hans they decide to take justice into their own hands. With the carnival on the road in a rainstorm, and with only the rain and the sound of a single pipe, the freaks attack Cleopatra and her lover with knives. The images are stark, with not-quite-recognizable shapes in the darkness, things moving in the mud, and the veil of the rain rent by lightning and thunder. What the freaks do to Cleopatra and her lover is never revealed graphically—by modern standards there is a lack of blood and body parts—but when seen again, Cleopatra has been savagely mutilated and is now the Chicken Woman, one of the freaks herself and the only one who is not accepted. I understand that in the original print there was a short scene that implied her lover had been castrated, but it was cut from the picture after its disastrous premiere.

The film was a financial and critical failure when it was released, and MGM took it out of circulation. It was banned in Britain for more than thirty years. Over the years it has had an unsavory reputation that is wholly undeserved.

Whether it was my reading, my age, my natural mental bent, or—as I suspect—some combination of all three, the film stuck with me as few others have. I not only recall the images of the film itself, I recall how I felt at fifteen, sitting in that cramped, drafty theater, so completely hooked by Browning's superb little morality play that I didn't notice how much it made my friends squirm.

Over the years, one aspect of the film continues to stand out: Throughout most of the film, Browning carefully avoids the grotesque. The abnormalities of the freaks are not dwelled upon; the concern and tenderness they have for each other, the ordinariness of their lives, reinforces the understanding that they are as human as anyone—it is how they live and behave that makes them real people, not how they look or how uncompassionate people react to them. Where another director might have made a mockery of the bearded lady having a baby, Browning treats it as what it is—a mother having a baby. Even when the freaks take their vengeance on Cleopatra and the strongman, it is a human reaction, the result of outrage on behalf of Hans, who has been the victim of heartless greed.

In all candor, I didn't realize all this on first viewing. I was too caught up in the film to be able to assess what Browning was doing, but those images were the ones I took away with me. That first time, I was compelled by the presence of the film, the utter reality he was able to evoke. My evaluations came later, when the film had soaked in.

Because of that first viewing, at the time when I was most receptive to what *Freaks* was, the window didn't close, but remained open enough to permit me to garner more from the film.

I saw it the second time in 1962, while I was at college. By that time I had a much larger store of horror fiction under my belt—works of Shirley Jackson, Henry and M. R. James, Arthur Machen, Algernon Blackwood, Richard Matheson, J. Sheridan Le Fanu, E.T.A. Hoffmann, E. Nesbit, Alexei Tolstoy, H.P. Lovecraft, among others—and therefore a greater scope of appreciation, and a keener critical sense. And, of course, I was older. I assumed that some of the mesmeric power of the film would be dissipated.

While it didn't have the impact of novelty—I knew the story and how it would end—it still sucked me into a world where I was persuaded to look through eyes other than my own, and to identify with the supposed monsters against the real monsters. It took me by surprise that the presence of the film was, if anything, stronger the second time around: *Freaks* continued to create a perspective that was unlike any other film I had ever seen.

And by that time I was already tending to be on the side of the monsters in any case. How much of that came from my first viewing of *Freaks* I really can't say, but I suspect it helped shove me in a direction

I was starting toward. It certainly helped clarify my thinking, and added to what I had been learning over the five years between shows. By my second viewing, I had played in *The Tempest* and *Richard III* and had had a firsthand crack at analyzing how monsters worked.

That second viewing also pointed out to me the skill of the camera work in the film, the use of lighting and the orientation of the camera to sharpen the story. The narrative power of Browning's camera was a revelation. When the freaks are together, the lighting is fairly direct and the camera seems to be on eye level. This serves to show more of the ordinary-life nature of the freaks. But when they are out in the world, the camera changes, watching them from the side or above, and the lighting heightens the light and shadow, prefiguring the surreal vision of the end of the film. Not until *The Haunting*, in the following year, did I see visual implication used to such a strong purpose.

Looking back, I suppose that my window closed after the second viewing. It didn't shut out anything, but the raw power of the film no longer had me at optimum receptivity. Too many other factors mitigated my response to the film, so that when I saw it the third time, I was better able to appreciate it without experiencing it to the degree I had before.

I didn't see *Freaks* again until 1974 at a private showing arranged by some movie-buff fans in the Bay Area. By then my reading in the horror and suspense field was very broad. I had developed an abiding interest in the films of Federico Fellini and François Truffaut. I had been selling stories for about six years and had written most of *Hotel Transylvania* and completed *False Dawn*. My critical standards had shifted again, requiring good work that has what I call consistency of vision, meaning a story that never breaks its own rules once it establishes them. Many horror films had come to disappoint me on precisely this point.

This time *Freaks* had few surprises, except that I remembered it so clearly. It continued to have the power to pull me into the world. There was no question of whether or not the freaks were accepted—by now they were on the side of humanity from frame one. And by now, Cleopatra had become more extreme in my eyes, someone who is too beautiful, a parody of what beauty is supposed to be. Hans had more stature than the strongman—he was short, not small. Oddly enough, because I knew what was coming, I wished that there might have been another way to end it, some means to show Cleopatra her real face without having to carve it into her body. Much as I might sympathize with revenge, I wished the freaks had not had to go to such lengths to achieve their vindication of Hans. But that was retrospect, the result of the two previous viewings and the years to think about it. And if I had been given the task of changing the ending, I wouldn't—and couldn't—have done it.

At the time I was struck by the many risks Browning took with the film. He was walking a tightrope, shifting the audience's natural tendency to ally itself with the outwardly attractive to a much more difficult—and potentially more moving—identification with the freaks. Had the freaks been the product of makeup and cinematic sleight-of-hand, it would not have taken so much to persuade the audience to side with them, because the audience would have the consolation of knowing that when the makeup and prostheses came off, the actors were just regular people like the rest of the world. By showing real freaks, people who stayed that way every day of their real lives, Browning was demanding an emotional stretch that might well have been greater than most viewers were willing to make. It is possible that this was one of the underlying reasons for the poor reviews the film received when it was first released.

The audience watching it that night was small, made up of knowledgeable film buffs, most of whom had an interest in the literature of the fantastic, whether science fiction, fantasy, or horror. It was very apparent when the film ended that several of those watching had found it disquieting. Only one other member of the audience had seen the film before. He and I had not discussed *Freaks* before the showing, so when the group started to talk about it after it was over, his insights were as new to me as they were to anyone in the audience.

His take on *Freaks* was much more political than mine. He felt the film was revolutionary in the literal sense. He felt that Cleopatra and her lover represented the oppressors of the world, those with wealth and power who took advantage of those lacking wealth and power. To him, the physical appearance of the characters was a metaphor for how they functioned in the political world. He felt that the poisoning of Hans was an analogy for the abuse of political and financial power and their deadly results for those who are victimized by the political system. To him, the mutilation of Cleopatra and her lover was an act of political revolution against those in power. By making the acrobat and the strongman freaks, social justice was achieved.

While I won't say I think he was wrong—if that's what he got out of it, that was what was in it for him—for me *Freaks* continued to be a psychological study, as much for the audience as the characters in the story. I was more sensitive than ever to the contrast between superficial assumptions and inner reality. Inhumanity, sadly, almost always wears as human a face as humaneness does. If anything, on this third viewing, the psychological strength of the film seemed greater than before. I could not protest my friend's assertion that the story was a metaphor, but to me the metaphor was psychological and spiritual, not political.

There was a debate that night among those who had watched *Freaks* if there would be an audience for it today that was more sympathetic than the one it encountered in 1932. The consensus was that it would probably be better received but might become one of those films, like *Night of the Living Dead* or *Phantom of the Paradise* with a large cult following of repeat viewers. It was also suggested that it might be more interesting to see a remake of *Freaks*. I was one of three holdouts against the idea. I doubted then—and I doubt now—that there was a director around who would have the courage to do the story straight, as Browning had, focusing on the humanity of the freaks and the monstrosity of the supposedly normal characters. I also doubted that a director who wanted to do it in the same spirit Browning had would be able to find financing for such a project. For all the advances in makeup and special effects, and with more ways to pull out the stops than Tod Browning would have known what to do with, I had the sneaky suspicion that those would be the elements that would steal the show, and the strength of the original would be lost in a welter of exploitive Grand Guignol, which would be calamitous to the story. I felt that it was a mistake to tamper with art, especially with the purpose of improving on it.

One of the tests of real art for me is how much the audience gets out of it. The members of the audience don't have to agree about what they get, so long as they get something, preferably something of personal value. In that sense, I think that *Freaks* is one of the most artistic American films of the thirties, because the images and the metaphors are so rich that even now, sixty years after it was made, it captures the audience and gives something of value. It also asks something of the audience. A response is required. It isn't safe. It is filled with unknown quantities. Like all good art, *Freaks* is dangerous.

I have no way of knowing how much *Freaks* has influenced my writing. That would require a level of self-wisdom I don't possess; and I can't go back in my life and unsee the film and then compare what that other version of my work might have been without the effect of *Freaks*. It tapped into a burgeoning interest of mine at a critical moment and provided impetus to my explorations of the genre, no doubt. It provided me with a number of compelling images that continue to affect me. Whether it also added fuel to what was to emerge as stories later on I have no way to assess. But I suspect that anything that has the power to remain so potently in my memory must have some impact on what I write, though what that impact is cannot be consciously identified.

It would be interesting to see the film a fourth time, now that so many years have gone by and I've had so much close literary contact with monsters. I wonder how risky it would seem to me now. There is a possibility that another window would be available that would create another range of insights. It might be that I might find another level of metaphor in the film, something I had not been ready to notice before. Just my being older might provide another reference point, and lead to a different slant on the story. Perhaps the images would touch off other perceptions than those I've already mentioned; I have no way of knowing, and would not know unless and until I see *Freaks* again.

If *Freaks* has had an identifiable influence on any of my work, it is probably most visible in the character of Lugantes, the dwarf jester in *The Godforsaken*. Lugantes is easily the most heroic man in the story, a humane, compassionate, courageous, loyal, loving man in a setting designed to squash those qualities out of all but the most resolute. And if Lugantes is anything, he is resolute. Horror that would turn others against the Infante does not daunt him. In the face of the most cruel oppression, he remains steadfast. He even makes jokes.

Not while I was working on the novel, but while I was correcting the galleys, I had a few flashes on *Freaks*, on the bizarre or oppressive made ordinary. Sixteenth-century Spain is a long way from a traveling carnival, but the environment in both is restricted and artificial. Was that the result of seeing *Freaks* or reading history? Or did both contribute? The exterior of many of the characters in the book did not reflect their true characters. Was there an echo of Cleopatra in the handsome, ruthless Gil? Was it there when I wrote the book or did I read it in later? I don't know how to determine that.

In retrospect, I'd venture to say that *Freaks* has had a very durable artistic credibility. Of the films I saw as a teenager, there are few that I have made an effort to see a second time, and of those, fewer still I have wanted to see a third, let along a fourth time. Since I know the story by now, it isn't the suspense that draws me. Given the flavor of my own writing, it is probably the way *Freaks* does a one-hundred-and-eighty-degree turn from most films of that vintage about physically abnormal people that accounts for its continuing attraction for me; I like doing one-hundred-eighty-degree turns on literary archetypes myself. I've seen other of Tod Browning's films (*West of Zanzibar*, *Dracula*, *The Mark of the Vampire*) and while I admire the skill with which he did them, they haven't the power that *Freaks* has.

Freaks is a disturbing film, an eerie film, evocative and affecting without resorting to sentimentality. Very few films—and very few books, for that matter—have been able to bring that combination off successfully. Unlike many other horror films of the thirties, the only things that look truly dated about *Freaks* are the cars and the clothes. The story itself and the characters have not been locked in time. It is strong enough, sufficiently itself that it has not been successfully imitated, nor has it been eclipsed by later efforts on the same theme.

In the long run, that may be the greatest achievement of Tod Browning's *Freaks*: that it continues, after all these years, to be a subgenre of one.